Voyages of Discovery

Voyages of Discovery

Essays on the Lewis and Clark Expedition

Edited with Introduction and
Afterword by James P. Ronda

MONTANA
HISTORICAL
SOCIETY
PRESS

Helena

Cover image: *Lewis and Clark, 1804*, by L. Edward Fisher, courtesy of the Missouri Bankers Association, Jefferson City

Cover and book design: Kathryn Fehlig

Typeset in Adobe Garamond and ITC Korinna

Printed by Thomson-Shore, Dexter, Michigan

Refer to credits to determine place of first publication for many of the articles. Those not included in the credits list first appeared in this volume.

© 1998 by Montana Historical Society Press,
P.O. Box 201201, Helena, Montana 59620-1201

98 99 00 01 02 03 04 05 06   9 8 7 6 5 4 3 2

Library of Congress Cataloging-in-Publication Data

Voyages of discovery: essays on the Lewis and Clark Expedition / edited by James P. Ronda

     p.   cm.

    Includes bibliographical references and index.

     ISBN 0-917298-44-6 (alk. paper).—ISBN 0-917298-45-4 (pbk. : alk. paper)

     1. Lewis and Clark Expedition (1804–1806) I. Ronda, James P., 1943–

F592.7.V69   1998   98-11224

917.804'2—dc21   CIP

For Don Jackson
with thanks for his life and his learning

Contents

Introduction

'So Vast an Enterprise': Thoughts on the
Lewis and Clark Expedition
James P. Ronda

Part One. Genesis

Jefferson's Instructions to Lewis
[June 20, 1803]

Geographical Knowledge and American Images
of the Louisiana Territory
John L. Allen

Jefferson, Meriwether Lewis, and
the Reduction of the United States Army
Donald Jackson

Part Two. The Corps of Discovery

73

Part Three. The Journey

109

Part Six. Looking Back

Afterword

Illustrations

Maps

Preface

THIS IS A BOOK FILLED WITH VOICES AND VISIONS. Some of the voices are from those who made the journey from Atlantic to Pacific waters; others are from those who took part by either watching or hosting the party. Still other voices are those who have studied the voyage and now bear witness to its significance. The visions revealed here come from the Corps of Discovery's many members—some of whom marched the route, and others who planned and plotted on the home shore. The power of print has made some voices, especially those of men both native and nonnative, seem louder and more important than others. We know with some measure of certainty what the Lemhi Shoshone headman Cameahwait said to Lewis and Clark. We can only guess at the thoughts and words of those Shoshone women who lugged expedition baggage over the Great Divide. But when listened to with a sensitive and discerning ear, the Lewis and Clark Expedition record speaks with the words and thoughts of a cast much larger and more inclusive than once imagined.

Whether written or spoken, language flows and changes like an unpredictable river. The waters of that river sometimes reveal noble ideals and at other times ill-concealed prejudices. Although spelling and capitalization have been standardized throughout the volume, none of the documents or essays has been sanitized or altered to fit current cultural standards. A number of the older essays are marked by language that a more reflective time now deems inappropriate or inaccurate. While regretting Bernard DeVoto's use of words like "savage" or "treacherous," it is also important to recall that DeVoto was the first Lewis and Clark historian to call for a fuller treatment of native perspectives on the journey.

Donald Jackson once said that the Lewis and Clark Expedition was "the product of many minds." The enterprise of this book has drawn inspiration and direction from many minds. Charles E. Rankin, Director of Publications at the Montana Historical Society, first suggested the venture and then gave it his wholehearted support. Chuck has been a guiding presence for so many historians of the American West. I remain deeply in his debt. Martha Kohl, Editor at the Montana Historical Society Press, has been editor, friend, and confidante. More than once, when it seemed as if this voyage might founder in deep water, Martha gave me her understanding, patience, and good counsel. I owe her more than she will ever know. In the spaces between thoughts, words, and print stand many creative people. At the Montana Historical Society and its press Brad Birzer, Eleanor Boviatsis, Glenda Bradshaw, Dorothy Carpenter, June Crofts, Kathryn Fehlig, Doris Hitt, Bergetta Hubbard, Marge Jacobson, Jeff Johnson, Pam Otto, Tammy Ryan, Randi Webb, and Doug Weber moved this book up the rivers, across the mountains, and on to the great Western Sea. For their creativity and dedication I offer my heartfelt thanks. As always, I am grateful to Sid Huttner, Lori Curtis, and Milissa Burkhart in Special Collections at McFarlin Library–The University of Tulsa, for coffee, good cheer, and a beautiful place to think and write. And despite her own scholarly commitments to everything from Oklahoma oil entrepreneurs to Tulsa philanthropists, Jeanne Ronda has been steadfast in her companionship. This book is dedicated to the late Donald Jackson. No one did more to revitalize Lewis and Clark scholarship in the twentieth century than Don Jackson. May his memory be ever green.

Introduction

'So Vast an Enterprise':
Thoughts on the Lewis and Clark Expedition

James P. Ronda

FOR MANY AMERICANS THE LEWIS AND CLARK EXPEDITION is a drama with only four actors—Thomas Jefferson, Meriwether Lewis, William Clark, and the Shoshone woman Sacagawea. But Clark knew better. He once described the expedition as "So Vast an Enterprise."[1] This was a venture that spanned a continent, touched countless lives, and affected in untold ways the future of the West. But no one appreciated the true size of the Corps of Discovery and its transcontinental mission more than Thomas Jefferson. Clark caught the sense of it just right when he called the president "that great Chaructor the Main Spring" of the expedition.[2] The president not only fashioned the expedition but was its most enthusiastic supporter. In early December 1806, just three months after Lewis and Clark returned to St. Louis, Jefferson boasted to Congress that his captains "had all the success which could have been expected."[3] The legislators, mired deep in both foreign and domestic troubles—and largely unaware of the expedition's many tasks—greeted the president's claim with bewilderment. Like those puzzled congressmen, we might ask: Where did the expedition come from? What were Jefferson's sources of inspiration and information as he launched the first American reconnaissance of the West? How did his explorers navigate through worlds beyond the Missouri already settled by generations of native people? What sort of community did the Corps of Discovery become on its way through the West? And finally, what were the enduring consequences of a venture held in so much affection by the president and his captains? This collection of essays and documents aims at answering those questions—or at least keeping alive the journey of discovery.

What Lewis and Clark often modestly called their "western tour" began in a swirl of dreams, schemes, illusions, and expectations. Generations of European explorers, cartographers, merchants, and monarchs had speculated endlessly about the interior of North America and what poet Walt Whitman later eloquently called "the passage to India." Dreams of personal wealth, national power, and perhaps even service to more holy causes fed such conjectures. Out of super-heated imaginations and long-surpressed desires came visions of golden cities, jewelled thrones, fantastic landscapes, and native people hungry for the Christian gospel. Before any exploring party left home there were journeys in the imagination. There was a "going out" into the territory of the mind that went before any leave-taking. And it was dreams of desire and voyages of the mind that gave all journeys vitality and direction. Long before saying farewell to St. Louis, the Corps of Discovery dreamed of the great river Ouragon and a way into and through the West. To that dream would be added Jefferson's vision of the West itself—a vision as fantastic and seductive as any called up by Columbus or Coronado.

From the Age of Columbus to the Age of Jefferson, Europeans had conjured visions of empire in the Americas. Each acquisitive nation, whether France or Spain, Great Britain or Russia, fancied itself master of some New World domain. Maps marked and charted those fantasies. *New* France, *New* Spain, *New* England, and even *New* Sweden—such were the names that danced across the cartographic stage. The kings, bureaucrats, merchants, and missionaries who dreamed of countries beyond the horizon believed that territorial acquisition would bring a whole treasure chest of prizes and rewards, some to be had on this earth and others in a promised land at the end of time. The chest only had to be pried open, whether by violent conquest, spiritual conversion, or the stealth of subtle diplomacy. These dreams of empire were not merely the stuff of idle speculation. Behind each dream was the power of a company, an individual, a nation, or even a church waiting to be unleashed.

Not all dreams of empire were the same. Each one tapped a different source for inspiration but all demanded decision and motion. By the time Jefferson pondered the future of an American empire in the West, he could draw on, and be inspired by, many brands of imperial dreaming. Three centuries of European invasion and conquest in the Americas had produced a long and often bloody legacy, one that the president and his republic found strangely compelling and sometimes painful.

These dreams inherited by Jefferson and his captains were tangled in a knot of paradoxes and contradictions; now at the distance of two more centuries the various strands seem clearer. One thread grew from the insatiable thirst for land. Territorial expansion was the most visible sign of empire. For Jefferson and his contemporaries the restless search for land meant two things. Land was the unmistakable mark of national prestige. Territorial area spelled power, a lesson well understood by those like Jefferson who read the history of the Roman Empire. Second, and equally important, land was the measure of personal status, economic opportunity, and stability. Landowners had what the eighteenth century called "a stake in society."

For Jefferson and his expansionist predecessors, the idea of territorial empire was never an abstraction. The geography of imperialism always grew from and looked toward the passion for wealth. At its beginnings in the epoch of Columbus, Cortez, and Coronado, that passion centered on gold. More than any other substance prized by adventurers sailing from Europe, gold symbolized things rare and precious. Gold was not only the accepted measure of value but its symbol as well. As a color it stood alongside (and for some, above) royal blue, imperial purple, and papal scarlet. For many Europeans, whether they ventured to the Americas or not, the new world was what seventeenth-century artist Albrecht Dürer called "the new golden land."[4]

By Jefferson's time there was less talk of gold to be found up Virginia's James River or west of the Appalachian Mountains in the Ohio country. But the dream that connected gold and wealth to America was not dead but only sleeping. As events in California barely two decades after Jefferson's death made plain, the dream of a "new golden land" remained a potent force to spark western adventure. For eighteenth-century Virginians like Jefferson, Lewis, and Clark, however, it was land rather than gold that summoned visions of personal wealth and national prosperity.

In a world that measured time by the seasons of planting, nurturing, and harvesting, land ownership represented the ideal of a stable, well-ordered agricultural society. Land was not only a unit of economic value, it was also the fundamental way to preserve the good life of the American republic. For many Jeffersonian republicans, gold symbolized wealth gained without work through chance, inheritance, or the oppressed labor of others. In the intensely anti-Catholic rhetoric of the day, gold was what the Spanish sweated out of the bodies of enslaved Indians. But wealth from land and the yield of that land came as the result of honest toil. Such work could be valued both for its own sake and for the usefulness of its products. Jefferson cherished the ideal of an empire built on farm land and rural life. The president and his westering captains could not escape both the desire for territory and the passion for wealth; the Virginia culture of land speculation and imperial expansion made that clear. That tradition would shape federal policy in general and the expedition in particular. But Jefferson believed that the republican ideals of simplicity, frugality, and rural living could somehow purify such passions, keeping Americans from the horrors of violence and conquest.

Empire builders—whether they stayed at home to plan or went on journeys to fulfill those plans—had long been inspired by dreams of territory, wealth, and power. To those familiar desires, Jefferson added something of himself, his time, and his place. His imperial dream for the West promised an empire of and for liberty. To other political philosophers of his age, the two words seemed utterly opposed. For generations historians and philosophers had argued that "empire" represented a polity based on violence, conquest, and oppression. Territorial expansion made tyranny the only effective means of government. On the other hand, "liberty" was imagined as a fragile political value, one that required peace and stability. Such social and political order could come only in a republic. And in Jefferson's time, political wisdom had it that republics were by their very nature small in geographic size and homogeneous in population.

For Jefferson, James Madison, and other republican expansionists, the intellectual-political problem was to create an imperial ideology that could somehow direct and purify the undeniable land hungers and restless energies of a young nation. Madison was the most systematic thinker and writer. His essay on the size of republics in *The Federalist Papers* represents a masterful analysis of the problem and a creative solution to it.[5] But it fell to Jefferson to actually link empire and liberty in public policy. While republicans often talked about the nation as a society of self-sufficient, small farmers, Jefferson knew full well that American farmers and merchants were increasingly part of an expanding global economy. Such economic expansion was irresistible; no sensible politician could stand in its way. But Jefferson did believe that agricultural societies—his cherished repositories of good values and the good life—could spread over large areas without loss of integrity. An expanding territorial empire was the only way to secure agricultural land, land that was the sure means to keep Americans on the farms and out of cities and factories. For Jefferson, empire was the only guarantee for liberty. Lewis and Clark could advance the cause of a noble empire, one that promised economic opportunity, political freedom, and cultural rejuvenation. And surely, thought Jefferson, those native people in the path of this empire would willingly give up their lands and gratefully accept liberty's blessings.

Visions of liberty's empire meant little unless they could find a place in some larger strategy for expansion and exploration. As with his other dreams, Jefferson was inspired by the past—especially his *reading* of the past. As Donald Jackson makes plain in his *Thomas Jefferson and the Stony Mountains: Exploring the West from Monticello*, the president became a geographer and an exploration patron thanks to his expansive library.[6] His ideas about exploration and the nature of western North America were shaped by his reading of the past. That reading taught him not only the particulars of individual expeditions but the lively tradition of geographic conjecture and speculation.

By the end of the eighteenth century, most scholars accepted a common understanding of North America's geography—its principle mountains, rivers, lakes, and other terrain features. That vision included not only the terrain itself but the relationship of one feature to another. And the vision offered its own yardstick for measurement. Land and water, plants and animals were valued by their potential usefulness to humans. Utility was the measure of real worth. The yardstick of utility did not mean that Lewis and Clark failed to appreciate what Lewis once called "seens of visionary inchantment."[7] But the aesthetic measure was more often fertility and order than romantic grandeur. Reflecting Enlightenment notions about balance in nature, geographers described North America in symmetrical terms. Mountains and rivers in the West were sure to be like those already familiar in the East. This meant that western mountains would be similar to the Appalachians with narrow ridges and many passes or water gaps. American rivers, whether in the East or the West, were imagined as navigable highways open to commerce in people and goods. As the East was accessible by river and trail, so the West should be as well. This was a geography of hope, one closely tied to ideas about a passage to India. That passage could be, so Jefferson thought, the commercial corridor linking an interior American empire to world markets.

While other geographers of empire had long thought about the Northwest Passage as a way *through* North America, Jefferson also inherited ideas about the passage as a way *into* the interior. Early ideas about the passage had devalued America. The continent was portrayed as a barrier, something that blocked the route to India and China. But another dream—one far more congenial to Jefferson's cultural patriotism—was growing in scholarly favor during the eighteenth century. This dream drew on ancient and biblical sources to describe the North American interior as Eden, the garden of the world. Increasingly, Jefferson's generation envisioned the West as a land of endless bounty. Here the soil was fertile, the water pure, and the climate temperate. Whether the West was in the Ohio Valley or beyond the wide Missouri, it was sure to be a farmer's paradise. And the passage might be the highway that could link this garden to the markets of the world. American farmers could till this garden, share in its republican virtues, and still profit from a capitalist economy. The passage and the garden would ensure the future of the republic. Exploration and expansion could save the nation by giving it room to escape urban-industrial doom. Jefferson's explorers were nothing short of agents for national survival. This was perhaps Jefferson's most appealing and most illusory dream.

The dreams and visions that inspired the Lewis and Clark Expedition were compelling and pervasive. But they were not unique to Jefferson and the American republic. Jefferson was not the only visionary who saw national wealth and cultural renewal in the West. He had spirited and aggressive rivals in Spain, Great Britain, and Russia. While Spanish empire builders and their already grand domain in North America should have worried Jefferson most, his profound distaste for Britain led him to cast the English and the Anglo-Canadians as the republic's most dangerous competitors. Although Jefferson tended to overestimate the long-term British threat in the West, the danger was nonetheless quite real. By the end of the eighteenth century—thanks in large part to the efforts of fur-trade geographers Peter Pond, Alexander Henry the Elder, and Alexander Mackenzie and the expansionist-minded North West Company—the British Empire seemed poised to reach across Canada to the Pacific. And that reach promised both a commercial and a political presence in the very region Jefferson hoped would preserve the American republic. The president wanted empire, not a shared domain.

Jefferson's thoughts about the West, exploration, and liberty's empire were all highly combustible. It would take only a small spark to set off an explosion. That spark came in the summer of 1802 when the president fled Washington's political heat and muggy weather for the mountain freshness of Monticello. Of the many books he ordered and read that summer, one captured his imagination. *Voyages from Montreal*, published in 1801, was Alexander Mackenzie's account of his 1789 and 1793 expeditions in search of a passage from Atlantic to Pacific waters. Mackenzie's book, in part ghostwritten by William Combe, was hardly compelling reading, even by eighteenth-century standards. But the final pages contained a message that even the drowsiest reader could not overlook:

But whatever course may be taken from the Atlantic, the Columbia is the line of communication from the Pacific Ocean, pointed out by nature, as it is the only navigable river in the whole extent of Vancouver's minute survey of the coast: its banks also form the first level country in all the Southern extent of continental coast from Cook's entry, and consequently, the most Northern situation fit for colonization, and suitable to a residence of a civilized people. By opening this intercourse between the Atlantic and Pacific Oceans, and forming regular establishments through the interior, and at both extremes, as well as along the coasts and islands, the entire command of the fur trade of North America might be obtained.[8]

Jefferson did not miss the promises and threats Mackenzie's words carried. The president immediately understood that Mackenzie had proposed a workable plan not just for territorial expansion and the fur trade but for permanent agricultural settlement as well. And considering how far Canadian traders had already penetrated into the West, the prospect of an expanded British West seemed both imminent and menacing. The Lewis and Clark Expedition, Jefferson's answer to Mackenzie's initiative, was born at that moment.

Visions, ideas, notions, and images—all must have danced in Jefferson's imagination during the fall and winter of 1802. Just as he had inherited a whole galaxy of conjectures and speculations about the West, the president was also heir to powerful ideas about the nature of exploration. By the time Jefferson began to make plans for the Corps of Discovery, there was already a well-defined design for large-scale exploration. The Pacific Ocean voyages of Captain James Cook (1768–71; 1772–75; 1776–80) and Captain George Vancouver (1791–95) represented the combined efforts of a national government and the scientific establishment. British imperial aspirations joined with the scientific ambitions of Sir Joseph Banks and the Royal Society to create expeditions aimed at political influence, economic advantage, and scientific knowledge. The president had no access to a force as large as the Royal Navy but he could call on officers of the United States Army. The American Philosophical Society and scientists living in and around

Philadelphia might play the role occupied by the Royal Society. And Jefferson himself could act as "the presiding genius," a phrase one biographer has used to describe Banks.[9]

Like Banks and other European exploration patrons, Jefferson understood discovery as a carefully planned, highly organized endeavor. To use the word most often employed by Jefferson, Lewis, and Clark, exploration was an "enterprise." To modern ears, the word has the ring of a commercial transaction or a corporate entity—a "business enterprise." But two centuries ago the term had a far broader meaning and enjoyed far wider usage. When Clark described the proposed journey as "this Vast Enterprise," he meant the word to stand for a large, thoroughly planned undertaking, one that recognized personal ambition and national pride as well as some measure of risk. "Enterprise" and "enterprising" were words that Clark, Jefferson, and Lewis used to signify individual energy, personal initiative, and the power of combined action.

Thomas Jefferson explored by reading, and his books taught him many of exploration's lessons. One of those lessons was that successful journeys of discovery demanded sound plans, plans that drew on the knowledge of many scholars in various disciplines. To accomplish the various missions proposed by a diverse group of scholars, these plans took shape and form in written instructions. Such written guidelines had been part of the European exploration strategy since the sixteenth century. But like his contemporary Sir Joseph Banks, Jefferson envisioned such instructions as a means to organize both exploration activities and the many kinds of information gathered by explorers. Written directions were to guide the journey and prepare the minds of those who made the trek.

The letter of directions that Jefferson prepared for Lewis in June 1803 was not the president's first venture into exploration planning. In late April 1793 Jefferson drafted guidelines for André Michaux's abortive journey to the Pacific. A decade before Lewis and Clark, Jefferson envisioned explorers studying everything from botany and ethnography to mineralogy and zoology. For Jefferson, exploration journeys required much more than simply a march to the end of the trail. Exploring meant making comprehensive surveys.

The distinguished Lewis and Clark scholar Donald Jackson once wrote that the expedition was the product of "many minds."[10] For Jefferson, the "many minds" he drew upon to write the letter of instruction included cabinet officers James Madison (State), Albert Gallatin (Treasury), and Levi Lincoln (Attorney-General). The president looked beyond his official family and recognized Philadelphia as the center for science in the nation. Jefferson enlisted support from prominent scientists including physician and scientist Benjamin Rush, University of Pennsylvania professor of natural history Benjamin Smith Barton, and astronomer and surveyor Andrew Ellicott. As it happened, the president received some of the most valuable advice from unexpected quarters. While Secretary of State Madison replied to Jefferson's request in an almost perfunctory manner, Gallatin and Lincoln made additions and suggestions that both refined and expanded the character of the expedition.

Few secretaries of the treasury and attorneys-general have had so wide a range of interests as Albert Gallatin and Levi Lincoln. From public policy and national finance to American Indian linguistics and physical geography, Gallatin and Lincoln spoke as both experienced administrators and amateur scholars. Gallatin's April 13 letter to the president reveals a man with a keen sense of the relationship between geography, imperial expansion, and the future of the American nation. Gallatin was every bit Jefferson's equal as an imperial visionary. And the secretary minced no words about American settlement in the West. The "great object" of the expedition, so Gallatin believed, was "to ascertain . . . whether from its extent and fertility that country is susceptible of a large population."[11] If Gallatin provided ideological substance for Jefferson's empire for liberty, Lincoln offered advice of a more political nature. Lincoln was a well-educated Massachusetts politician and one of the president's most astute advisors. Painfully aware of mounting tensions between Congress and the president as well as Federalist partisan opposition to any territorial expansion, Lincoln felt certain that an unsuccessful expedition would be a political disaster. Long before the phrases "spin doctor" and "damage control" entered the national vocabulary, Lincoln knew what they meant. He wanted an expedition with so many missions that even if one failed, the administration could still claim some success. Because the preliminary instructions evidently did not detail the scientific and ethnographic dimensions of the journey, the attorney-general urged Jefferson to be very specific on those matters. The president had spelled out what Lincoln aptly called "a knowledge of the country." Now he pushed Jefferson to "add more explicitly those articles which have for their object the improvement of the mind and the preservation of the body." As Lincoln cleverly put it, "if the enterprise appears to be an attempt to advance them, [missions relating to science and ethnography] it will by many people, on that account, be justified, however calamitous the issue."[12]

Lincoln also worried about Meriwether Lewis's temperament and his reputation for impetuousness. Like others who knew the president's private secretary, Lincoln recognized the young officer's disposition to court danger and perhaps even stand in harm's way. Lewis shared a trait common among eighteenth-century military officers—an almost obsessive sense of personal as well as national honor that allowed for neither retreat nor compromise. The attorney-general suggested that the instructions counsel prudence and survival over bravado and glorious death. Martyrdom might satisfy one aspect of Lewis's complex personality but it would surely defeat the whole enterprise. Both Gallatin and Lincoln regarded the journey as "an enterprise of national consequence." Lewis's passion for daring and danger could not be allowed to threaten something so important.[13]

What Jefferson's circle of "many minds" produced by the end of June 1803 was a document of enduring "national consequence." Modern readers of the instructions meet a document that can be understood and appreciated in several ways. One reading might picture Jefferson's letter to Lewis as a map, a description of what the president expected his explorers to encounter in the West. Like all exploration planners, Jefferson had carefully charted the "unknown" long before launching the voyage. The instructions for Lewis contained expectations about three vital aspects of the journey's likely discoveries: the West as a geographic place; the West as an inhabited place; the West as an unfolding and perhaps hazardous experience. Each of those categories presented a complex mixture of hope and faith, science and fantasy.

When Jefferson prepared exploration directions for André Michaux in 1793 the West as a place still had the hazy outlines of fantasy. The West was sure to be home for many things—plants, animals, peoples, and terrain features—"things very curious." And among those curious things, Jefferson hoped that Michaux might learn about mammoths and perhaps herds of llamas. Ten years later the presence of such animals seemed either less possible or less important. But the West as place was no less wonderful or attractive. Its terrain remained a geography of hope. That hope promised both a water passage "for the purpose of commerce" and a farmer's paradise destined to constantly renew the republic. Jefferson's West of 1803 promised a place "interesting" and "remarkable," a place well suited for the weighty transactions of the American republic.

Neither Jefferson nor his explorers expected the West to be empty. While the president never fully grasped the ways native people had already settled the West as "home," he did recognize the presence of indigenous cultures and communities. In 1793 Indians played a relatively small part in Jefferson's exploration expectations. Michaux was simply to record "the names, numbers, and dwellings of the inhabitants, and such particularities as you can learn of their history, connection with each other, languages, manners, state of society, and of the arts and commerce among them." Of the potential troubles or possible misunderstandings between Michaux and western Indians, Jefferson expected little and said even less. His only thought in 1793 was that Michaux might well put his observations on birch bark, "a substance which might not excite suspicions among the Indians."[14]

A decade later, Jefferson's expectations, hopes, and fears about native people in the West were far larger and far better defined. Lewis's instructions prepared the Corps of Discovery to live with native people as subjects for scientific inquiry, as possible military and diplomatic allies, as potential commercial partners, and certainly as subjects of a new American empire. But beneath all these expectations lay profound fear and suspicion—feelings born from generations of violent frontier conflict. Jefferson admitted that it was "impossible for us to foresee in what manner you will be received by those people, whether with hospitality or hostility." But the president and his advisors expected trouble. They expected violence, not hospitality; misunderstanding, not cooperation. Prudence, experience, and Jefferson's own understanding of Indian-white relations dictated what became the expedition's governing principle in dealings with western Indians. "In all your intercourse with the natives, treat them in the most friendly and conciliatory manner which their own conduct will admit."[15] Not all expectations become self-fulfilling prophecies. The journey witnessed its share of suspicions and tensions. And the Corps of Discovery did take the lives of two young Indian men. But most often the expectation of trouble gave way to the promise of at least guarded friendship.

Cut to its essentials, the instructions for the Corps of Discovery advanced one fundamental expectation. When Lewis suggested during the winter of 1803 a side-trip from St. Louis to Santa Fe, Jefferson snapped back that the expedition had but one objective— "the direct water communication from sea to sea formed by the bed of the Missouri and perhaps the Oregon."[16] But Jefferson never thought his captains would make their way to the Pacific wearing blinders. Exploration journeys were as much about the going as the goal. The Corps of Discovery was not just to put its collective head down and follow its nose to the western sea. Instead, the explorers were directed to scout the country and meet its inhabitants. The captains were to be participant-observers, writing, describing, collecting, and labeling the world of the West.

Jefferson's letter to Lewis can also be read in light of two centuries of American history since the expedition. The instructions defined in precise and enduring terms the relationship between the federal government and journeys of discovery. What the president fashioned in 1803 was a national strategy for the exploration of the West. Scientific exploration now had a place on the national agenda and perhaps a line in the federal budget. For its time, the Lewis and Clark Expedition was what has come to be called "big science," an enterprise involving several institutions, many specialists, and substantial funding. Jefferson initiated the practice of "big science" in western exploration. The creation of the U.S. Army Topographical Engineers in 1838, the Pacific Railway Surveys of the 1850s, and the post–Civil War territorial surveys continued the Corps of Discovery tradition. And today one might see scientific exploration on more distant frontiers in the journeys of NASA and in the investigations undertaken by the National Science Foundation and the National Institutes of Health.

By the time Lewis and Clark reached St. Louis at the end of 1803, their proposed journey was already the "Vast enterprise" Clark had called it months before. What Jefferson had first imagined as an exploring party led by one officer commanding some ten or twelve men had now grown to twice that size and then some. But the dimensions of this enterprise went well beyond an enlarged Corps of Discovery. The expedition had already touched the lives of politicians, bureaucrats, and scientists. The journey was aided and abetted by clerks working for the military storekeeper at Philadelphia, gunsmiths hammering away at the Harpers Ferry arsenal, and boat builders laboring at their craft in Pittsburgh. The expedition counted on the efforts of innkeepers, hunters, and teamsters. Americans of all sorts and conditions were involved in the life of the expedition community. To the ranks of Jefferson's many minds we should add the names of those who quietly worked to move the enterprise from dream to reality. We might put on the expedition roster the names of shirtmaker Matilda Chapman, druggist David Jackson, tinmaker Thomas Passmore, and tailor Francis Brown. And months later, as the explorers nearly starved in the bitter snows of the Lolo Trail, they would struggle to eat the "portable soup" made by Philadelphia cook François Baillet. This too went up the Missouri, across the mountains, and on to the western sea.

CO

THANKS TO MODERN HIGHWAYS AND AUTOMOBILES it is now possible to retrace the Lewis and Clark route in fairly short order. From beneath the Gateway Arch in St. Louis to Fort Clatsop and back seems just a matter of gasoline and credit cards. But such modern motion loses track of the original expedition's rhythm. Thinking about the character of the journey itself can bring us closer to it not just as static "history" but as something of lived experience.

Consider the weather. Jefferson always watched the weather, recording rainfall and temperature. But it was climate that really interested him. Climate is a scientific abstraction, something to study at a distance. But weather was what the explorers had to live in and through. Jefferson took it for granted that his captains would make a seasonal journey. They would travel from spring to fall and fort up during the winter. As they did so, Lewis and Clark observed climate, that scientific abstraction, but kept a keen eye on the weather, its gradual shifts and sudden changes. Weather was immediate, direct, and personal. William Clark never forgot how he felt struggling through the snowy weather of the Lolo Trail. "I have been wet and as cold in every part as I ever was in my life."[17] Even in a sheltered camp like Fort Clatsop, the weather could not be ignored. Lewis constantly lamented the cold, wind, and rain. "It continued to rain and blow so violently," he reported, "that there was no movement of the party today."[18] Wind, snow, rain, fog, and sun—these could delay an Indian council, detain an anxiously awaited departure, threaten life in a narrow gully, or open an ice-choked river channel.

And there were the rivers. Like the weather, they set the pace and direction of much expedition progress. For centuries European geographers and exploration patrons envisioned a North America cut through by great rivers. Rivers were highways for conquest and commerce. They were the trails of empire. But in the West that greeted Lewis and Clark those trails could be confusing, unpredictable, and even treacherous. Jefferson's captains soon discovered that the Missouri was not the Ohio, that the Salmon was not the Potomac, and that the Columbia was a demon at The Dalles. Mostly seasonal in flow and often unnavigable, western rivers were hardly the broad "communications" Jefferson envisioned in his instructions for Lewis. As the Corps of Discovery struggled to climb the western ladder of rivers, Lewis and Clark perhaps guessed that in later years the rhythm of American expansion would not be bound to rivers but to the trails along their banks.

Weather and water set the framework for the expedition's tour to the Pacific. But in the end it was human muscle and animal energy that made it happen. The Corps of Discovery made its journey propelled by the sweat and strain of men, women, and horses. Geographers' dreams and imperialists' visions could not drag boats against rushing currents, haul supplies over broken ground, or give courage to endure moments of great fear and days of crushing boredom. What progress the expedition made day by day depended on strong backs and ready hands. Some of the most compelling images of the journey focus on work—the labor of men sometimes knee-deep in freezing water or the strength of Shoshone women packing expedition goods over the Lemhi Pass. The passage across the continent began in the mind of Thomas Jefferson but found fulfillment only through toil. The pace of the route was the stretch of an arm, the gait of a horse, or the step of tired feet.

There are many ways to imagine the Corps of Discovery's voyage to the Pacific. Looking at a modern map, the route seems a great arc sweeping and inscribing its way across the northern plains to the bar of the Columbia. There is something attractive, almost reassuring about this linear image. Its confident lines link the route to the certainties of the transcontinental railroad and the interstate highway system. We might imagine the journey as an exercise in going out and coming back, a field reconnaissance by an infantry company. Or we might, with a more Native American sensibility, envision the journey as a great circle—not the circumnavigation of a Magellan but a circle something like an imperial noose. But none of these images bring us closer to the way the president and his captains understood the voyage.

If the word "enterprise" helps us appreciate the larger meanings and implications of the expedition as a human organization, the word "tour" can be equally useful for thinking about the journey itself. Jefferson repeatedly called the expedition "Mr. Lewis's tour" or "the tour of Lewis and Clark." In modern usage the word "tour" has come to connote nothing more than a well-organized sight-seeing vacation. Guided tours promise exotic views without danger, exciting adventures without hazard. Modern tours are planned as diversions, with knowledge and experience as incidental attractions. But in the eighteenth century the word "tour" carried quite different meanings. One meaning centered on the Grand Tour, the sojourn that young English gentlemen (and some gentlewomen) took to gain a sense of civilization and good taste. Under the watchful eye of a skilled "gouvernor," unpolished aristocrats were shuttled from

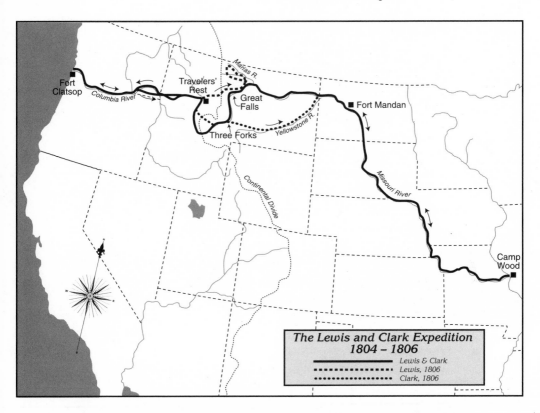

one palace and gallery to another, all in the quest for the veneer of gentility and high culture. In the eighteenth century, the idea of a tour increasingly took on another meaning. In an age of scientific investigation and the Enlightenment, travel for scenery and good manners seemed both frivolous and irresponsible. Sir Joseph Banks summed up the new idea of a tour for serious inquiry. When friends criticized him for joining Cook's expedition to the Pacific, Banks replied: "My Grand Tour shall be one round the whole globe."[19]

By the time Lewis invited Clark to join his tour, the word carried a powerful set of expectations. Those expectations included careful planning, sound organization, and a reasoned search for knowledge. The word implied, at least for Jefferson, no hint of pleasure seeking or escapism. At its center, the Enlightenment exploration tour was what historian Eric J. Leed calls "disciplined observation."[20] Military organization combined with Jefferson's detailed instructions gave the Lewis and Clark

Expedition just that character. The Lewis and Clark tour had a unique shape and sequence. Combining the motion of travel and the stops for rest and reconsideration, the Jeffersonian tour might look to modern eyes like the dots and dashes of Morse code. We might imagine the dashes as the trek itself while the dots represent times at places like Fort Mandan, Fort Clatsop, and Camp Chopunnish. Framed by weather, rivers, and human energy, the code rhythm made the Lewis and Clark tour just what Clark called it—a "Vast enterprise."

A VAST ENTERPRISE AND A GRAND TOUR OF DISCOVERY, the journey was also a profoundly personal one—one that counted days of motion and courage in swift waters and long, warm afternoons for storytelling and perhaps adventures of a more intimate nature.

It is difficult to imagine the Lewis and Clark journey without thinking about motion, the motion of men and boats and water. One of those days of motion was Saturday, June 9, 1804. The Corps of Discovery had been on the Missouri less than a month, having left Camp Dubois outside St. Louis on May 14. The explorers already knew about the river's sawyers and snags, its sudden twists and treacherous currents. The rainy morning of June 9 found the expedition in camp—perhaps on an island—near the Cooper-Saline county line in present-day north-central Missouri. The night's hard rain had slacked off to a miserable cold drizzle, promising a wet and uncomfortable day. But the real worry that morning was the river, its swift current and hidden dangers.

No sooner had the expedition flotilla set out than the keelboat struck and hung up on a log snag. In the high water of the June rise, snags and sawyers (logs hidden just beneath the surface with one end impaled in the river bottom and the other just below the surface) were a constant threat. The morning's first snag was more annoyance than hazard, and the French *engagés* had the keelboat cleared in something less than half an hour. Once again nosing up the river, the expedition passed Arrow Rock, future site of an important American settlement. If Lewis and Clark thought that the danger had passed, the river soon taught them a harsh lesson.

A small island split the Missouri into two narrow channels. Those passages were choked with debris, and the fast current made maneuvering difficult. As the keelboat came around the trailing edge of the island, the boat's stern struck a hidden log. The current seized the bow and swung the boat broadside in the narrow channel. The vessel then slammed hard against driftwood and more snags. With typical understatement, Clark recorded that "this was a disagreeable and Dangerous Situation." Looking up stream, the captains could see "imense large trees" drifting toward the helpless boat. Rescue came when several members of the party leaped into the water, swam ashore, and then used the cordelle or towrope to secure the boat. The surviving journals neither name the heroes of the day nor make it clear whether they acted on their own or at the officers' command. But Clark proudly declared that his men were "not inferior to any that was ever on the waters of the Misssoppie."[21] Several days later, when the crew saved the keelboat in a similar circumstance, Clark was even more generous with his praise. The boat was saved "by Some extrodany exertions of our party ever ready to incounture any fatigue for the promotion of the enterprise."[22]

JUNE 9, 1804, WAS A DAY OF DASH AND MOTION, a time to discover hidden springs of courage and initiative. Above all it was a day to advance the enterprise, to mark courses and count the miles. In the expedition's calendar of days, Thursday, November 22, 1804, spent in winter camp at Fort Mandan in present-day North Dakota, was more notable for its commotion than its motion.

In the early morning hours on Thursday there was no hint of trouble to come. Just two days before, the captains had finally moved into their own quarters. And only the day before the whole party was "in high Spirits." A bright, clear day on the northern plains seemed in the offing and Clark pronounced it "a fine morning." The work routine that shaped every day at Fort Mandan began with a trade detail—Sergeant Nathaniel Pryor, five men, and a pirogue—bound upriver to the Mandan village of Ruptáre. René Jusseaume, sometime-trader and now employed as an expedition interpreter, had arranged a deal for some Indian corn. Pryor's trip was just one more tie that bound Fort Mandan to its native neighbors.

At about ten o'clock, the morning routine was broken by an alarm from the post sentry. What Clark learned after questioning the guard sent the captain hurrying to the nearby interpreters' lodge. Toussaint Charbonneau, the then-pregnant Sacagawea, Charbonneau's other Indian wife, and Jusseaume's native family had established camp just south of the fort. The sentry reported that "an Indian was about to kill his wife." Once at the Charbonneau-Jusseaume home, Clark stumbled into a nasty marital squabble, one that had already turned violent. What Clark soon heard was a sordid story of jealousy, confusion, and blood. As he understood it, about a week before there had been a bitter argument between a Mandan woman from Ruptáre and her husband. The quarrel was evidently about a night she spent with someone from Fort Mandan. When the argument headed toward blows, the woman had fled to the Charbonneau-Jusseaume household. After a few days the potential for trouble seemed less and the Indian woman returned to her spouse. What had only been simmering before now boiled over in a fury of violence. Toward evening the woman staggered back to the interpreters' camp, "apparently much beat, and Stabed in 3 places." Now two days later the angry husband seemed ready to press the argument to a fatal end.

Clark's reaction to the whole affair led him to attempt the roles of investigator, negotiator, and peacemaker. His first thought was to berate the Indian husband for his "rash act" and "forbid any act of the kind near the fort." But Clark soon recognized that the incident and its passions had gone too far for a simple scolding. Working through Charbonneau or Jusseaume, Clark questioned the furious husband. The Indian claimed that a sergeant had slept with his wife. But the suspicion that now fell on John Ordway may have been misplaced. Several weeks later, when the still-fuming husband paid another visit to the interpreters' camp, Clark recorded that the guilty lover was an interpreter—perhaps either Jusseaume or Charbonneau.[23] For the moment all Clark knew was that a sergeant from his command was the cause for considerable trouble.

And the angry native husband went even further, saying that "if he [the sergeant] wanted her he would give her to him." Ordway had no intention of taking a Mandan wife, whether he was involved with this particular woman or not. In an attempt to make amends, Clark ordered Ordway "to give the man Some articles." Clark knew that members of the expedition had regular sexual contacts with Indian women. Both captains had expected such liaisons from the beginning, laying in assorted medical supplies to deal with venereal complaints. And in this particular case Clark seemed to recognize the existence of a different sexual code when he asserted that no member of the Corps of Discovery had been intimate with the woman in question "except the one he [the husband] had given use of for a nite." But a now-defensive Clark rashly promised that in the future no expedition member would have relations with any married Indian woman. In the complex world of personal relationships, the boundaries of intimate territory seemed ever shifting, ever suspect.

Clark had been drawn into this controversy by a desire to stop violence and reestablish harmony. Now he was tempted to go deeper and play the marriage counselor. Assuming an authority he never possessed, the officer "advised him [the husband] to take his Squar home and live happily in the future." But neither the goods from Ordway nor the bromides from Clark satisfied the unhappy husband. And to make matters even more confusing, Mandan headman Black Cat appeared at the camp and added his advice to the kettle. Black Cat's lecture provided just enough heat to make the pot boil over. The aggrieved husband stalked off, dragging his wounded wife, both "apparently dissatisfied."[24]

Jefferson's instructions never contained any precise guidelines for exploring the dimensions of courage or the boundaries of intimate behavior. Despite warnings about Lewis's penchant for danger and bravado, the president offered only the most general directions about survival in the face of hostile opposition. When Jefferson came to write his obituary-as-biography of Lewis, he praised the captain for "enterprise, boldness, and discretion."[25] And surely Lewis deserved such praise. But on countless days like the one near Arrow Rock on the Missouri it was the uncommon courage of common men that saved the enterprise. Jefferson was even less forthcoming in his guidance about the expedition as a personal endeavor. The spirit of Enlightenment exploration pointed travelers outward into a wider world. It was the English statesman Edmund Burke who described exploration as preparing "the Great Map of Mankind."[26] Making that map demanded outbound journeys. The notion of exploration as an interior voyage, a probing of the self, was an idea that would have to wait for other times and other patrons. But the reality of exploring inner space and the self, the boundaries of behavior and values, was a reality that happened on November 22, 1804, as it did on so many other days. Almost as an afterthought in his journal record for that troubled day, Clark noted that Black Cat shared "many Indian anickdotes." The Lewis and Clark Expedition was the "Vast enterprise" that Clark had once called it. But it was also a profoundly personal one—one that counted days of motion and courage in swift waters and long, warm afternoons for storytelling.

Those days along the Missouri were like so many on the Beaverhead, the Columbia, or the Yellowstone. They were not times for important scientific discovery or momentous Indian diplomacy. The days held no grizzly bear terror, no wonder at countless buffalo black on the plains. No latter-day scholar or historical society would find either days or sites worthy of a marker or a museum. But June 9, 1804, and November 22, 1804, were the days of common experience. They represent expedition daily life and the emblematic places of discovery. They were and remain the real stuff of the Lewis and Clark story. These events—the otherwise small things forgotten—remind us that the journey was all about one community moving through the lives and neighborhoods of other communities. The Lewis and Clark enterprise was something more than a traditional tour and something less than an armed invasion by a conquering horde. On those ordinary days, the Corps of Discovery brought together the worlds of native and newcomer long separated by time and space. On those days the realm of the West became both larger and smaller, both promising and forbidding.

IT IS NOT EASY TO RECOGNIZE THE LAST DAY of the expedition's journey. For some adventurers the journey ended at the first sight of the Pacific Ocean. For others the circle was complete once back at the Mandan villages. And for Sacagawea the voyage was never fully finished until her death in 1812. But perhaps September 26, 1806, is as good a choice as any. It was surely as revealing a day as June 9, 1804, and November 22, 1804. That September day in St. Louis held both the end of one journey and the beginning of another. The last entry in Clark's official journal is both cryptic and revealing, obscure and tantalizing. "We commenced Wrighting."[27] Students of the expedition have long debated just what the captains were writing in their rented St. Louis room. Were they busy drafting letters home to friends and relatives? Was Clark laboriously recopying some final journal entries? Were they puzzling over how to tell Jefferson that his "water communication" from the Atlantic to the Pacific was as elusive as ever? Whatever the exact character of the "Wrighting," the larger meaning of the act is now plainer. Having made the journey, Lewis and Clark were now preparing to shape their personal experiences into formal history. The travelers began a new venture into the territory of narrative and commentary. Donald Jackson once called the Corps of Discovery "the writingest explorers of their time."[28] That writing was more than a simple recounting of miles and camps, courses and distances. By their words the explorers fashioned not only a description of the West but a sense of its possible meanings. In their letters, journals, and maps, the explorers created a landscape as vast and as personal as the expedition enterprise itself. That September day in 1806 is a bridge between them and us, between their journey and ours. It is where, at least for a moment, time and distance are erased and we join with the Corps of Discovery in a common enterprise. Lewis and Clark moved from being explorers to being explainers. Like them, we continue the explaining. And that is an enterprise every bit as vast as the one that took the Corps of Discovery into the West.

Notes

1. Donald Jackson, ed., *Letters of the Lewis and Clark Expedition with Related Documents, 1783–1854*, 2d ed. (Urbana, Ill., 1978), 1:113.

2. Ibid., 1:111.

3. Ibid., 1:352.

4. Hugh Honor, *The New Golden Land: European Images of America from the Discoveries to the Present Time* (New York, 1975), 28.

5. Garry Wills, ed., *The Federalist Papers* (New York, 1982), nos. 9, 10.

6. Donald Jackson, *Thomas Jefferson and the Stony Mountains: Exploring the West from Monticello* (Urbana, Ill., 1981); see also John L. Allen, "Imagining the West: The View from Monticello," in *Thomas Jefferson and the Changing West: From Conquest to Conservation*, ed. James P. Ronda (Albuquerque, N. Mex., 1997), 3-23.

7. Gary E. Moulton, ed., *The Journals of the Lewis and Clark Expedition* (Lincoln, Nebr., 1983–97), 4:226 (hereafter JLCE); see also Albert Furtwangler, *Acts of Discovery: Visions of America in the Lewis and Clark Journals* (Urbana, Ill., 1993), 23-51.

8. W. Kaye Lamb, ed., *The Journals and Letters of Sir Alexander Mackenzie* (Cambridge, U.K., 1970), 417.

9. J. C. Beaglehole, *The Life of Captain James Cook* (London, 1974), 291.

10. Jackson, *Letters*, 1:v.

11. Ibid., 1:33.

12. Ibid., 1:35.

13. Ibid.

14. Ibid., 2:671.

15. Ibid., 1:64. Jefferson's Instructions to Lewis are also reprinted in this volume, 31-38.

16. Ibid., 1:137.

17. JLCE, 5:209.

18. Ibid., 6:347.

19. Barbara Maria Stafford, *Voyage into Substance: Art, Science, Nature, and the Illustrated Travel Account, 1760–1840* (Cambridge, Mass., 1984), 4.

20. Eric J. Leed, *The Mind of the Traveler* (New York, 1991), 188.

21. JLCE, 2:289.

22. Ibid., 2:300.

23. Ibid., 3:260.

24. Ibid., 3:239.

25. Thomas Jefferson, "Memoir of Meriwether Lewis," in *The History of the Expedition under the Command of Lewis and Clark, to the Sources of the Missouri River, Thence across the Rocky Mountains and down the Columbia River to the Pacific Ocean, Performed during the Years 1804–5–6, by Order of the Government of the United States,* ed. Elliott Coues (1893; reprint, New York, 1964), 1:xvii.

26. George H. Guttridge, ed., *The Correspondence of Edmund Burke* (Chicago, 1958–78), 3:350-51.

27. JLCE, 8:372.

28. Jackson, *Letters,* 1:v.

*Missouri River at Bear Gulch, date and photographer
unknown. Elk Head Rock is in the distance.*

Part One

Genesis

WE ALL LIKE SIMPLE STORIES FROM THE PAST, especially those with plots that run in a straight line from noble beginnings through dramatic middles and finish at satisfying ends. These are tidy stories, cherished national parables with often reassuring meanings and morals. There is something comforting and just plain "right" about the picture of the Founding Fathers wisely accepting the Declaration of Independence and then confidently marching out to fight the Red Coats. Never mind that Lexington and Concord became battlegrounds nearly a year before Thomas Jefferson offered the Continental Congress his lawyerly brief for rebellion.

There is a similar sort of plot line wisdom for the Lewis and Clark Expedition. An all-knowing President Jefferson, so the story goes, bought Louisiana and then sent his captains to inspect the goods. In easily memorized shorthand, the story might go "first the purchase, then the expedition." But all of this manages to ignore the weight of chronology—that the expedition was planned well before the purchase and that the two events had quite distinct origins.

The essays and documents in this opening section reveal a more complex story, in fact, a whole set of stories remarkably rich in meanings and deep in the reach of time. In the largest sense, the Corps of Discovery grew from some of the most compelling events and ideas in world history. Just as the American West was always part of a wider world, so the expedition sprang from expansive dramas on wide stages.

Thinking about the origins of the Lewis and Clark Expedition, we are taken back to a world of dreams and schemes, a world alive and magnetic long before Thomas Jefferson read Alexander Mackenzie's *Voyages from Montreal* or worried about Napoleon's designs on Louisiana. This was a world of geographic images, Enlightenment theories, and national rivalries. The maps drafted by Samuel Lewis (no relation to Meriwether) and Peter Pond embody many of the key geographic ideas alive in the world of Lewis and Clark. Jefferson's detailed instructions prepared for Lewis open yet another window into the past—a window through which we can begin to see the president's exploration strategies and goals. The maps and the instructions reveal the West as Jefferson hoped it would be—a region of navigable rivers, easily portaged mountains, and vast, empty, fertile spaces. The Lewis and Clark journey was shaped by ideas and events deep in the past and, as a blues singer once put it, "a long time coming."

This map of the Northwest, drawn by British fur-trade geographer Peter Pond and published in Gentleman's Magazine, *in 1790, illustrates the state of geographic knowledge and conjecture before Lewis and Clark.*

Samuel Lewis, map of Louisiana, 1804. This map—a reflection of geographic expectations before the Lewis and Clark Expedition—overextends the Missouri-Platte drainage system and provides the Rocky Mountains several openings near the source streams of the Missouri. Had it existed, such a Louisiana, with its navigable water routes, would have perfectly suited the growing agrarian republic.

Jefferson's Instructions
to Lewis
[June 20, 1803]

*To Captain Meriwether Lewis esq. Capt. of the 1st
regimt. of Infantry of the U.S. of A.*

YOUR SITUATION AS SECRETARY OF THE PRESIDENT OF THE U.S. has made you acquainted with the objects of my confidential message of Jan. 18, 1803 to the legislature; you have seen the act they passed, which, tho' expressed in general terms, was meant to sanction those objects, and you are appointed to carry them into execution.

Instruments for ascertaining, by celestial observations, the geography of the country through which you will pass, have been already provided. Light articles for barter and presents among the Indians, arms for your attendants, say for from 10. to 12. men, boats, tents, & other travelling apparatus, with ammunition, medecine, surgical instruments and provisions you will have prepared with such aids as the Secretary of War can yield in his department; & from him also you will recieve authority to engage among our troops, by voluntary agreement, the number of attendants above mentioned, over whom you, as their commanding officer, are invested with all the powers the laws give in such a case.

As your movements while within the limits of the U.S. will be better directed by occasional communications, adapted to circumstances as they arise, they will not be noticed here. What follows will respect your proceedings after your departure from the United states.

Your mission has been communicated to the ministers here from France, Spain & Great Britain, and through them to their governments; & such assurances given them as to it's objects, as we trust will satisfy them. The country <*of Louisiana*>[1] having been ceded by Spain to France, <*and possession by this time probably given,*> the passport you have from the minister of France, the representative of the present sovereign of the country, will be a protection with all it's subjects; & that from the minister of England will entitle you to the friendly aid of any traders of that allegiance with whom you may happen to meet.

The object of your mission is to explore the Missouri river, & such principal stream of it, as, by it's course and communication with the waters of the Pacific ocean, whether the Columbia, Oregan, Colorado or any other river may offer the most direct & practicable water communication across this continent for the purposes of commerce.

Beginning at the mouth of the Missouri, you will take <*careful*> observations of latitude & longitude, at all remarkeable points on the river, & especially at the mouths of rivers, at rapids, at islands, & other places & objects distinguished by such natural marks & characters of a durable kind, as that they may with certainty be recognised hereafter. The courses of the river between these points of observation may be supplied by the compass the log-line & by time, corrected by the observations themselves. The variations of the compass too, in different places, should be noticed.

The interesting points of the portage between the heads of the Missouri, & of the water offering the best communication with the Pacific ocean, should also be fixed by observation, & the course of that water to the ocean, in the same manner as that of the Missouri.

Your observations are to be taken with great pains & accuracy, to be entered distinctly & intelligibly for others as well as yourself, to comprehend all the elements necessary, with the aid of the usual tables, to fix the latitude and longitude of the places at which they were taken, and are to be rendered to the war-office, for the purpose of having the calculations made concurrently by proper persons within the U.S. Several copies of these as well as of your other notes should be made at leisure times, & put into the care of the most trust-worthy of your attendants, to guard, by multiplying them, against the accidental losses to which they will be exposed. A further guard would be that one of these copies be on the paper of the birch, as less liable to injury from damp than common paper.

The commerce which may be carried on with the people inhabiting the line you will pursue, renders a knolege of those people important. You will therefore endeavor to make yourself acquainted, as far as a diligent pursuit of your journey shall admit, with the names of the nations & their numbers;

the extent & limits of their possessions;

their relations with other tribes of nations;

their language, traditions, monuments;

their ordinary occupations in agriculture, fishing, hunting, war, arts, & the implements of these;

their food, clothing, & domestic accomodations;

the diseases prevalent among them, & the remedies they use;

moral & physical circumstances which distinguish them from the tribes we know;

peculiarities in their laws, customs & dispositions;

and articles of commerce they may need or furnish, & to what extent.

And, considering the interest which every nation has in extending & strengthening the authority of reason & justice among the people around them, it will be useful to acquire what knolege you can of the state of morality, religion, & information among them; as it may better enable those who may endeavor to civilize & instruct them, to adapt their measures to the existing notions & practices of those on whom they are to operate.

Other objects worthy of notice will be

the soil & face of the country, it's growth & vegetable productions, especially those not of the U.S.

the animals of the country generally, & especially those not known in the U.S.

the remains or accounts of any which may be deemed rare or extinct;

the mineral productions of every kind; but more particularly metals, limestone, pit coal, & saltpetre; salines & mineral waters, noting the temperature of the last, & such

Jefferson Peace Medal—front
Oregon Historical Society, Portland ORH138090

Jefferson Peace Medal—back
Oregon Historical Society, Portland ORH138091

circumstances as may indicate their character;
volcanic appearances;
climate, as characterised by the thermometer, by the proportion
of rainy, cloudy, & clear days, by lightning, hail, snow, ice,
by the access & recess of frost, by the winds prevailing at
different seasons, the dates at which particular plants put forth
or lose their flower, or leaf, times of appearance of particular
birds, reptiles or insects.

Altho' your route will be along the channel of the Missouri, yet
you will endeavor to inform yourself, by enquiry, of the character
& extent of the country watered by it's branches, & especially on
it's Southern side. The North river or Rio Bravo which runs into

the gulph of Mexico, and the North river, or Rio colorado which runs into the gulph of California, are understood to be the principal streams heading opposite to the waters of the Missouri, and running Southwardly. Whether the dividing grounds between the Missouri & them are mountains or flat lands, what are their distance from the Missouri, the character of the intermediate country, & the people inhabiting it, are worthy of particular enquiry. The Northern waters of the Missouri are less to be enquired after, because they have been ascertained to a considerable degree, & are still in a course of ascertainment by English traders, and travellers. But if you can learn any thing certain of the most Northern source of the Missisipi, & of it's position relatively to the lake of the woods, it will be interesting to us.

<*Two copies of your notes at least & as many more as leisure will admit, should be made & confided to the care of the most trusty individuals of your attendants.*> Some account too of the path of the Canadian traders from the Missisipi, at the mouth of the Ouisconsing to where it strikes the Missouri, & of the soil and rivers in it's course, is desireable.

In all your intercourse with the natives, treat them in the most friendly & conciliatory manner which their own conduct will admit; allay all jealousies as to the object of your journey, satisfy them of it's innocence, make them acquainted with the position, extent, character, peaceable & commercial dispositions of the U.S.[,] of our wish to be neighborly, friendly & useful to them, & of our dispositions to a commercial intercourse with them; confer with them on the points most convenient as mutual emporiums, and the articles of most desireable interchange for them & us. If a few of their influential chiefs, within practicable distance, wish to visit us, arrange such a visit with them, and furnish them with authority to call on our officers, on their entering the U.S. to have them conveyed to this place at the public expence. If any of them should wish to have some of their young people brought up with us, & taught such arts as may be useful to them, we will receive, instruct & take care of them. Such a mission, whether of influential chiefs or of young people, would give some security to your own party. Carry with you some matter of the kinepox; inform those of them with whom you may be, of it's efficacy as a preservative from the smallpox; & instruct & encourage them in the use of it. This may be especially done wherever you winter.

As it is impossible for us to foresee in what manner you will be recieved by those people, whether with hospitality or hostility, so is it impossible to prescribe the exact degree of perseverance with which you are to pursue your journey. We value too much the lives of citizens to offer them to probable destruction. Your numbers will be sufficient to secure you against the unauthorised opposition of individuals or of small parties: but if a superior force, authorised, or not authorised, by a nation, should be arrayed against your further passage, and inflexibly determined to arrest it, you must decline it's farther pursuit, and return. In the loss of yourselves, we should lose also the information you will have acquired. By returning safely with that, you may enable us to renew the essay with better calculated means. To your own discretion therefore must be left the degree of danger you may risk, and the point at which you should decline, only saying we wish you to err on the side of your safety, and to bring back your party safe even if it be with less information.

As far up the Missouri as the white settlements extend, an intercourse will probably be found to exist between them & the Spanish posts of St. Louis opposite Cahokia, or Ste. Genevieve opposite Kaskaskia. From still further up the river, the traders may furnish a conveyance for letters. Beyond that, you may perhaps be able to engage Indians to bring letters for the government to Cahokia or Kaskaskia, on promising that they shall there recieve such special compensation as you shall have stipulated with them. Avail yourself of these means to communicate to us, at seasonable intervals, a copy of your journal, notes & observations, of every kind, putting into cypher whatever might do injury if betrayed.

Should you reach the Pacific ocean inform yourself of the circumstances which may decide whether the furs of those parts may not be collected as advantageously at the head of the Missouri (convenient as is supposed to the waters of the Colorado & Oregan or Columbia) as at Nootka sound, or any other point of that coast; and that trade be consequently conducted through the Missouri & U.S. more beneficially than by the circumnavigation now practised.

On your arrival on that coast endeavor to learn if there be any port within your reach frequented by the sea-vessels of any nation, & to send two of your trusty people back by sea, in such way as <*they shall judge*> shall appear practicable, with a copy of your notes: and should you be of opinion that the return of your party by the way they went will be eminently dangerous, then ship the whole, & return by sea, by the way either of cape Horn, or the cape of good Hope, as you shall be able. As you will be without money, clothes or provisions, you must endeavor to use the credit of the U.S. to obtain them, for which purpose open letters of credit shall be furnished you, authorising you to draw upon the Executive of the U.S. or any of it's officers, in any part of the world, on which draughts can be disposed of, & to apply with our recommendations to the Consuls, agents, merchants, or citizens of any nation with which we have intercourse, assuring them, in our name, that any aids they may furnish you, shall be honorably repaid, and on demand. Our consuls Thomas Hewes at Batavia in Java, Wm. Buchanan in the Isles of France & Bourbon & John Elmslie at the Cape of good Hope will be able to supply your necessities by draughts on us.

Should you find it safe to return by the way you go, after sending two of your party round by sea, or with your whole party, if no conveyance by sea can be found, do so; making such observations on your return, as may serve to supply, correct or confirm those made on your outward journey.

On re-entering the U.S and reaching a place of safety, discharge any of your attendants who may desire & deserve it, procuring for them immediate paiment of all arrears of pay & cloathing which may have incurred since their departure, and assure them that they shall be recommended to the liberality of the legislature for the grant of a souldier's portion of land each, as proposed in my message to Congress: & repair yourself with your papers to the seat of government <*to which I have only to add my sincere prayer for your safe return*>.

To provide, on the accident of your death, against anarchy, dispersion, & the consequent danger to your party, and total failure of the enterprize, your are hereby authorised, by any instrument signed & written in your own hand, to name the person among them who shall succeed to the command on your decease, and by like instruments to change the nomination from time to time as further experience of the characters accompanying you shall point out superior fitness: and all the powers and authorities given to yourself are, in the event of your death, transferred to, & vested in the successor so named, with further power to him, and his successors in like manner to name each his successor, who, on the death of his predecessor, shall be invested with all the powers & authorities given to yourself.

Given under my hand at the city of Washington this 20th day of June 1803.

TH: J. Pr. U.S. of A.

Notes

1. Words and phrases set between carets and italicized were deleted from the manuscript, presumably by Jefferson.

Geographical Knowledge and American Images of the Louisiana Territory

John L. Allen

ON JULY 4, 1803, THROUGH THE MEDIUM OF THE PUBLIC PRESS, the news that the United States had gained possession of that vast territory comprising much of the western drainage of the Mississippi River and known as Louisiana burst upon an American populace almost totally unprepared to understand what they had acquired.[1] One observer, writing to a major Washington newspaper, said of Louisiana geography that "all is vague conjecture and uncertain calculation."[2] And another writer of the same time noted that "there are vast regions . . . of which no nations know anything . . . there is no certainty whether it be land or sea, mountain or plain."[3] Even Thomas Jefferson, unwitting architect of the purchase, could say only that the "information as to the country is very incomplete."[4]

Despite the fuzziness and inadequacy of geographical lore on Louisiana, the experience of more than a century of exploration in that area was not completely lost to literate Americans of 1803–4. Ever since the French missionary-explorer Jacques Marquette discovered the Missouri River and named it as the logical pathway to the Pacific Ocean, explorers operating with the sanctions of French, British, and Spanish colonial authority had penetrated the trans-Mississippi region—hoping to find, by way of the Missouri River and its hypothetical connections with westward-flowing waters—the fabled passage across North America that had been the goal of exploration since the New World was first recognized as a barrier in Europe's path to the Orient.[5] Other rivers of the territory, such as the Red and Arkansas, were partially explored, often with the hope that they might provide trade connections with the assumed rich Kingdom of New Mexico. This drive of the European colonial powers toward the west provided experiences and literature which were vital in establishing the images or patterns of belief about the nature and content of Louisiana in American minds.

Geographical lore that was characteristically American was mingled with the French, British, and Spanish geographical knowledge of the continent.[6] Like the European powers, the young republic was interested in the Passage to India.[7] Her motives were both commercial and territorial. While the explorers of France, Britain, and Spain had sought the will-o'-the-wisp that was the Northwest Passage, the frontier society that became the United States had been "realizing westward." By the time of the purchase of Louisiana, the vanguard of the American migration had already reached the eastern border of that new territory. Looking toward the west, this vanguard saw the future possibilities of the commercial passage to the Pacific through the eyes of a people with a two-hundred-year heritage of hacking homes from a wilderness and saw, with optimism and desire and longing, the vision that the poets would record:

> Towards the desert turn our anxious eyes,
> To see 'mong forest statelier cities rise;
> Where the wild beast now holds his gloomy den,
> To see shine forth the blessed abodes of men.
> The rich luxuriance of a teeming soil,
> Rewards with affluence the farmer's toil,
> All nature round him breathes a rich perfume,
> His harvest ripens and his orchards bloom.[8]

The way that men perceive or understand their environment is significant for explanations of human spatial activity. At no time in the history of the United States had this statement been more true than it was at the opening of the nineteenth century. By the time that American acquisitions of a major portion of the trans-Mississippi West became a reality through the purchase of Louisiana, many elements of the American population were already advocating expansion of the republic into that territory.[9] What would later be called "manifest destiny" was becoming a force in American thought and action; the expansion of America into the West, hesitant at first and then gaining momentum, began. In all its phases, this expansion was conditioned by the geographical images that had formed in American minds relative to the lands beyond the frontier of the Mississippi, particularly those images that dealt with the agricultural potential of the West and with the prospects of an easy transcontinental communication system via the western rivers.

As is the case with so many geographical ideas, those images of the West that formed first were among the last to fade. An examination of American geographical thought about Louisiana for the period during which Americans were beginning to articulate their views of the area may help to interpret the conditioning influence of the initial images of the West on later exploration and settlement.

The year 1804 is a particularly good one for source material from which to derive the images of the West as they might have appeared in the minds of literate Americans.[10] American interest in the entire trans-Mississippi area took a great upward surge after news of the purchase, and a great flow of geographical information on the West began. Editors of newspapers and magazines, government officials, land speculators, and publishers in general dredged up and reprinted every available piece of information on the territory of Louisiana. The transmission of that lore to the reading public took a number forms: travel accounts or journals, available either in book form or in "extract" form in periodicals, based on the experiences of the European and American explorers in the West before the purchase; published debates on the worth and value of the western lands (usually in regard to the purchase itself); correspondence from Americans living on the western frontier to eastern newspapers, and the geographies and maps of ateliers.[11]

The accounts mentioned most frequently by booksellers and with the greatest coverage in the periodical literature were those of the British explorers in the Old Northwest and Canada.[12] Second in volume and in popularity, judging from the number of extracts, was travel literature from the period of the French occupation of Louisiana, 1673 to 1763.[13] Apocryphal travel accounts by Americans were also popular but of lesser importance.[14] Original narratives of Spanish-sponsored exploration in Louisiana between 1763 and 1803 were virtually nonexistent, although references to Spanish activity did appear in correspondence between American residents of the borderlands and the eastern periodicals.[15]

The information content of the travel literature was highly variable. Those of the British were the least mythical in nature. Although British explorers had made very few entries into Louisiana, their reports included Indian information on parts of the area. Even when the British accounts did not apply directly to Louisiana, the information they contained on western Canadian geography—particularly that relative to an interior mountain range as a source region and drainage divide of rivers—was interpolated by Americans to fit within the purchase lands. But the most important feature of the British travel narratives was their emphasis on the commercial water route to the Pacific.[16]

Considerably different in character and quality of information were the chronicles of French Louisiana. Like the British journals, the French accounts presented information on the hypothetical height-of-land in the interior which served as a divide of Atlantic and Pacific waters. In contrast to British literature, this height-of-land was associated with features of myth and legend, and the French chronicles told tales of inland seas, of great rivers that flowed in two directions at once, of cities of gold and white Indians. Even French comments on the all-water passageway were encrusted with fantasy. An oft-repeated story related the spectacular journeys of Indians who had traversed the glories of the interior and reached the Great South Sea by the river systems of western North America.[17]

American accounts, because of their apocryphal nature, contained much the same kind of information, combined with over-enthusiastic estimates of the agricultural potential of the western lands. Whether accurate or inaccurate, the sometimes-fictional French and American travel literature exerted as much influence on American images of the West as did completely factual accounts. Unable to separate reality from unreality, Americans drew from the literature ideas of an area exceeded by no other in "fertility of soil and temperature of climate," traversed by magnificent natural highways that could carry commerce to the very shores of the western ocean.

The spirited public debates that followed the news of the cession of the Louisiana territory to the United States were an additional source of information for American concepts of western geography. During the summer and fall of 1803 and throughout 1804, both positive and negative opinions on the nature of Louisiana were published. On one side of the debate were those critics who agreed with "Watty Watersnake" that "then there is Louisiana—a mighty matter indeed! an absolute barren that nobody knows the bounds of or cares."[18] Such opinion was in the minority and most writers tended to support the contention of "Providence Peacemaker" who wrote, "No country enlightened by the sun has a better soil to expose to its rays; or a soil capable of higher cultivation, or of richer or greater variety of produce."[19] This description, and others like it, was probably applied to lower portions of Louisiana territory—below the mouth of the Ohio. Because of the general lack of understanding of regional variation throughout the West, comments such as those of "Peacemaker" seem to have been accepted by most Americans as describing the entirety of the area acquired from France.[20] Therefore, if the sheer weight of favorable opinion on the purchase lands is any indication, all of Louisiana was—in the mainstream of American opinion—considered perfect for agriculture. Nearly two centuries of wilderness experience had apparently not served to quell the Americans' unshakable belief that to the west there was an area where life was happy and blissful, where sickness, disease, and poverty were unknown, where people did not die; the West was a garden, and the fact had been known for centuries.

A third source of information aiding in the formation of American images of Louisiana was correspondence from the West that appeared in contemporary news media. Letters from American residents of Louisiana to friends and relatives in the eastern states often worked their way into the eastern periodicals, and many were written with the public in mind and often contained items that the writer thought might prove interesting or descriptive.[21] With few exceptions, this published correspondence spoke of the newly acquired lands in glowing terms, fixing in the mind's eye the picture of all Louisiana as a land of great beauty and fertility.[22] The exception to the rule was the correspondence relative to recent Spanish-sponsored exploration in Louisiana which transmitted the desert concept of the West that seems to have been a feature of French and Spanish attitudes toward Louisiana in the late eighteenth century and described the land quality of Louisiana in less than enthusiastic terms.[23] Even among these items appeared the notion that the western lands were of great value. Tales were still told, relayed by the Spanish fur trade, of Indians who had traveled across the continent by way of the mighty western rivers—all the way to the South Sea—and on its shores were wonders and mysteries and black dwarfs.[24] Beyond was the open passage to the Orient.

A fourth source for the images of the Louisiana territory in 1803–4 was the works of the geographers and cartographers.[25] A considerable range of information on the West may be found in the geographical writings of the time, but this information is brief, highly generalized, and very contradictory from one volume to the next, with some elements of western geography, such as land quality, not being mentioned at all in the geographies.

Most of the geographical references described rivers like the Mississippi, Missouri, Columbia ("Oregan" or "great river of the West"), and Rio Grande ("Rio Bravo" or "Rio del Norte") in detail and with a fair degree of accuracy for their lower portions. Other western rivers such as the Platte, Arkansas, and Yellowstone were seldom referred to or described. Descriptions of the mountain ranges of the interior were also sketchy and indefinite. It was an accepted fact that interior ranges—usually called the Stoney or Shining Mountains—existed, although there was great disagreement as to their size, location, or physical characteristics.

Even greater controversy and contradiction appeared in the geographers' descriptions of the region where the mountains and rivers came together to form the divide that parted the continental waters. Few of the geographies presented the divide as one created by the existence of a major mountain range that ran the length of the continent.[26] A more common view, if a much less accurate one, was that of a drainage divide in the form of a pyramidal height-of-land or upland plateau from which rivers flowed in several directions and which, for many geographers, did not take the form of a mountain range at all but was represented as a level and extensive plains region lying between more mountainous regions on the north and south.[27] This seems to have been the fundamental principle of western geography, the core of misconception as stated by the geographers. The drainage divide between eastward and westward flowing streams need not be a range of mountains but might just as well be a high plateau, an area of extensive plains, a theoretical "height-of-land." The Rockies, Shining Mountains, or Stoney Mountains were there, but their size, extent, and nature as a continental divide were not understood. The heads of rivers like the Missouri and Columbia were near to one another and located in an area that just might be relatively level. If the heads of the Missouri and Columbia were in the same area, and if that area were a level upland rather than a major mountain barrier, then only a short and easy portage would be necessary to link the seas of the East and West and bring all the commerce of the Orient to the republic.

The confusion in American geographical information was illustrated nowhere more clearly than in the works of the ateliers. *A New and Elegant General Atlas* (published in 1804 to accompany Jedidiah Morse's *American Universal Geography*), coauthored by Samuel Lewis of Philadelphia and Aaron Arrowsmith of London, provides excellent examples of the contradictory nature of the source material for images of the West. The relevant section from the general map of North America drawn by Arrowsmith presented a fairly accurate picture of the major features of Louisiana, including a representation of a north-south range which acted as a continental divide. By way of contrast, Lewis's map of Louisiana, which appeared in the same atlas, provided a much less accurate (if more detailed) view of western geography.[28] The two major distinguishing features of the Louisiana map were the great over-extension in a westerly direction of the Missouri-Platte drainage system and the representation of broken mountain ranges west of the Missouri's headwaters with several openings in the mountain barrier near the source streams of the Missouri—openings which may, perhaps, be viewed as cartographic modifications of theories on the plateau-plains nature of river source regions.[29] Of the two views of the West presented in the *Atlas*, the Lewis representation of Louisiana was larger than life. The Stoney Mountains were close to the Great South Sea, and through the breaks in those mountains the representatives of the ideal agrarian republic could flow down to the shores washed by waves from China.

The United States in 1804 was an agricultural nation with an administration in Washington based on the Jeffersonian assumptions of the ideal agrarian republic. In spite of the fact that among some segments of American society—particularly in the urban centers of the Northeast—agrarian expansionism was viewed with disfavor, most American images of the Louisiana territory seem to have been colored by the feeling that the United States must maintain vast areas for the expansion of an agricultural population if she were to remain a republic.[30] The majority opinions among Americans on the land quality of the West, then, were based on hope and optimism—a hope that the lands to the west would provide a firm base for the agrarian republic and an optimism that this must be the case.

Detractors had put forth the view that the West was "an absolute barren" or a "dreary tract" and, indeed, some of the reports of the most recent explorers in the West (insofar as these reports were available) could have substantiated this notion. But these critics were not in the majority. The predominating concept of the West was that it was indeed a garden, with extremely fertile soil, climates benign, soft, and salubrious.[31] Immense plains might, as many accounts put it, stretch as far as the southern ocean, but these plains were not barren, sandy nor even partially arid. They were verdant, lush, teeming with game and, most important, available for the spread of an agricultural population. The rivers flowed among the most beautiful dales; the Mississippi and other rivers of Louisiana were analogous to Niles which diffused the fertility of Egypt from their banks. The West was full of hope.

Like the views of the land itself, the ideas on what the land contained were seemingly based on this agrarian tradition. For centuries, wealth in gold, gems, and other precious minerals had been sought toward the sunset, but in the American images of the West in 1804, few elements of the El Dorado remained. The choicest luxuries of the West were the lush vegetation and the salubrious climate. Some authorities might have held that the lands of the West contained precious minerals in their bowels but the folk emphasis on mineral wealth was more practical.[32] The West contained lead, iron, and salt, basic needs of a frontier agricultural people; gold and silver and gems could come later.

According to what seems to have been the majority opinion, the area of Louisiana was a well-watered region, with many streams available for millsites, and rivers available for transportation.[33] Little was actually known about major rivers such as the Red, the Arkansas, the Missouri or the Columbia; virtually nothing was known of the Kansas, Platte, Yellowstone, Snake, and others.[34] Americans tended to think about the western rivers in general terms, and all the rivers of Louisiana were apparently accorded the same characteristics of length, size, and navigability that had been mentioned in accounts of the Mississippi and Missouri.[35] Like the many other things in the West, the rivers were seen as having majestic proportions: "Each step which one takes from East to West, the size of all objects increases ten fold in volume. It seems that nature has made this corner of the terrestrial globe the most favorite of its immense sphere. The products which one discovers there in proportion as one goes into the interior are more majestic, more beautiful than elsewhere."[36]

There was also a gap in American geographic knowledge relative to the lakes of western North America. The concepts of great lakes or inland seas in the western interior, an important feature in the geographical lore of earlier times, does not seem to have formed a major element in the American images of Louisiana.[37] The fact that some few Americans held to the earlier notions of huge inland seas was important to the overall nature of the patterns of belief about the territory, for from the inland lakes emanated the mythical and the fantastic. Associated with the inland seas of earlier lore and still a partial feature of American thought about the West were tribes of white Indians, bearded Indians, civilized Indians, Welsh Indians, golden cities, alabaster cities, mythical beasts, and all the hosts of fancy that have always been part of the literature of the American West.

American ideas about the symmetrical drainage patterns of North America were more important. The tenets of theoretical geography had provided a common source area for the major North American rivers somewhere in the interior, and it is possible that this concept was widely accepted.[38] When it was combined with the theoretical assumptions of the long-range navigational possibilities of the western rivers, it provided a rational basis for the hope of establishing an all-water communication from the Atlantic to the Pacific.[39] This all-water communication, like the notions of land quality, was an important feature of the optimism with which Americans viewed the newly acquired territory. Through the channels of communication with which the West was blessed, the agricultural produce that was a necessary adjunct of the great fertility of the western lands might find new outlets—even into the shores of China and Japan:

> Rejoice, ye too, rejoice ye swains,
> Increasing commerce shall reward your cares.
> A day will come if not too deep we drink
> The cup which luxury on careless wealth
> Pernicious gift bestows; a day will come
> When through new channels we shall clothe
> The California coast, and all the realms
> That stretch from Anian's Streights to proud Japan.[40]

Certain agreements might have prevailed in the images regarding the fertility of the West or the size and navigability of western rivers. No such agreement pertained to the view of the western mountains. Called by various names, the western mountains were shifting, misty, and illusory features. They were viewed as an unbroken chain running three thousand miles north from Mexico. Or they terminated around the forty-seventh or fifty-eighth parallel of latitude and left the way open to the Pacific. They were a very high range of mountains, perhaps highest on the continent or maybe even in the world. Or they were simple ridges or hills of no great size and extent. The concept of the mountains as a continental divide which separated the "rivers and streams, sending some to the Atlantic and others to the Pacific," seems to have been grasped by some.[41] But even this notion was a contradiction in the face of the conflicting view that the major rivers of the continent had their sources in an area that could best be described as a pyramidal height-of-land.

The opposing views on the mountains as either source or separator of the western rivers were made less contradictory by

several theories on the nature of the mountains themselves. Some
believed it possible that the Shining Mountains ran without break
from north to south. Alexander Mackenzie, the British explorer
whose widely read journals fixed the nature of the mountains in
the minds of many, admitted that he did not know how far south
of this crossing the mountains extended, and that it was therefore
possible that breaks in the backbone of the continent might be
found below the fiftieth parallel.[42] Jonathan Carver, another traveler
and also a primary source of information, reported (and American
geography books relayed the information) that a southern range
of mountains called "the mountains of New Mexico" terminated
between forty-seven and forty-eight degrees north latitude and that
between them and the Shining Mountains on the north there might
be an area of level ground.[43] It was in this area of level ground
that, in Carver's theoretical scheme, the common source area for
the "capital" North American rivers—including the Columbia and
Missouri—would be found. This view, probably accepted by many
Americans, including some of the best informed, made possible
both the recognition of a range of mountains that acted as a
continental divide and the retention of the concept of a common
source area for the major rivers of the West.[44] The implications of
such a rationalization for those who desired the all-water route to
the Pacific are obvious.

Perhaps the most inaccurate notions about the western
mountains were those relative to size, extent, and location. The
altitude of the Shining Mountains was a matter of great conjecture
and although some unreliable sources had reported extreme
elevation, few specific measurements were available. The most
widely read and reliable scientific periodical of the day, the *Medical
Repository*, reported that the Shining Mountains were "in some
places as much as 3250 feet high above the level of their base which
is, perhaps, 3000 feet above the sea."[45] It is clear that the true
height of the Rockies (either in terms of their vertical rise or of
their base height above sea level) was not even remotely grasped.

Also inaccurate was the popular conceptualization of the
mountains as a single ridge. Most of the travel accounts which had
reported the crossing of the mountains—and it matters not whether
those reports were fictional, as most of them certainly were—

described the passage as one of relative ease. Even the accurate and factual journals of Alexander Mackenzie who had indeed crossed the Rocky Mountains spoke in terms of a simple portage of 817 paces across a slight ridge of land as the only break in water transportation from the Atlantic to the Pacific drainage. Mackenzie's information was accurate for the area between the headwaters of the Mackenzie-Athabasca and the Fraser River, but Mackenzie and virtually everyone else believed the river he discovered on the western side of the divide to be the upper Columbia. If only a simple ridge separated the Peace River from the Columbia, so the theoretical reasoning went, then it was likely that only a simple ridge lay between the head of the Missouri and the source region of the southern branches of the Columbia. In the minds of many Americans, the crossing of the Shining Mountains would certainly not be an insurmountable or even difficult task, and if the great navigability of the streams which flowed from the mountains were considered, then the crossing could be viewed with even more optimism.[46]

The location of the mountains relative to the Pacific Coast was a matter for conjecture also, and the Shining Mountains shifted from east to west and back again, depending on the authority. From much of the British information, it was clear that the mountains lay somewhere between the 112th and 115th meridians, and this view appeared on many available maps, including those by Arrowsmith. But other popular sources of information pushed the mountains farther west, toward the Pacific. Reports from the Spanish officials in Louisiana during the last decade of the eighteenth century had entered American geographical lore through correspondence from Americans living on the western frontier, and many of those reports indicated that the western ranges could not be far from the shores of the South Sea—perhaps as close as forty leagues or about one hundred miles. Alexander Mackenzie, always the primary authority on western geography, added that the mountains he had crossed in Canada closely paralleled the coast.[47] The generalized image of the Shining Mountains was of a low, single ridge which was fairly close to the Pacific and which might well have breaks in the chain where the sources of the Atlantic waters approached those of the Pacific. If one view were held in common about the mountains of the West, it was that they provided no great barrier to the expansion of American commerce and population toward the Pacific.

If geographical knowledge of the West can be envisioned as three dimensional, then the Louisiana territory in American lore of 1804 can best be described as a basin, surrounded by ridges of better knowledge and grading into a fast, flat interior surface of pure conjecture, broken here and there by peaks of better understanding or more information. Exploration by the French and Spanish in the lower reaches of the Mississippi's western tributaries, by the British across the continent north of the lands encompassed in the purchase, and by the British and Spanish along the coast of the Pacific Northwest meant that fairly reliable geographical information was available for the periphery of Louisiana. The quality of absolute knowledge graded downward swiftly toward the interior, into those areas contacted briefly by the fur trade or partially known through Indian information and finally into those areas of the interior that were virtually unknown. Some islands of better information, such as the Great Bend of the Upper Missouri that was reached by both the British from the north and the Spanish-sponsored explorers from the south, appeared as enclaves of higher quality knowledge within the partially known or unknown area.

From this geographical lore, literate Americans developed patterns of belief about the nature and content of Louisiana, images that were accurate for some sections of the territory but imperfect when applied, as they were, to the Northwest as a whole.[48] If Americans tended to view the Louisiana territory as a garden, it was because the greatest volume of geographical information— that obtained from the lands bordering the Mississippi—presented such a picture. If the rivers were considered as oversized, it was because they had been observed only in their lower reaches. If the mountains were seen as low, single ridges that were close to the Pacific, it was because the only mountains with which most Americans were familiar fit such a description, as did the mountains which were crossed by the British fur trade in Canada. Like geographic knowledge itself, the images can be graded for quality. In the gradation can be seen the impact of the geography of hope and desire.

When Americans first began to think seriously about the lands west of the Mississippi, following the cession of Louisiana, their thoughts were colored with the teleology which conditions knowledge. Louisiana was outsized, and it stretched to the shores of the Pacific. Its rivers were wide, deep, long, and navigable to their sources. The things that were to be seen in Louisiana were more majestic, more beautiful than elsewhere. The soil was the best in the world, the climate was easy, and the native inhabitants resembled races of Homeric proportions. In the very beginning of American thought about the West, those lands were lands of opportunity. Louisiana would provide the home for the expansion of the ideal agrarian republic and through its vast river systems, connecting with short portages all the way to the Pacific and the Orient beyond, that republic might achieve what would soon be spoken of as her "manifest destiny."

Notes

1. Although neither term is completely accurate in a purely historical sense, "Louisiana" and "Louisiana territory" will be used to refer only to that portion of the Mississippi basin between the Continental Divide and the Mississippi itself.

2. Washington, D.C. *National Intelligencer*, August 10, 1803.

3. Charles B. Brown, *An Address to the Government of the United States on the Cession of Louisiana . . .* (Philadelphia, 1803), 16.

4. Thomas Jefferson to Governor Breckinridge, August 12, 1803, folios 23144-46, vol. 134, Jefferson Papers, Manuscripts Division, Library of Congress, Washington, D.C. (hereafter Jefferson Papers).

5. Marquette began the chain of exploration up the Missouri when he described that river as heading in an area close to another river which flowed to the Pacific. See Reuben Gold Thwaites, ed., *The Jesuit Relations* (Cleveland, Ohio, 1907), 59:87-163.

6. This lore was not necessarily different in content from other lore on the West. It was, however, "geoamerican" knowledge, interpreted by Americans in ways that were distinctly different from the interpretations given it by other peoples. See John K. Wright, "What's American about American Geography," in *Human Nature in Geography: Fourteen Papers, 1925–1965* (Cambridge, Mass., 1966), 124-39.

7. American interest in the passage is nowhere more evident than in the objective of the Lewis and Clark Expedition of 1804–6 as stated by Jefferson:

"The object of your mission is to explore the Missouri river, & such principal stream of it, as, by it's course and communication with the waters of the Pacific ocean, whether the Columbia, Oregan, Colorado or any other river may offer the most direct & practicable water communication across this continent for the purposes of commerce." Jefferson to Meriwether Lewis, June 20, 1803, fols. 22884-87, vol. 132, Jefferson Papers, reprinted in this volume, 31-38.

8. W. M. P., *A Poem on the Acquisition of Louisiana: Respectfully Dedicated . . . in this City* (Charleston, S.C., 1804), 20. The term "desart" is not used in a climatic sense but refers to a country devoid of settlement.

9. An authority on America's attitudes about manifest destiny wrote that "soberminded elements in both political parties in the period prior to the War of 1812 consigned such revealers of God's purpose [those who favored western expansion as the natural right of the Republic] to the outer edge of the lunatic fringe." Frederick Merk, *Manifest Destiny and Mission in American History* (New York, 1963), 13. This might well be an accurate statement but it is misleading. Many historians have failed to recognize the difference between the opinion of the elite, which was nonexpansionist, and the opinion of the nonelite or folk opinion, which tended to be expansionist in nature.

10. The qualification of "literate" is necessary since the nature of images for this period can be examined only in written documents. The qualification does not imply that "nonliterate" images were different from the "literate" ones—although there is virtually no way to test this. If all the various types of images were described, it probably would be found that there was much greater similarity between the "literate" and "nonliterate" images than between the elite and folk views of the western lands.

11. In examining the source material, the author consulted virtually all hardcover publications containing information on Louisiana that would have been available at the time of the purchase and a representative sample of the 1803–4 periodical literature. Although the total volume of this information was considerable, the actual content was limited since items on Louisiana found their way not only into one or two papers or magazines, but were reprinted in most major newspapers and many other periodical publications. In addition, material from the travel accounts, correspondence, and geographies was extracted and printed in periodicals. Therefore, whereas a total count of items on the geography of Louisiana might list between five hundred and six hundred titles, the actual number of items is only about one-quarter of that amount. The references below include only a few selected titles from this mass of data. A full listing may be found in the bibliography of John L. Allen, "Geographical Images of the American Northwest, 1673–1806" (doctoral diss., Clark University, 1969), particularly 779-83 and 789-95.

12. The accounts of Jonathan Carver, *Travels through the Interior Parts*

of North America (London, 1781); Robert Rogers, *Concise Account of North America* (London, 1765); and Alexander Mackenzie, *Voyages from Montreal . . . to the Frozen and Pacific Oceans*, 2 vols. (London, 1801), were of primary importance, being more widely advertised than any comparative volumes and appearing more often as extracts in such periodicals as Boston's *Weekly Magazine*, Washington, D.C.'s *National Magazine*, New York's *American Magazine*, and Philadelphia's *American Museum*. Extracts also appeared in important geographies, including Jedidiah Morse, *American Universal Geography* (Boston, 1803); and John Pinkerton, *Modern Geography* (Philadelphia, 1804).

13. The most popular French travel narratives were those of the La Salle expeditions such as Henri Joutel, *A Journal of the Last Voyage Performed by Monsr. de la Salle* (London, 1714); various editions of the relations of Father Louis Hennepin and the geographies of the French Jesuit traveler, Pierre Charlevoix in *A Voyage to North America* (Dublin, 1766). While not reprinted in America, the above volumes were available from booksellers in the major cities of the Northeast. Furthermore, the authors of these narratives were cited as the best authorities on the geography of Louisiana in such American works as Thomas Hutchins, *An Historical Narrative and Topographical Description of Louisiana and West Florida* (Philadelphia, 1784); William Winterbotham, *An Historical Geographical, Commercial and Philosophical View of the United States . . .* , 4 vols. (New York, 1796); and *A Topographical and Statistical Account of the Province of Louisiana* (Baltimore, 1803). Of additional importance were the relations of Le Page du Pratz, *History of Louisiana* (London, 1763); Daniel Coxe, *Carolana* (London, 1741); Louis Lahontan, *New Voyages to North America* (London, 1703); and Jean Bossu, *Travels through That Part of North American Formerly Called Louisiana* (London, 1771).

14. Only one of the American accounts came from an actual expedition. This was Thomas Hutchins, *Historical Narrative and Topographical Description for Louisiana and West Florida*, a journal of a surveying trip in the Mississippi valley by Hutchins—"the official geographer to the United States." The remainder of the American accounts consisted of Don Alonzo Decalves, *Travels to the Westward* (Keene, N.H., 1794); John Vandelure, *Narrative of a Voyage . . . to the Western Continent* (Windsor, Conn., 1801); and numerous extracts of the western travels of a Captain Isaac Stuart (*American Museum*, August 1787) were purely fictional. In spite of their apocryphal nature they exerted considerable influence on American images.

15. The more important Spanish-sponsored explorers in Louisiana—Jean Truteau, James Mackay, and John Evans—did contribute to American literature on the West, but their accounts were not published until after 1804.

16. The best example is Alexander Mackenzie *Voyages from Montreal*, the

central theme of which was the establishment of such a route. The popularity of this account—advertised more than any other contemporary travel volume—suggests that Americans were interested in his comments on the topic.

17. Such tales appear throughout French Louisiana chronicles, but the most frequently referred to is the story of an Indian traveler named Moncacht-Apé. The most contemporary account appeared in du Pratz, *An Account of Louisiana* (Newburgh, N.Y., 1803).

18. Washington, D.C. *National Intelligencer*, September 26, 1803.

19. Ibid., October 24, 1803.

20. It is no surprise that Americans tended to think of Louisiana in uniform geographic terms. Out of a total of eighty-seven separate newspaper articles dealing with the value of the purchase in 1803–4, only three make any distinction among various parts of Louisiana and only one provides any distinguishing geographical information that sets the area above the mouth of the Ohio apart from the rest of the territory. A related question deals with the American conception of the size and boundaries of the territory as acquired from France. Like the problem of regional variation, the question of limits and bounds was simply not soluble given the limited amount of information.

21. Since nearly all American citizens resident in Louisiana or in the eastern borderlands of the Mississippi lived below the mouth of the Ohio, most descriptions applied to the area known as "lower" Louisiana.

22. Typical of this type of correspondence was that of Dr. John Sibley of Natchitoches, Louisiana, whose descriptive letters found their way into at least a dozen major newspapers in 1803 and 1804. The letters dealt almost exclusively with the climate of Louisiana, described as being "akin to that of China or India," and with the abundance of game animals in western lands comparative to "the finest countries in the world, abounding with rich prairies stocked with buffaloes, wild horses, mules, hogs, antelopes, &c. and no hostile Indians to contend with." See, for example, Sibley's letters in the Baltimore *Federal Gazette*, January 10 and 12, 1803.

23. The journals of Jean Truteau, James Mackay, and John Evans contain frequent references to barrenness and sterility. The fact that these accounts were not available in 1804 may have been partially responsible for the lack of a similar tradition in the American views on the West.

24. The best example is the correspondence of "Viator," which first appeared in the Cincinnati *Western Spy* and later in several eastern papers, including the Washington, D.C. *National Intelligencer*, October 21, 1803. "Viator" not only described major portions of the West as "sterile or sandy" but also repeated the legends of continental traverses by Indians.

25. There were two types of geographical references—textbooks designed for grammar school use and general geographies written for the public.

The former included Benjamin Workman, *Elements of Geography* (Philadelphia, 1803), and Robert Davidson, *Geography Epitomized* (Norristown, Pa., 1803); the latter consisted of Morse, *American Geography*, and John Pinkerton, *Modern Geography*.

26. This view was illustrated in one of the elementary geographies which described the Continental Divide as, "Another vast range, far-reflecting the sun,/ Three thousand miles northward from Mexico run,/ Dividing the waters which flow far to the west,/ From those that roll on to the Atlantic in haste." Davidson, *Geography Epitomized*, 50.

27. The concept of a pyramidal height-of-land appeared in geographical writings as early as the sixth century, A.D. It was applied to North America by the Canadian French and appeared in geographical lore in the United States through the travel accounts of Jonathan Carver. By 1803, the concept was firm enough to be stated by Pinkerton: "The four most capital rivers on the continent of North America, viz., THE ST. LAWRENCE, THE MISSISSIPPI, THE RIVER BOURBON [NELSON], AND THE OREGON [COLUMBIA] OR RIVER OF THE WEST, have their sources in the same neighbourhood . . . within thirty miles of each other . . .," Pinkerton, *Modern Geography*, 1:414. America's premier geographer, Jedidiah Morse, held to the height-of-land theory but saw it as an upland plateau between northern and southern mountain ranges, "in about 47 and 48 N lat., where a number of rivers rise and empty themselves into either the N. Pacific ocean, into Hudson's Bay, into the waters which lie between them, or into the Atlantic Ocean." See Morse, "Shining Mountains," Boston *American Gazetteer*, 1803. Detailed discussion of the pyramidal height-of-land concept may be found in Allen, "Geographical Images," relevant sections of chapters 1-5.

28. The contrast between the two maps seems to be the result of different source materials. Where the North America map is most probably drawn following the information of the British fur trade circa 1800 and resembles nearly all other maps drawn by Arrowsmith, the Louisiana map, drawn by Samuel Lewis of Philadelphia, seems to be an offshoot of French and Spanish manuscript materials. It is probable that the Louisiana map is more representative of the American view of the West than is the general map of North America.

29. The most obvious reason Lewis would have drawn an overextended Missouri system is that he apparently followed a map drawn around 1795 by Antoine Soulard, the surveyor-general of Spanish Louisiana. The Soulard map—very similar in appearance to the Lewis map—showed such lengthening and represented the widespread view among Americans that the Missouri was a much longer river than it actually is. For an expansion of this idea and its importance for American attitudes see Allen, "Geographical Images," 256-58.

30. The greatest volume of criticism of the administration's action in acquiring Louisiana was found in the newspapers and pamphlets of Boston, Hartford, New York, and Philadelphia. Slightly less than 25 percent of the references to the territory in those papers commented on any advantages to be gained by an expansion of American population into the purchased lands. The picture is different for newspapers from rural locations in the same general area of the Northeast. More than two-thirds of the references to the value of the purchase in those papers viewed the acquisition of new agricultural territories favorably.

31. Out of a total of 134 items related to Louisiana or the West in the materials consulted from 1804, 54 items made direct reference to land quality. Within those 54 items, the word "fertile" appeared thirty-six times; "benign," fourteen times; and "salubrious," twenty-seven times. "Verdant," "fine," and "beautiful," each appeared between five and ten times, and "lush" was used three times. By contrast, the words "barren," "sterile," or "waste" appeared twice, three times, and once respectively. The word "desert" was not used in any of the 54 land quality descriptions.

32. In spite of the fact that some of the more important source materials mentioned the wealth of precious and semiprecious minerals to be found in the West, only five out of twenty-nine references to minerals in the 1804 publication referred to precious metals or stones.

33. A total of twenty-one items provided some description of the rivers and streams of Louisiana and of these twenty-one items, the term "well-watered" appeared thirteen times. In none of the twenty-one items was it suggested that Louisiana was water deficient. Fifteen of the items mentioned either long-range navigation or mill site location as advantages of the rivers of Louisiana.

34. A total of eighty-six items mentioned (although not necessarily described) rivers by name; in each of these items the Mississippi was mentioned. The Missouri was mentioned in all but four, the Red River appeared in thirty-two items and the Arkansas River in nineteen. The Columbia or "Oregan" was mentioned eleven times, and the Kansas and Platte once each.

35. The overenthusiastic estimates of the size and navigability of western rivers did not begin to erode until after the Lewis and Clark Expedition and even then slowly. Even such careful observers as Lewis and Clark consistently overestimated the length and degree of navigability of the rivers they passed. Allen, "Geographical Images," chaps. 6-8.

36. From a letter written by Louis Vilemont, a traveler in Spanish Louisiana during the opening years of the nineteenth century. Cited in A. P. Nasatir, ed., *Before Lewis and Clark: Documents Illustrating the History of the Missouri, 1785–1804* (St. Louis, 1952), 2:690-703.

37. Great lakes or huge inland seas in the lands west of the Mississippi were mentioned in only 4 of the 134 items consulted.

38. Only 4 items out of the 134 that related to Louisiana or the West described the source area of the major rivers; each of these 4, however, gave a description based on either Morse or Pinkerton. In spite of the lack of commentary on the common source area in the 1804 material, it would seem logical to assume that the notion was well fixed since the common source area was described in so many of the geographical writings of the period.

39. This type of rationalization led Thomas Jefferson to plan and sponsor the Lewis and Clark Expedition of 1804–6. Prior to his first term as president, Jefferson had made several attempts to locate the connection between the Missouri and the Columbia for the purpose of establishing an all-water transportation route between the Atlantic and Pacific. His plans were never carried through until he dispatched Lewis and Clark to find "the most direct & practicable water communication across this continent for the purposes of commerce" via the Missouri and Columbia rivers.

40. This poem, possibly by Isaiah Thomas of Worcester and Boston, first appeared in Boston's *Royal American Magazine*, January 1774. During 1803 and 1804 it was reprinted in broadside form and circulated widely, particularly in New England.

41. *The Medical Repository*, 1 (second hexad, 1804), 393.

42. Mackenzie, *Voyages from Montreal*, 2:346-48.

43. Jonathan Carver, *Travels through the Interior Parts of North America* (London, 1781), 121.

44. A close examination of the correspondence among Thomas Jefferson, Albert Gallatin, and the members of the American Philosophical Society indicates such a conception among the best scientists of the day. Allen, "Geographical Images," 401-8.

45. *The Medical Repository*, 5 (first hexad, 1802), 462. The same information is noted in caption form on Aaron Arrowsmith's maps of North America published in 1796 and 1802.

46. It is true that, in many cases, only a slight height-of-land separates the furthermost sources of the western rivers. But in 1804, the notion that mountain rivers, such as the Missouri, might be navigable nearly to their sources was an idea set forth and followed by theoretical geographers. Once western exploration commenced, however, such illusions were destroyed.

47. Mackenzie, *Voyages from Montreal*, 2:346.

48. People do not like blank spaces in their images any more than cartographers like blank spaces on maps and therefore tend to take information from "known" areas and expand it into areas for which information is not available or is nonexistent.

Jefferson, Meriwether Lewis, and the Reduction of the United States Army

Donald Jackson

THE AMERICAN PEOPLE HAVE ALWAYS DISLIKED THE IDEA of a large regular army in peacetime. In the early days of the Republic, however, America began to discover that some kind of standing army was essential; militia was not always enough.

Immediately after the Revolution, the Congress began to divest itself of the army that had defeated Cornwallis at Yorktown. Despite some dissenting voices, soldiers who had enlisted to serve for the duration of the war were discharged. By January 1784, Major General Henry Knox, the new commander, could report that only about 620 men were still in service—and the bottom figure was still to come. In June of that year, Congress discharged all but 25 men who were to be posted to Fort Pitt and West Point to protect materiel. No officer above the rank of captain was retained in service.[1]

Almost at once, the thinking of Congress had to change. Indian hostilities in the Old Northwest, and the refusal of Great Britain to vacate certain garrisons, necessitated new enlistments and the building of new forts on the frontier. When these threats were lessened somewhat by the signing of Jay's Treaty with England in 1794, and the Treaty of Greenville with the Indians in 1795, tensions were eased—and then another new threat appeared. Misunderstandings between the United States and France, eventually to result in the standoff now called the Quasi-War, prompted Congress to authorize a provisional army of 10,000 men for a period not to exceed three years.[2] When the excitement cooled without any land confrontation with France, that temporary quantum jump in the number of armed forces was reversed. In the final months of the John Adams administration, in 1800, the United States forces consisted mainly of four regiments of infantry, two of artillerists and engineers, and two of light dragoons.[3] This was the army that Jefferson took over as commander-in-chief, upon his assumption of office in 1801.

Jefferson had run for the presidency on a platform calling for even greater reductions; the discharge of the provisional army was not enough to satisfy the Republican demand for a minimum standing army. When he took office, Jefferson commanded an authorized force of 5,400 officers and men. By the end of his first year, he and the Congress were to eliminate the cavalry, cut back the number of artillerists and engineers, and thus pare the army enrollment to about one-half.[4]

The new president did not know the military as well as he might have. He knew the army, but that was a different thing. The army was that great force in government about which he could talk knowledgeably with generals and cabinet officers, discussing balance of power, regimental strength, deployment, and logistics. The military were the officers and men of that army, and Jefferson had never been one of them; he had never worn a uniform.

Reducing the number of enlisted men would be no problem, for actually the maintaining of regiments up to authorized strength had always been difficult. But reducing the officer corps required a different approach. These career professionals must be dealt with as individuals, some to stay and some to go.

By midsummer following his election, Jefferson had received from the War Department a roster or roll of all his commissioned officers, listed with their rank and the units they commanded or to which they were assigned.[5] Most certainly there were men on the roster who were longtime friends and associates of Jefferson: Brigadier General James Wilkinson, the commanding general; Major Thomas H. Cushing, the adjutant and inspector; and such familiar names as John F. Hamtramck, commanding the First

Infantry, and old Major Zebulon Pike, of the Third Infantry, the father of the famous explorer.

But most of the officers on the roster were strangers to Jefferson, and he would need to rely upon someone else to tell him who the potential leaders were, as well as the incompetents, and to identify those officers as Republican or Federalist. That the Federalists would be in the majority he could have no doubt, for party patronage had become an aspect of military policy under the administration of John Adams.

The measure that Jefferson took to obtain a profile of the army is shown upon the roster, dated July 24, 1801. After each officer's name, one or more symbols appear. They are mysterious marks—circles, crosses, and combinations of dots—intended to be understood only by someone who possessed a key to the symbols. That key, written on a single sheet of paper, is present with the roster in the Jefferson papers at the Library of Congress. On it the symbols are given such meanings as these: officers who are superior; those who are respectable but not superior; those unfit to serve; officers who are Republicans, or Federalists, and—the ultimate downgrading—those "most violently opposed to the Administration and still active in its vilification."

These symbols, and the sheet explaining their meaning, have until recently been described as being "in an unknown hand."[6] They are, in fact, in the hand of a young man whose name is a familiar one today wherever American history is read. It is the hand of Meriwether Lewis, of the Lewis and Clark Expedition.

While we cannot assume with certainty that Lewis made the evaluations, merely because the symbols are in his handwriting, a reexamination of his relationship with Jefferson renders this assumption quite tenable.

Nothing in the Lewis and Clark story is more firmly believed than the tradition that Jefferson hired Meriwether Lewis in 1801, not as a secretary or aide, but as a trainee for a transcontinental expedition. Lewis was a hometown boy whom Jefferson had known since childhood. He had received some conventional grammar-school education with classical overtones and had absorbed a greater than average interest in natural history. Much of his knowledge was self-acquired. He seemed born to rise, in the agricultural-

Explanation of the notes set opposite (in the column of remarks) to
to the names of the several officers composing the Army of the
United States. ———

o — Denotes such officers as are of the 1st Class, so esteemed from
         superiority of genius & Military proficiency.

: — Ditto   Ditto second class, respectable as Officers, but not
         altogether entitled to the 1st grade ——

oo — Ditto   Ditto. Republican.

‖ — Ditto Officers whose political opinions are not positively ascertained

‡ — Ditto Political apathy

X: — Ditto opposed to the administration, otherwise respectable officers.

†† — Ditto opposed to the administration more decisively. ———

†††††† Ditto   Ditto most violently to d°. and still active in its vilification

:: — ditto professionally the soldier without any political creed ——

#. — Ditto. unworthy of the commissions they bear ——

——— .— ditto unknown to us. ———

Key to the symbols used by Meriwether Lewis in evaluating officers

mercantile circles of Virginia, and he chose one of the most
routinely traveled routes; a career in the United States Army.

Joining the militia during the Whiskey Rebellion in 1794, Lewis
moved north and languished in various cantonments in western
Maryland and Pennsylvania, deciding the following year to try life
in the regular army. He was appointed ensign in the second
sublegion in 1795, transferring the next year to the First Infantry
Regiment. This was to be his outfit for the duration of his military
career. His active duty was spent partly in the recruiting service
and partly as a paymaster. As a special messenger for General
Anthony Wayne, and as paymaster to his regiment, he traveled

much. During a furlough he went to Kentucky on family business, and his duties took him from post to post in the Ohio Valley: Fort Wayne, Detroit, Pittsburgh, and Cincinnati.

Soon after Jefferson learned the results of the election that made him president, he wrote young Lewis and offered him a position as his secretary. Sending the request through channels, he told General Wilkinson that he thought it would be advantageous "to take one who possessing a knolege of the Western country, of the army & it's situation, might sometimes aid us with informations of interest, which we may not otherwise possess." He used similar language in his letter to Lewis himself, saying "Your knolege of the Western country, of the army and of all it's interests & relations has rendered it desirable for public as well as private purpose that you should be engaged in that office."[7]

At this point, historians go astray by stacking one conjecture upon another. They reason that Jefferson had long wished for an expedition to the Pacific; that he was at last in a position to carry out such an operation; and that he placed Lewis on his staff so that he could personally guide the study and preparation necessary for such an expedition. Dozens of books and articles on the expedition contain these assumptions.

To accept this easy train of events is to sidestep several matters about which we can never be entirely informed. It is true that Jefferson had since 1783 shown specific signs that he valued the idea of a transcontinental exploration. He had asked George Rogers Clark in that year how he would like to lead such an enterprise, and Clark had declined. He had helped the American Philosophical Society to raise the money and draw the plans for botanist André Michaux, who proposed to visit the Pacific Coast but whose plans were canceled. In both these instances, Jefferson apparently was acting as a private citizen. But during the seven years he served in the federal government, in the 1790s, he did nothing whatsoever to press for a government-sponsored expedition. His correspondence during the last half of the 1790s contains almost nothing about the American West.

Perhaps what brought Jefferson's thoughts back to hemispheric geography was the publication of a book in London. Late in 1801, Alexander Mackenzie's *Voyages . . . Through the Continent of North*

America, to the Frozen and Pacific Ocean was published; copies were available in Philadelphia and New York within a short time. Jefferson already knew something of Mackenzie's travels, but his first knowledge of the book probably came in a letter from Dr. Caspar Wistar, of Philadelphia, who frequently sent the president bits of new information. In January 1802, he wrote: "Have you seen McKenzie's account of his journeys across the Continent & to the Northern Ocean?"[8] He was referring, of course, to Mackenzie's expedition across Canada—during which he reached the Pacific. At the end of Mackenzie's narrative, he had urged the British government to lose no time in establishing a trading post in the Pacific Northwest, to gain control of the very profitable trade with the Orient in sea-otter skins. Mackenzie's suggestion was filled with implications for the control not only of the fur trade but of an enormously important part of the continent.

Jefferson ordered a copy of Mackenzie's book, probably receiving it in the summer of 1802.[9] During August he had as a house guest his old Philadelphia friend, and member of the American Philosophical Society, Benjamin Smith Barton. Barton's travel diary for the period is missing or was not kept, so we have no record of his stay at Monticello. The two men might well have discussed the Far West, as Barton had been a participant in the earlier plan to send Michaux to the Pacific. It is not likely, however, that Jefferson mentioned a specific new western enterprise; we may suspect this because, when he finally informed Barton that he was sending Lewis and Clark to the Pacific, some months later, he wrote in terms that suggest he was then advising his friend for the first time.[10]

Sometime within the weeks immediately following Barton's visit, Jefferson must have decided to act. By early December 1802, he had approached the Spanish minister to the United States, Carlos Martínez de Irujo, setting forth his plan to explore the course of the Missouri River, cross the Rocky Mountains, and descend the western watercourses to the Pacific.[11] It appears, then, that Jefferson's decision to set on foot what was to become the Lewis and Clark Expedition was made about a year and a half after he had hired Lewis as a member of his staff.

In reviewing the wording of Jefferson's first letter, offering Lewis the post of secretary, perhaps we have been paying attention to the wrong phrase. The two key phrases in the message are: *Your knolege of the Western country* and *the army and of all it's interests & relations.* By "western country" Jefferson meant the Ohio Valley. Lewis had traveled there and knew what the westerners were thinking—a matter of deep concern to Jefferson, who had to be alert to the separatist elements on the outer edge of his constituency. An intelligent young officer who had recently traveled as far as Kentucky could be useful, especially if he were someone long known and trusted by Jefferson.

The phrase mentioning "the army and all it's interests & relations" may be the more important one. Here was a young military man who could be expected to evaluate for Jefferson, in complete candor, the officers of high and low rank whom he had come to know so well as he traveled his paymaster's route. If one can read into Lewis's knowledge of the "western country" the potential for a transcontinental expedition, it is equally logical to see in Jefferson's reference to "the army and all it's interests" an assignment to help him with the task of reshaping the military forces.

Below is the list of qualifications which Lewis set forth on his sheet of symbols, then transferred to the roster. For simplicity the symbols have been converted to letters of the alphabet, and the wording slightly altered. Lewis called the listing: "Explanation of the notes set opposite (in the column of remarks) to the names of the several officers composing the Army of the United States."

[a] Denotes such officers as are of the 1st Class, so esteemed from a superiority of genius & Military proficiency.

[b] Officers of the second class, respectable as officers, but not altogether entitled to the 1st grade.

[c] The same. Republican.

[d] Officers whose political opinions are not positively ascertained.

[e] Political apathy.

[f] Opposed to the Administration, otherwise respectable officers.

[g] Opposed to the Administration more decisively.

[h] Most violently opposed to the administration and still active

in its vilification.

[i] Professionally the soldier without any political creed. ·

[j] Unworthy of the commissions they bear.

[k] Unknown to us.

Tables 1 and 2 present some data compiled from the roster of officers and the evaluations added by Lewis. Table 1, showing distribution of officers by state, would have come as no surprise to Jefferson; a large proportion of his officers came from the more heavily populated Federalist states in the Northeast. In Table 2, the data have been adapted and simplified; for example, Lewis's three categories of Federalist, ranging from mild to unregenerate, have been combined under a single heading.

It is clear that in the winnowing process, military qualifications

TABLE 1			
DISTRIBUTION OF OFFICERS BY PLACE OF ORIGIN*			
Connecticut	14	Pennsylvania	46
Delaware	2	Rhode Island	3
Georgia	4	South Carolina	8
Kentucky	5	Tennessee	3
Maryland	32	Vermont	6
Massachusetts	34	Virginia	36
Mississippi	1	Canada	1
New Hampshire	4	France	5
New Jersey	12	England	3
New York	26	Ireland	7
North Carolina	9	Scotland	1
Northwest Terr.	1	Switzerland	1
	Germany	4	

*Names on the roster total 269, but 1 officer, Richard Skinner, is not listed by place of origin. States or countries on the roster do not always correspond with those in Francis B. Heitman, *Historical Register and Dictionary of the United States Army* (Washington, 1903).

	TABLE 2 EVALUATION OF OFFICERS IN SERVICE*	
	In service July 24, 1801	Retained June 1, 1802
Superior [a]		
Republican [c]	9	4
Federalist [f, g, h]	23	18
Nonpolitical [e, i]	11	9
Undetermined [k]	24	18
Acceptable [b]		
Republican [c]	4	4
Federalist [f, g, h]	18	7
Nonpolitical [e, i]	20	12
Undetermined [k]	25	14
Unfit [j]	44	6
Qualifications unknown [i]	91	39
Total	**269**	**131**

*Letters in brackets correspond to Lewis's key. The total of 6 unfit officers retained does not include 1 who died after the evaluation was made.

were given greater consideration than party preference. There are, however, two ways to state this conclusion. We can say that Jefferson and his advisors followed the practice of ignoring party preference, selecting the officers to be retained on the basis of military proficiency. It may be more realistic to phrase the conclusion in a different way: no matter how much Jefferson might have wished for any army heavily weighted with Republicans, there was no way that he could have it in the early years of his administration.

In converting to a non-Federalist army, Jefferson had to pay attention first to his small general staff, all but one of whom had multiple crosses after their names to denote their category as "most violently opposed to the administration." Of the seven officers on the general staff, three were discharged within a year after their evaluation. Two old officers who had served honorably in the Revolution were retained, despite their Federalist leanings: Thomas H. Cushing, the adjutant and inspector, and Caleb Swan, the paymaster general. Edward D. Turner, brigade inspector, was retained as a captain but resigned three years later. In assigning political ranking to the men of the general staff, young Captain Lewis had a problem about the commanding general himself, James Wilkinson. Lewis placed no symbols at all after Wilkinson's name, perhaps because he felt it presumptuous to evaluate him, or because he felt that Jefferson knew Wilkinson's strengths and weaknesses all too well. Wilkinson was retained as commanding general, and in later years when he was implicated in the Aaron Burr conspiracy and other intrigues, Jefferson defended him—though not without some equivocation.

Jefferson wanted Republicans in his top civilian posts, military and naval, as well as in the commissioned ranks. His appointment of Henry Dearborn, of Maine, to be secretary of war was a gesture to the strongly Federalist Northeast, as was his appointment of Attorney General Levi Lincoln, of Massachusetts. He offered the post of secretary of the navy to four Republicans before filling it with Benjamin Stoddert, who soon resigned to be replaced by Robert Smith.[12]

The conversion of the army was no secret. In June 1802, the attorney general warned Jefferson that much unrest was evident in the Northeast, although he believed that federalism was losing ground. He wrote, "General Dearborn & myself endeavored to prepare a list of names this morning, for commissions for Massachusetts, to submit to your consideration. As soon as we have done the best we can do, we will wait on you with it."[13] When the secretary of the navy recommended that Robert Gamble, of Pennsylvania, be appointed a midshipman, he was careful to remind the president that the young man was highly recommended by John P. G. Muhlenberg, an active Republican. And when Alexander Dallas came up for his midshipman's commission, his only character reference was his father, Alexander J. Dallas, another influential Republican who was secretary of the commonwealth of Pennsylvania.[14]

Jefferson's patronage policy was personally a moderate one, but he was subject to conflicting pressures. Secretary of the Treasury Albert Gallatin favored a completely nonpartisan appointment policy in some areas of government. On the other hand, Henry Dearborn was unrelenting in his insistence on removing Federalists. He told House speaker Joseph B. Varnum: "We have been much more liberal towards them, than they would be towards us, and in future I think we ought to give them measure for measure."[15]

In remaking the regular army, Jefferson was more successful in controlling its size than its political complexion. After Congress passed the act fixing the military peace establishment in 1802, there was no increase in the regular army for six years—until a conflict with England began to seem likely.[16]

To summarize, it seems probable that Jefferson hired Captain Meriwether Lewis for quite another purpose than to train him for a transcontinental expedition, and that he decided on that expedition much later than has previously been believed. And so when Lewis set out from Washington and Philadelphia, in the spring of 1803, to begin the nation's most enduring tale of exploration and adventure, he had the satisfaction of knowing that he already had served his president and his party in a rather unusual way.

Notes

1. *Journals of the Continental Congress, 1774–1789*, ed. Worthington C. Ford et al. (Washington, D.C., 1904–37), 25:703; 27:513-24. Two sound works on the post-Revolutionary army are Francis Paul Prucha, *The Sword of the Republic: The United States Army on the Frontier, 1783–1846* (Bloomington, Ind., 1969); and Richard H. Kohn, *Eagle and Sword: The Beginnings of the Military Establishment in America* (New York, 1975).

2. Prucha, *Sword of the Republic*, 39-40. The Federalists, determined to base their appointments on political considerations, delayed the completion of the new army by at least three months. Kohn, *Eagle and Sword*, 244.

3. Under an act reducing the size of the army, these discharges were effective June 5, 1800. See *U.S. Statutes at Large*, 2 (June 5, 1800), 85-86.

4. "An act fixing the military peace establishment of the United States," *U.S. Statutes at Large*, 2 (March 16, 1802), 132-37. As of June 1, the army was to consist of two regiments of infantry each comprising ten companies, one regiment of artillery (five battalions of four companies each), and a corps of engineers.

5. Roster of Officers, July 24, 1801, microfilm, series 1, reel 24, folios 19697-705, Jefferson Papers, Manuscripts Division, Library of Congress, Washington, D.C. (hereafter Jefferson Papers).

6. For example refer to Noble E. Cunningham, Jr., *The Jeffersonian Republicans in Power* (Chapel Hill, N.C., 1963), 66. He has later recognized Lewis's hand in Cunningham, *The Process of Government under Jefferson* (Princeton, N.J., 1978), 127.

7. See Jefferson to General James Wilkinson, February 23, 1801, and Jefferson to Meriwether Lewis, February 23, 1801, microfilm, series 1, reel 22, Jefferson Papers.

8. Caspar Wistar to Jefferson, January 8, 1802, microfilm, series 1, reel 25, Jefferson Papers.

9. Cheetham's bill shows June 21, 1802, as the date of the order. See James Cheetham's bill for the book, February 22, 1803, microfilm, series 1, reel 28, Jefferson Papers. Cheetham was also a journalist, publishing the bi-weekly New York newspaper, *The Republican Watch-Tower*.

10. "You know we have been many years wishing to have the Missouri explored & whatever river, heading with that, runs into the Western ocean. Congress, in some secret proceedings, have yielded to a proposition I made them for permitting me to have it done; it is to be undertaken immediately, with a party of about ten, & I have appointed Capt. Lewis, my secretary, to conduct it." Jefferson to Benjamin Barton, February 27, 1803, microfilm, series 1, reel 27, Jefferson Papers. See also W. E. McAtee, ed., "Journal of Benjamin Smith Barton on a Visit to Virginia, 1802," *Castanea: Journal of the Southern Appalachian Botany Club*, 3 (1938), 85-117. Manuscript fragments from Barton's trip to Virginia are in the American Philosophical Society Library, Philadelphia, Pennsylvania.

11. Carlos Martínez de Irujo to Pedro Cevallos, Decembre 2, 1802, legajo 5630, apartado 2, Papeles de Estado, Archivo Histórico Nacional, Madrid, España.

12. Jacob E. Cooke, *Tench Coxe and the Early Republic* (Chapel Hill, N.C., 1978), 394, 395 n. After Stoddert resigned April 1, 1801, Dearborn occupied the post along with his own until July 15, when Smith accepted the appointment.

13. Levi Lincoln to Jefferson, June 28, 1802, microfilm, series 1, reel 26, Jefferson Papers. These proposed commissions probably included civilian posts as well as military appointments.

14. Robert Smith to Jefferson, May 9, 1803, microfilm, series 1, reel 28, Jefferson Papers.

15. Cunningham, *Jeffersonian Republicans*, 68-69. Cunningham deals briefly with Jefferson's coded roster and its implications.

16. Cooke, *Tench Coxe*, 427. On April 12, 1808, Congress approved an addition of eight regiments to the regular army.

Missouri River at La Barge Rock, 1965, photographed by Merrill J. Mattes

Part Two

The Corps of Discovery

JUST AS CHARLES DICKENS's *Tale of Two Cities* gave generations of readers a lopsided, highly colored version of the French Revolution, a host of lesser novelists, biographers, and journalists have fashioned what one historian calls "the myth of the explorer." A central part of that myth asserts that exploration journeys were undertaken by solitary adventurers—typically white males—trekking through desolate and often threatening landscapes. Such a picture, whether in print or paint, reveals more about romantic and heroic ideals than exploration realities.

Jefferson, Lewis, and Clark recognized exploration as the work of many hands and many minds. The eccentric John Ledyard (1751–1789) might propose walking across America with only his dog for company, but his journeys were always more visionary than practical. By the time Captain James Cook made his epochal Pacific voyages, it was clear that a successful exploration required a large company of sailors and scientists, a set of clearly defined duties and relationships, and a system of command drawn largely from military models. The Lewis and Clark Expedition began firmly set in that military pattern. Jefferson's Corps of Discovery was first in the field as an infantry company. And not an especially distinguished company at that. As Lewis, Clark, and Sergeant John Ordway learned at Camp Dubois, their recruits and "volunteers" were a rough and rowdy crew. Resentful of authority, these men gloried in their own aggressive individualism.

But gradually, and not without a little pain, this factious bunch became a remarkably cohesive community. As the essays in this section make plain, months of travel and living together—often in close quarters—created a community more like a family than a collection of squads and messes. Diverse in ethnicity, race, gender, age, and language, the expedition community grew closer by a common purpose and shared experiences. Expedition members as different as Patrick Gass, Sacagawea, George Drouillard, John Ordway, and York did not lose their distinctive habits of speech and ways of life. Instead, they seemed to gain a larger sense of purpose, an identity that transcended but did not deny the individual.

John Ordway to His Parents St. Louis, Missouri

∞

Honored Parence.   *Camp River Dubois*
                                       April the 8th 1804

I NOW EMBRACE THIS OPPERTUNITY OF WRITING TO YOU once more
to let you know where I am and where I am going. I am well thank
God, and in high Spirits. I am now on an expidition to the
westward, with Capt. Lewis and Capt. Clark, who are appointed
by the President of the united States to go on an expidition through
the interior parts of North America. We are to ascend the Missouri
River with a boat as far as it is navigable and then to go by land, to
the western ocean, if nothing prevents, &c.

   This party consists of 25 picked Men of the armey & country
likewise and I am So happy as to be one of them pick'd Men from
the armey, and I and all the party are if we live to Return, to
Receive our Discharge when ever we return again to the united
States if we chuse it. This place is on the Mississippi River oppisite
to the Mouth of the Missouri River and we are to Start in ten days
up the Missouri River. This has been our winter quarters. We
expect to be gone 18 months or two years. We are to Receive a
great Reward for this expidition, when we Return. I am to Receive
15 dollars pr. month and at least 400 ackers of first Rate land, and
if we make Great Discoveries as we expect, the united States, has
promised to make us Great Rewards more than we are promised,
&c. For fear of exidants I wish to inform you that I left 200 dollars
in cash, at Kaskaskias. Put it on interest with a Substantial man by

the name of Charles Smith &c. pertnership which were three[?] more Substantial men binding him and Capt. Clark is bound to See me paid at the time and place where I receive my discharge and if I Should not live to return my heirs can git that and all the pay Due me from the U.S. by applying to the Seat of Government. I have Recd. no letters Since Betseys yet, but will write next winter if I have a chance. Yours, &c.

John Ordway Sergt.

'A Most Perfect Harmony'
The Lewis and Clark Expedition as an Exploration Community

James P. Ronda

THE TRUTH ABOUT OURSELVES OFTEN COMES in unremarkable and unexpected ways. A casual phrase, a quick word, a hasty "hot damn" can often reveal more than a carefully constructed sentence or paragraph. So it was in early August 1805. Thrashing about in the brush, Sergeant Patrick Gass lost Meriwether Lewis's favorite tomahawk. It might have prompted an angry word or a cold glare. Lewis was surely capable of such fury. But instead, the captain put the following lines in his journal: "Accedents will happen in the best families."[1] He was right on both counts. Accidents do happen and the members of the expedition had become the best of families. Lewis had acknowledged that fact some months before. On April 7, the day the Corps of Northwestern Discovery pulled out of Fort Mandan, Lewis described his men as enjoying "a most perfect harmony."[2]

But it had not always been so. The members of the expedition began their journey as a wild bunch of hard-drinking, brawling, and insubordinate rowdies. It is easy for us to forget that at their beginnings the explorers were not clean-shaven, keen-eyed Eagle Scouts. They did not leave Wood River with the "right stuff." They were not the John Glenns and Neil Armstrongs of their day. But somehow this passel of rough and tumble galoots became the best of families, willing to share the risks and hazards of a common life in pursuit of an important goal. How did all that happen? What were the experiences that, at least for a time, transformed ordinary man into an extraordinary band of brothers?

To see what they became we must understand who they were. What we know about the lives of those who ventured up the Missouri "Under a Jentle Brease" makes for thin reading. There are just hints and scraps about men like John Thompson, Moses Reed, and Silas Goodrich. They have their moments in time and then, for the most part, they are lost to us. Because we know so little, we fall back on convenient stereotypes. Here is Drouillard the hunter, Gass the carpenter, Shields the blacksmith, and Shannon the forever lost. But none of these cardboard cutouts satisfies, and we long to know these men as flesh and blood.

We might get to know them better by dividing them into three distinct groups. First, there were the soldiers. In the years after the American Revolution soldiering in the ranks was not an especially honorable profession. The young American republic promised opportunity in the civilian world. Soldiers were viewed with suspicion. In the Jefferson years the small frontier army was a refuge for failures, misfits, and troublemakers. Officers often found their men to be raucous, bad-smelling, foul-mouthed troopers. For every John Ordway—a man of superior ability—there were dozens ready to drink and brawl at a moment's notice. Zebulon Montgomery Pike recognized as much when he described the soldiers of his Mississippi expedition as a "Dam'd set of Rascels."[3]

William Clark, always an astute judge of character, knew as much about the troops that came to him from several frontier companies. He had enough military experience to guess that officers might easily be tempted to "volunteer" their most troublesome men for a distant mission. Clark said as much when he noted that the men detailed from Captain John Campbell's company of the Second Infantry Regiment were not quite the quality he had hoped for.[4] Campbell had pawned off on the expedition some of his outfit's notorious drinkers, including Privates Thomas Howard and Hugh Hall. Soldiers like John Boley, John Newman, and John Potts were a rough lot. Clark once called boozer and hog thief John Collins a "black gard."[5] Perhaps their officers and home companies breathed a sigh of relief to see such men off post and headed west.

The fabled young men from Kentucky, toting their long rifles, were not much better when it came to orders and discipline. Their world, the dark and bloody ground of Kentucky and Tennessee, put the highest premium on individualism and personal survival. No man worth his powder and shot would stoop to take orders from others. That individualism was matched by a history of terrible violence between native people and their new white neighbors. The border world of John Colter and George Drouillard had as its fundamental code—me and mine first, and the Devil take the hindmost.

French boatmen, the *engagés*, made up the third of the expedition's social groups. In the mythology of the West, French Canadian voyageurs represent all that is daring, bold, and colorful. Singing "À La Claire Fontaine" at the top of their voices, the voyageurs paddled the lakes and rivers in relentless pursuit of beaver. But the jaunty, devil-may-care voyageurs of Montreal and the Great Lakes were not the same as those Lewis and Clark hired at Laclede's Landing. The French boatmen of St. Louis, known as the men of the southern trade, were quite a different breed. Alexander Henry the Younger, an experienced fur trader and Lewis and Clark contemporary, described the southern men in quite unflattering terms. They were, he wrote, "insolent and intriguing fellows" driven by greed. Henry blasted them as "undisciplined, impertinent, ill-behaved vagabonds."[6] The expedition got a taste of such behavior when the boatmen bitterly complained about hard work and short rations.[7] La Liberté's decision to leave the expedition was just a visible statement of what some of his comrades may have been thinking.

Hard-bitten soldiers, scrappy frontiersmen, and unpredictable boatmen—this was hardly a crew to inspire confidence. Lewis and Clark expected trouble, but they hoped that a winter at Camp Dubois might iron out the difficulties. On at least one score the captains were right. Life at Wood River was an endless round of drinking, fighting, and short-term desertion. Insubordination was everywhere. One corporal was busted to buck private for fighting and another man was sent packing for theft. There were surreptitious trips to taverns and probably some womanizing. Clark and top sergeant John Ordway did their best, but those efforts were often in vain.

Two incidents reveal just how deep the troubles ran in expedition life. On the frontier, Christmas and New Year's were important holidays. They were times to break out of the winter doldrums. Feasting, dancing, and drinking were at the center of those festivals. Christmas 1803 at Camp Dubois showed the rank and file at their worst. The day began at dawn with a traditional gunfire salute. From then on it was all downhill. Too much whiskey and too much frolic led to swinging fists.[8] In the modern vocabulary of MTV, these men were determined to "fight for your right [to party]."[9]

A year later Sergeant Ordway would describe Fort Mandan's Christmas as all "peace and tranquility" but at Dubois it was anything but peace and quiet.

But no single event more fully reveals the expedition's early tensions than the near-mutiny in February 1804. Late in that month both captains were away from camp on business in St. Louis. Sergeant Ordway, an experienced professional soldier, was left in command. Once Lewis and Clark were gone all hell broke loose. Reuben Field refused to pull guard duty. His insubordination was aided and abetted by John Shields. Shields "excited disorder and faction among the party." But it was more than just backtalk. When Ordway attempted to quiet an ugly situation, Shields threatened to kill the sergeant. Others joined the rebellion, including Colter, Wiser, Boley, and the recently demoted John Robertson. These men had been secretly visiting a local tavern while claiming to be out hunting.[10] When the captains announced sentences for some of those involved, they kept loaded pistols nearby. Perhaps it was a measure of how little had been resolved.[11]

On May 14, 1804, Sergeant Ordway recorded the expedition's departure from Dubois, saying that the party had thirty-eight "good hands."[12] He must have been joking! The Dubois troubles snapped at the expedition's heels. No sooner had the Corps reached St. Charles than the lure of town and tavern proved as powerful as ever. Privates Werner and Hall took off without permission for a night on the town. John Collins went further. He attended a St. Charles dance, behaved in "an unbecoming manner," and then spoke with considerable scorn about orders not to leave camp.[13]

And the troubles did not slacken as the expedition moved

upriver. Clark boasted that his men were "ever ready to inconture any fatigue for the promotion of the enterprise."[14] It was an idle claim and just two weeks later Collins and Hall were again before a court martial, once more accused of drinking on duty.[15] The current of discontent kept rolling, and on July 12 Alexander Willard was sentenced to one hundred lashes "on his bear back" for sleeping on guard duty.[16] Trouble reached flood stage in late summer and early fall. The stories of Moses Reed's desertion and John Newman's "mutinous expression" are familiar ones.[17] The tales are worth remembering if only to recall that they were both the severest and last personnel troubles the expedition experienced. We know they were the last. Lewis and Clark, not blessed with the fortune-teller's art, probably thought the worst was yet to come.

Heading into a winter at close quarters, the captains had every reason to worry about cabin fever and sudden outbursts of uncontrolled fury. For every reliable Drouillard or Ordway there were others as unpredictable as the northern plains weather. Had Lewis and Clark looked at the post journals of the Hudson's Bay Company, they would have found a disturbing record of violence bred by isolation, boredom, and just plain cussedness. Was Fort Mandan going to be a Camp Dubois made worse by harsh weather and possibly unpleasant neighbors?

Those nagging fears were not realized. At Fort Mandan the expedition settled in and settled down. With the minor exception of Thomas Howard's brush with post rules, there were no more angry eruptions. During the Mandan winter the Corps of Northwestern Discovery found itself and became a family. It was a family that could grouse and complain—as every family must— but it was a community now willing to submerge individual desires for the good of the whole. How did that happen? How did these prickly characters create and then enjoy "a perfect harmony?"

The Fort Mandan experience gave the expedition what it needed most—a sense of unity and common purpose for the journey ahead.

At least part of the explanation rests with the actions of Lewis and Clark themselves. Their years of military service had taught them the value of order and discipline. From the beginning they envisioned the expedition not as some wandering band of trappers but as an infantry company with all the regulations dictated by the Articles of War. Drills, parades, inspections, and court-martials—all these were efforts to impose a sense of unity from above. That effort had some success. Young adventurers like John Colter and George Shannon were no longer about to leave camp without permission. But discipline from above could not build a sense of common purpose and shared destiny. Lewis and Clark wanted men who were reliable, not resentful. The journey called for men willing to take responsibility for their own lives as well as the lives of others. The Articles of War, no matter how scrupulously enforced, could not produce that kind of man and that sort of community.

Military regulations might make for proper mess organization. Those rules could not foster a sense of mutual trust. That would demand a set of shared experiences. The captains seemed to understand that. As much as possible, sergeants and enlisted men were brought into the active chain of command. Disciplinary proceedings that involved sentences short of death were administered by the soldiers themselves. When the expedition needed a new sergeant to replace the deceased Charles Floyd, the captains did not make the choice themselves. Instead they fell back on the militia tradition and held an election for the post.[18] That precedent continued and at important places throughout the journey Lewis and Clark took time to involve their men in the decision-making process.

But shared experiences meant more than voting for a new NCO or selecting a site for Fort Clatsop. What really mattered were those moments when all had to pull together for the common good. It was the feeling of community that came out of surviving a terrible storm, pushing over a treacherous place on the Missouri, and just squeaking through a confrontation with the Teton Sioux. By the time the expedition reached the Mandans, it had its own supply of stories to draw upon. The stories we tell about each other remind us who we are. Now in firelight and shadow there were stories to share—stories about prairie dogs, buffalo, and the charms of Arikara women. You can almost hear the voices. Remember that sudden July storm that nearly capsized the keelboat, remember Sergeant Floyd's death, and remember how good that Arikara corn tasted.

Military discipline and the expedition's own folklore were beginning to tame rowdy spirits. But it was really the winter at Fort Mandan that made the difference. What happened that winter is a testimony to the power of routine, to the way shared work binds people one to the other. There was a rhythm of life at the fort that gave all who were there a sense of common identity. Building the fort demanded cooperative effort. Men who had once snarled at each other now put arms and shoulders together lifting and setting heavy sixteen-foot eave beams. Soldiers and hunters who never gave a thought to the comfort of someone else now dug latrines to preserve the health of all. Clark recognized how hard all were laboring, noting that on one cold night the men worked until one in the morning.[19] Toil—the joining of hands in the common task—bonded the explorers together. Cooking, cleaning, and rough fun were equally important in fostering that sense of harmony. What holds any day together are its predictable rituals of eating, washing, and household chores. Fort Mandan had those rituals and they gave the post a feeling of home. And just how much at home men of the expedition felt can be judged in a telling line from John Ordway. He described the Fort Mandan rooms as "warm and comfortable."[20] The fort was a home and its inhabitants were becoming a family.

What a family does for fun says much about that family. Life at Fort Mandan was not all hard work and daily chores. There was plenty of time for good times. We should remember that the fort's walls rang with the sounds of light-hearted music. Pierre Cruzatte's fiddle scratched out ancient French airs. Perhaps the walls also heard a Shoshone lullaby or an English ballad. A brass sounding horn and a tambourine rounded out Mandan's ensemble. Dancing was a common frontier pleasure. François Rivet danced on his hands while his comrades pranced and whirled many a fancy set and reel. In a feat not generally recognized, the expedition became the first federally funded transcontinental dance troupe. And there were games. Quick fingers and nimble minds enjoyed backgammon. Lewis called it "the good old game."[21] There were also games played by native neighbors. On a cold December evening John Ordway and two friends watched as some Mandan men played the popular hoop and pole game. The sport basically involved throwing a short spear or shooting an arrow at a hoop or ring. Scoring depended on the accuracy of the strike toward the ring. Because the throwing sticks looked like billiard cues, later white observers insisted that the earthlodge people played pool. Ordway was interested enough to want to play the game, but his efforts were thwarted when he could not understand the scoring system.[22]

The expedition family always took note of holidays. Birthdays, the Fourth of July, Christmas, and New Year's never went uncelebrated. At Camp Dubois the December and January festivals had been occasions for rowdy drinking and fighting. Fort Mandan's Christmas showed the change. There was dancing, a bit of hunting, and a merry disposition all around. Sergeant Ordway caught the mood in a memorable phrase—"All in peace and quietness."[23]

There was a bit more unbuttoned merrymaking when the party celebrated New Year's 1805. Both French and English traditions tended to put more emphasis on New Year's than Christmas. On January 1, after firing two swivel guns to mark the occasion, the captains allowed sixteen men "with their Musick" to visit the Mandan village of Mitutanka "for the purpose of Dancing." The merry men of the expedition had told Clark that their visit was made at "the particular request of the Chiefs of that Village." Led by John Ordway, the party left the fort carrying a fiddle, a tambourine, and a brass horn. At the entrance to Mitutanka the Americans fired their weapons and played a brisk tune. Welcomed into the village, they marched to the central plaza, fired another round, and began to dance. The Mandan onlookers were especially charmed by Rivet's ability to dance upside down on his hands. All joined in a circle around the Frenchman, dancing and singing. After some time all the revelers were invited into the lodges for food and gifts of buffalo robes. Late in the afternoon the eating and dancing finally played out and most of the men went back to Fort Mandan. But some few did stay in Mitutanka overnight to enjoy other kinds of Mandan hospitality.[24] It is a testimony to the good cheer of that day that the following day Lewis took a group to the village for an encore performance.

That delightful New Year's celebration, bringing together explorers and Indians, represents what I think was the fundamental

National Museum of American Art, Smithsonian Institution, Washington, D.C., gift of Mrs. Joseph Harrison, Jr.

Birds-Eye View of Mandan Village, 1800 Miles Above St. Louis, *oil on canvas, 1837–39, by George Catlin. The Corps of Discovery learned to work and live harmoniously with one another at Fort Mandan, in part due to the good example of their Mandan neighbors, who lived in a village much like the one captured by George Catlin in the 1830s.*

fact of life at Fort Mandan. The expedition was a community living alongside other communities. The Lewis-and-Clark tribe now joined other tribal peoples struggling to survive on the northern plains. Fort Mandan was never an isolated frontier outpost, caught in the grip of a Dakota winter and cut off from the simple pleasures of human companionship. Long before Lewis and Clark came to the Upper Missouri, Mandan and Hidatsa villagers had brightened their winters with a steady round of visits to the lodges of friends and neighbors. Life in the winter camps could be harsh and hungry, but there were also times for storytelling and gossip. Once the fort was built, the Americans simply became part of the social web. Nothing seemed more natural than the desire of explorer and Indian alike to see each other at home and share some food and friendship.

The days of Fort Mandan added up to five months. And on most of those days Indians and whites met for all sorts of dealings. Business, diplomacy, hunting, sex, and simple curiosity made for daily encounters. Lewis and Clark's hospitality was well known; Indians often came early in the day, slept overnight inside the fort if invited, and left the next morning. Indian visitors brought to Fort Mandan's rooms a sense of friendship and good company. The arrival of native neighbors usually meant sharing food and enjoying a dance or some music. There must have been time to appreciate a fine bow, a good gun, or a skillfully decorated pair of moccasins. The sheer numbers of Indian tourists sometimes tested everyone's patience. Lewis called his neighbors "good company" but in the same breath complained that they sometimes overstayed their welcome. Sergeant Ordway peevishly recalled that on one day in mid-December he had fourteen Indians all eating in his squad room at the same time. It was enough to stretch the seating capacity of any small town Dakota cafe. Frayed nerves and misunderstandings were inevitable. When an Indian guest did something to annoy Private Joseph Whitehouse, the soldier struck him on the hand with a spoon.[25]

All these comings and goings had a profound effect on the expedition. It would not be wide of the mark to say that the earthlodge people civilized some of their more obstreperous white neighbors. That happened in two ways. From the earliest contacts between Europeans and Native Americans, the white strangers used Indians as a kind of foil for themselves. We know, said the French or English, who you Indians are and thus we know ourselves. The fancy anthropological term is counter cultural image but the idea is a simple one. I know my own self because I am either like or unlike you. Being surrounded by other tribes, the Lewis-and-Clark tribe formed its own distinct identity. To put it another way, at Fort Mandan the expedition found an in-group personality. Second and equally important, the villagers provided a good example of a life that was remarkably harmonious. The explorers could not have remained unaffected by the good company around them. The Fort Mandan experience gave the expedition what it needed most—a sense of unity and common purpose for the journey ahead.

So much western history is written like a John Wayne movie or a Louis L'Amour novel. Powerful individuals, so we are told, tamed a wild and savage land. But what happened to the men of the Lewis and Clark Expedition gives the lie to such a distorted vision. The explorers began their journey as individuals, boozing and brawling, threatening and storming. Along the way they learned a fundamental lesson—a lesson the earthlodge people learned generations before. It was a lesson about cooperation and community. Once learned, it was not soon forgotten. Lewis was right. Here at Mandan the expedition had come to know a perfect harmony.

Notes

1. Reuben G. Thwaites, ed., *Original Journals of the Lewis and Clark Expedition, 1804–1806* (New York, 1904–5), 2:299-300.

2. Gary E. Moulton, ed., *The Journals of the Lewis and Clark Expedition* (Lincoln, Nebr., 1983–97), 4:10 (hereafter JLCE).

3. Donald Jackson, ed., *The Journals of Zebulon Montgomery Pike with Letters and Related Documents* (Norman, Okla., 1966), 2:114.

4. JLCE, 2:139.

5. Ibid., 2:148.

6. Elliott Coues, ed., *New Light on the Early History of the Greater Northwest: The Manuscript Journals of Alexander Henry the Younger and David Thompson* (1897; reprint, Minneapolis, 1967), 2:889-90.

7. JLCE, 2:306.

8. Ibid., 2:141.

9. Beastie Boys, "Fight for Your Right," on *Licensed to Ill*, Def Jam/ Brooklyn Dust, 1986.

10. JLCE, 2:178-88, 194.

11. Ibid., 2:183.

12. Milo M. Quaife, ed., *The Journals of Captain Meriwether Lewis and Sergeant John Ordway* (Madison, Wisc., 1916), 79.

13. JLCE, 2:234-37.

14. Ibid., 2:300.

15. Ibid., 2:329-30.

16. Ibid., 2:369-70.

17. Ibid., 2:488-89; 3:169.

18. Ibid., 2:500-501.

19. Quaife, *Lewis and Ordway*, 163; JLCE, 3:237.

20. Quaife, *Lewis and Ordway*, 171.

21. JLCE, 3:265.

22. Quaife, *Lewis and Ordway*, 172.

23. Ibid., 174; JLCE, 3:261.

24. Quaife, *Lewis and Ordway*, 174; JLCE, 3:266-67.

25. Quaife, *Lewis and Ordway*, 172; JLCE, 2:261, 288, 315. See also James P. Ronda, *Lewis and Clark among the Indians* (Lincoln, Nebr., 1984), 98-107.

Passage to India
From Christmas to Christmas
with Lewis and Clark

Bernard DeVoto

Monday 24th Decr. Some Snow this morning. we finished Setting pickets & arected a blacksmiths Shop. the afternoon pleasant. the Savages came as usal we fired our Swivels as tomorrow is cristmas day &. C.

THUS WROTE SERGEANT JOHN ORDWAY, sixteen hundred miles up the Missouri River, in 1804, with the expedition that President Jefferson had sent to traverse the lands purchased from France and discover a route to the Pacific. The pickets and the blacksmith shop meant the completion of a triangular, bulletproof fort a mile or two below the Mandan villages, where Captains Lewis and Clark had halted their company for the winter some seven weeks before. The snow which fell that morning marked the end of a cold wave during which temperatures of thirty and forty below zero were common and the sentinel had to be changed every half hour. The river had long since frozen over and buffalo were crossing it in great herds. Captain Clark and eighteen men went hunting them, and had to spend a night on the snow with only the fresh hides for covering. Northern lights blazed almost to the zenith, many of the men had their hands and feet frostbitten, sunlight on snow produced a blindness which could only be treated by holding the face in the steam created by pouring water on heated stones. That was a Mandan remedy, but the Indians had already learned to call upon the expedition's medicine chest, which had cost the government $55, or rather less than the kit you would take on a vacation in Egypt. "A Womon brought a Child with an abcess on the lower part of the back, and offered as much Corn as she Could Carry for some Medison," Clark writes, and such entries had become common.

Those medicines, among which the favorite was Dr. Rush's famous pills, were one of the most valuable assets the expedition had, but a more valuable one had been added on November 4, when Toussaint Charbonneau was hired as interpreter on the condition that one of his Indian wives should come with him. This was Sacajawea, "the Bird Woman," a Shoshone girl whom a Hidatsa war party had captured four years ago and brought east. Her husband was a bungler, a coward, and a bully, but Sacajawea at once became indispensable to the expedition. She had to be dauntless to share the labor and privation of the journey, but she was more than dauntless—she had an integrity and sweetness of personality unique among the women of her race whom history knows. Her services to the United States can hardly be overvalued; she saved the expedition at its crucial moment, and if, as the "Dictionary of American Biography" says, more memorials have been erected to her than to any other American woman, it is clear that she earned them.

The day before Ordway's note, Little Crow's wife had brought to the fort a present of corn and a "kittle of boiled Cimmins [summer squash], beens, Corn & Choke Cheries, which was palitable." On Christmas Eve, Sergeant Gass says, "Flour, dried apples, pepper and other articles were distributed in the different messes to enable them to celebrate Christmas in a proper and social manner." Christmas morning was cloudy.

> we fired the Swivels at day break, [Ordway says] & each man fired one round. our officers Gave the party a drink of Taffee [Taffia, West Indian rum]. we had the best to eat that could be had, & continued firing dancing & frolicking dureing the whole day. the Savages did not Trouble us as we had requested them not to come as it was a Great medician day with us. we enjoyed a merry christmas dureing

the day & evening untill nine oClock—all in peace and
quietness.

Private Whitehouse notes plaintively that this festival was "all
without the compy. of the female Seck, except three Squaws the
Intreptirs wives and they took no part with us only to look on."
The enlisted personnel had not lacked comfort, however, for the
Mandans and most other tribes hospitably offered their wives and
sisters, and when this honor was suspended the "squars" were both
generous and cheaply purchasable. The black skin and kinky hair
of York, Captain Clark's bodyservant, were marvelously attractive
to women and had already given him an enviable eminence.

It was the *voyageur* Cruzatte, a mighty waterman, who played
this irrecoverable Christmas music on a fiddle, while the fires blazed
and the north wind howled round the fort. Boating songs, probably,
and minuets and carols that had crossed the Atlantic to New France
and traveled the rivers for two centuries, to be sung never more
incongruously than at the Mandan villages. He played them
through the long winter and the men danced to them, and delighted
Indians looked on—the chiefs swaggering in the laced and
epauletted coats that had been formally presented to them, with
dress swords, feathers, and medals of the President, of domestic
animals, or of farmers sowing grain, distributed according to their
degree. And Cruzatte's fiddle, like the serene loyalty of Sacajawea,
had its part in making this the most successfully managed expedition
in the history of exploration, as it was one of the most important.

That the company could spend Christmas "in peace and
quietness" at the Mandan villages meant that Meriwether Lewis
and William Clark had already proved their greatness as diplomats,
no less than as commanders and explorers. The Osages frankly
disbelieved that the Great White Father now dwelt in Washington
rather than London or Paris, and this skepticism was shared by
more important tribes—among whom the British interests were
nurtured by traders adept in the management of savage minds. As
the keelboat and the pirogues moved up the river, rumors shaped
in the interest of the crown ran ahead of them. To pacify the tribes
while asserting American jurisdiction over them was one of
Jefferson's prime objectives, and a crisis of world polity turned on

this handful of soldiers, a force so fragile that the slightest mismanagement must have wiped it out, would have given the Indian problem a wholly different shape, and might have changed the map of North America. Both the Arikaras and the Teton Sioux had listened to the double tongues, and Lewis magnificently served his nation by compelling the latter into respect and good behavior by a show of force. That episode was the last clash with the Indians until, on the journey home, Lewis was forced to shoot a Blackfoot and so created an implacable hostility which lasted for many years and made that tribe the greatest obstacle to the development of the interior West.

The conflict with the Sioux was behind them when they built their fort. So was the single fatality the expedition suffered, the death of Sergeant Floyd from "bilious fever." So were all infractions of discipline and all discord. The twenty-nine enlisted men, three sergeants, and two interpreters, who with Lewis and Clark and York and Sacajawea were to compose the final party, were welded into a superb, and unexcelled instrument for the exploration of the wilderness.

So they passed the winter among the Mandans, traditional friends of the whites, whose two villages stood where the Missouri turned southward, athwart a principal trade route of the tribes and fur companies. John Floyd, the blacksmith, mended tools for the Indians, and from the iron of a burnt-out camp stove forged tomahawks that enraptured them. The captains practiced medicine, York enlarged his conquests, and chiefs from many tribes came to smoke with the agents of the White Father, to receive gifts from them, and to appraise their power. Traders of the North West Company came also and were ordered to abandon their propaganda on American soil, or charged with suaver messages for their headquarters. And always, from the Mandans, from the traders, from the visiting chiefs, the captains sought information about the country they must traverse. For a few miles still they would be on waters sometimes traveled by whites, but beyond the mouth of the Rochejaune even rumor would cease. So while the ice groaned and shuddered by night, they sat with blanketed braves before the great fires in the fort, and patiently drew from them all they had seen or heard about the western waters.

One sees that firelight on intent faces as the Indians draw river courses on the puncheon floor, scrawling with bits of charcoal the known bends and rapids, and the bearings of distant peaks, shaping a handful of ashes to show how a range loops down from the north, grunting and disputing, sending to the village for a brave whom chance may have led up some unknown creek. The captains listened, trying to check their informants by one another, never sure how much was guessed or rumored or perhaps merely invented about the uncharted waste, so many of whose rivers and summits they were to christen in the months ahead. The Mandans had never crossed the main range or journeyed to the Spanish lands. They had heard of the great westward-running river whose mouth the captains had been ordered to find, and of the big, stinking salt pond it emptied into, but how far away it was or by what route it might be reached not even Sacajawea, who had been born beyond the divide, could tell them.

On February 11, Sacajawea's first child was born, "a fine boy," writes Lewis, who eased her labor by grinding a rattlesnake's rattle and administering a little of it dissolved in water. He was named Jean Baptiste; before long Clark was calling him "Pomp" and offering to educate him among the whites; strapped on his mother's back, the infant was to cross the continent and come back in safety. . . . Already they were trying to get the boats out of the ice, but did not succeed until the 26. Then the ice shivered and splintered, northing swans arrived, the larger flights followed them. They packed cases with animal and Indian mementos for Mr. Jefferson, wrote a last report to him, and sent all off together in the keelboat with the discharged men under Corporal Warfington. About five in the afternoon of April 7, 1805, in "six small canoes and two large periogues," they started upstream toward the unknown.

Stripped to the waist, they were in ice water most of the time, pulling the boats off the Missouri's fiendish sandbars. They had seen the country change many times and now it changed again, for they were in the high plains, the semiarid region of the real West. They encountered the alkali for the first time; it made the water bitter and purgative, as thousands were to learn who followed after them. It also gave the whole party sore eyes, which the captains correctly treated with "a solution of two grains of white vitriol," and may have in part accounted for the boils that now became common. There was a new danger also in the "white bears," the grizzlies for whose ferocity the Indians had tried to prepare them. The first one they saw set out after Lewis after it had been shot and chased him till killed by another hunter; a few days later, another one furiously pursued Private Bratton for over half a mile, though it had a bullet "through the center of the lungs"; three days later, two hunters had to dive into the river to escape one that had been shot seven times.

Peril, of course, was nothing new. A mere dot of sentient, vigilant skill, they had moved through an immensity of multiple and unintermitted danger. But now, in the untrodden country, the journey becomes something simple and immortal—a tableau of courage and endurance in clear light, one of the world's heroic stories that seem like myths. They toiled westward on the sun's path, toward the fourth house of the sky, fulfilling a dream which Meriwether Lewis had had in his boyhood, fulfilling an older, more complex dream of Thomas Jefferson's, and by strength and skill and valor they rolled the unknown back before them. The country ahead of them was an untraveled chaos, the boundary of man's knowledge moved with them, they passed and the map was made forever. The day's march lay between walls of the capricious and treacherous wilderness and walls of a capricious and malevolent race of savages; the day's march ended and the walls had been moved farther back.

Past the Little Missouri, past the Rochejaune which they were the first to call the Yellowstone, past the Big Muddy and the Milk River and the Musselshell. On May 26, Lewis climbed the highest neighboring hill and looking westward saw lines lift and waver above the horizon and sun flash on distant snow—"the object of all our hopes and the reward of all our ambition," the Rocky Mountains. On June 2 they reached a large river coming down from the north and faced a decision on which success or utter failure hinged. For nothing in their data sufficed to tell them which fork was the true Missouri and would lead them to the Continental Divide. The north fork, which Lewis was to call Maria's, looked far likelier than the other, and even after both had been reconnoitered the whole party except the captains thought that it was the Missouri. The process by which they determined on the other one might serve as a model of scientific analysis and must be granted a high place in the history of thought. The decision made, Lewis hurried up the south fork to be sure, and was sure when he heard the thunder of the great falls, felt the spray borne by the wind for several miles to fall for the first time on a white man's cheeks, and finally stood deafened and dazzled above the gorge.

They got the boats round the falls by a gigantic labor, and went on. A cloudburst nearly destroyed them and, not for the last time, Sacajawea owed her life and her child's to William Clark. Navigation would soon be impossible, game began to fail, the summer was shortening, and ice formed in the buckets overnight. Whether they would do Thomas Jefferson's will or fail and probably perish on the continental crest depended on their finding the Shoshones at their accustomed hunting ground—on their being friendly—on their having horses to sell. Clark, the more skillful frontiersman, ranged ahead but did not meet them; then Lewis went and it was he who finally found them, unfriendly, suspicious, disposed to flight or murder. The Shoshones feared that this prodigy, the first white man they had ever seen, might be working some corrupt device of their enemies and might betray them into ambush. Failure of the great adventure now hung by a single thread above the commander's head, but, telling them about the party of white men to the eastward, of the woman of their nation who was with it, of the marvelous black-skinned man, Lewis managed to allay part of their distrust and they turned back with him. They might have killed him, as in fact he thought they would; they might have gone on to overwhelm the party that was toiling on with Clark— and came later than Lewis had promised. But they did not. The arrival of Clark proved Lewis's tongue straight, and at once history soared into that purer ether where fiction dare not venture. For Lewis, wanting clearer speech with the chief Cameahwait, who had accompanied him, sent for Sacajawea to interpret. A moment later she threw her blanket round the chief and was weeping violently. Just below the Continental Divide, after five years of separation, she had met her own brother, from whose tent she had been ravished. "After some conversation between them she resumed her seat and attempted to interpret for us; but her new situation seemed to overpower her and she was frequently interrupted by her tears."

They now reached the limit of strain and exhaustion. There was no game to be found, all of their flour had been used up, and they had only a little corn. They had long since learned to like dog meat, which at first had nauseated them, but after they left the Shoshones there were no dogs to buy. Every day's travel among the peaks cost a fatigue of man and beast alike that amounted to collapse. They ranged widely for game but found none, ate the three colts they had, at last had to kill some of the horses for food. They killed a coyote, then another horse, and the remnants of this fed two of their hunters the next day, returning to the party without game—who "roasted the head of the horse, which even our appetites had spared, and supped on the ears, skin, and lips of the animal." At last, on westward-running waters, they found Indians who had dried salmon and berries and camas root to sell. But hearty meals after weeks of privation sickened them, and the camas, besides, was both purgative and emetic when prepared badly. Various of the men, then Clark, and finally Lewis fell ill. They dosed themselves with Rush's pills and pressed on. The cold thin air of the mountains yielded to sweltering heat as they descended, and this too weakened them. "Today he [Lewis] could hardly sit on his horse, while others were obliged to be put on horseback, and some, from extreme weakness and pain, were forced to lie down alongside of the road [trail] for some time."

But in the mountains circumstance and the impersonal malice of the wilderness had done their utmost, and the expedition now reached navigable water again, the Kooskooskee River. They camped on its bank and while the sick recovered, the well made canoes for the last stage of the appointed labor. Reverting to a water route, they had no more to face than a daily, routine hazard of skill against destruction. Down the Kooskooskee to the Snake they went, and down the Snake till at last they reached the river for which they had set out. Two years and three months before, the Columbia had been just a dead reckoning in Thomas Jefferson's study, just a hole pricked in blank white paper with the point of his dividers. And now, forever, a known line was drawn in ink across that white paper from Jefferson's study in Washington to the great river of the West.

There were dangerous rapids still to pass, and the food failed sometimes, and wood for fires was scarce. The Indians too were different, treacherous, occasionally dangerous; they were greater thieves, having been more in contact with white men, whose pea jackets, hardware, and venereal diseases came up the Columbia along the immemorial trade route. They shot the last rapid of the Cascades and came on November 2 to tidewater. The journey now added one climactic indignity: as they floated down the river a storm rose and, after crossing the Continental Divide and breaking a trail across the arid wilderness, they must be seasick. It was the rainy season, too, and they were hardly to be dry again till next spring. The river widened, high winds made the waves furious, at night their camp was nearly washed from under them. Almost at journey's end, they had to stop on November 10, and for two days gales, thunder, and hailstorms buffeted them. There was a final precarious moment with some anonymous Indians and, on November 14, Captain Lewis rounded a last point and saw the open sea.

They were too uncomfortable, too waterlogged, too weary, and much too seasoned to rejoice. The journal says, "Ocian in View! O! the joy," and says little more. A campsite must be found and preparations for the winter must be begun—better to think of such urgent things than of significances that hovered above that stormy promontory. But the continent had been crossed and was no longer unknown. The trail was blazed, the Americans had occupied their country, the Republic had reached its farthest frontier. An idea with which the restless mind of Thomas Jefferson had wrestled through many nights had been given flesh, Meriwether Lewis's dream had come true, and the thing was done. It was November 14, 1805, and the journey of Lewis and Clark to a foreseen but unknown end had reached that end on a rainy Pacific beach. Another, older, more dreambound journey ended too. The passage to India was achieved, and three ships made harbor that had sailed from the port of Palos on Friday, the third of August 1492, at about eight in the morning.

They were still looking for a campsite when one of the captains carved a legend on a large pine tree. "William Clark December 3d 1805. By Land from the U. States in 1804 &5." One reads the legend, seeing that inked line move westward across blank paper. "By Land from the U. States." Yes.

They found their campsite, up Netul River from Meriwether Bay, where wood was plentiful and game abundant. They began building their fort, in the endless rain. It was not finished till after the new year and in fact was never satisfactory or even watertight, but within a few days it had a roof. They established an outpost on the beach, where salt would be made for the winter and the homeward journey—and whence word came that evoked the only selfish request Sacajawea is known to have made. A whale had stranded there, and she asked leave to go see it, to behold a marvel and take word of it back with her to her own people. About this time, too, she sacrificed a treasured gaud. The captains wanted, so that they might send it to Mr. Jefferson, a magnificent sea otter coat that a visiting chief wore. But they could not buy it, for their stock had been depleted, in part lost, in part cached in the mountains, and they had no blue beads, which alone its owner valued. Sacajawea had a necklace of blue beads—and so Mr. Jefferson in due time was able to see for himself the principal article for which his merchants would contend with the Russians in these waters. Her generosity must have cost William Clark a pang. He had come to feel for her not only a complete respect but a tenderness compounded of shared hazards and proved trust. He called her "Janey," in utter comradeship and had named a great rock Pompey's Pillar after her infant son. And once, after the mountains were passed, she had secretly given him a small piece of bread which she had saved and carried heaven knows how long to feed the child.

So they came to their second Christmas, with no salt and the rain rapidly spoiling the meat they shot. "we would have spent this day the nativity of Christ in feasting," Clark says, "had we any thing either to raise our Sperits or even gratify our appetites, our Diner concisted of pore Elk, so much spoiled that we eate it through mear necessity, some Spoiled pounded fish and a fiew roots." Sergeant Ordway speaks:

Wednesday 25th Decr 1805. rainy & wet disagreeable weather. we all moved in to our new Fort, which our officers name Fort Clatsop after the name of the Clatsop nation of Indians who live nearest to us. the party Saluted our officers by each man firing a gun at their quarters at day break this morning. they divided out the last of their tobacco among the men that used [it] and the rest they gave each a Silk handkerchief, as a Christmast gift, to keep us in rememberance of it as we have no ardent Spirits, but are all in good health which we all esteem more than all the ardent Spirits in the world.

They were of the world's great adventurers, they had come up the Missouri, over the mountains, and down to the Pacific, by ways no white man had ever taken before, and they had kept their health. They had the winter before them, and the back trail at its end—shirts and leggings and hundreds of pairs of moccasins to make, more than three months of wind and rain, of short rations, of salt making and wood gathering, of yarning and singing and dancing to Cruzatte's fiddle at night, within sound of the Pacific sea. No ardent spirits were left, there was only a pound or two of tobacco and a silk handkerchief apiece to symbolize Christmas for this crew of a greater Argosy. But they had reason enough to be content.

And Captain Clark fared better: "I recved a pres[e]nt of Capt. Lewis of fleece hosrie [hosiery] Shirt Draws and Socks, a pr. Mockersons of Whitehouse a small Indian basket of Gutherich [Goodrich], two Dozen white weazil tails of the Indian woman, & some black root of the Indians before their departure."

A hero's Christmas presents, on the edge of the Pacific, with the now traversed continent behind him and the dream achieved. They attest an immortal deed, the affection of his comrade, the respect of his men. And the warm heart of Sacajawea, whose ailments he had treated with niter and zinc sulphate and Rush's pills, whom he had delivered from her husband's blows, whose child also he had nursed and doctored, whom he had several times snatched from death, whom he had come to think of not as an Indian squaw but as a woman of extraordinary fineness and staunchness. And whose gratitude and loyalty were his. She had but inadequate words to give him on Christmas, the great medicine day of his race, but, accepting the custom she could not comprehend, knowing that he had been kind to her and that this was a day of kindness, she gave him what she had. History will remember William Clark as one of the greatest of its captains, and, remembering him, it will not forget the twenty-four white weasel tails that Janey gave him on Christmas Day.

Faces to Voices

Portraits of the Lewis and Clark Expedition

James P. Ronda

WE LIVE IN A TIME THAT DEMANDS, AND OFTEN OVERVALUES, visual images. The vast film and television industries reflect a passion for the visual—whether in a photograph or a painting. For all its powerful and potentially graphic moments, the Lewis and Clark Expedition story remains deeply rooted in the world of words and writing. Through the journals, maps, and other records we are asked to fashion our own portraits of those on the journey and along the way. The Corps of Discovery voyaged the West before the advent of photography and video tape. Awed by the sight of the Great Falls of the Missouri, Meriwether Lewis wished for a camera obscura to help him capture the scene. The device he had in mind would have only enhanced the work of his own sketching. Lewis's camera could not by itself make lasting impressions of the falls. The face of the country at that moment and the faces of those who saw it seem lost to those intent on the visual experience.

But in a handful of cases there are visual representations of some key figures in the larger expedition story. Of course, Lewis and Clark had their portraits done by Charles Willson Peale, the young republic's semiofficial court painter. And later the French artist Charles B. J. F. de St. Memin executed somewhat romanticized profile portrayals of the two captains. But as this gallery of images suggests, other actors in the expedition drama had their faces matched to their voices either on canvas or paper. At least three expedition participants—Sergeant Patrick Gass, Private Alexander Willard, and the Piegan Blackfeet Wolf Calf— lived into the age of photography. As for those who did not, George Catlin painted the elderly Hidatsa chief Black Moccasin. While not a contemporary image, Charles M. Russell offered his sense of York and the Hidatsa chief Le Borgne in a memorable but oddly mistitled painting. No contemporary images of Sacagawea exist, either; but the Shoshone woman captured the imagination of supporters of woman suffrage at the turn of the century, and so became one of the most commemorated women in American history, with statues erected in her honor across the United States.

The pictures reproduced here are reminders of both the incomplete nature of the historical record and the enduring reality of the Lewis and Clark story. These images are what another age called "remembrancers," ways to recall that these persons were flesh-and-blood people with genuine lives, great hopes, and sometimes tragic disappointments.

Meriwether Lewis, *by Charles Willson Peale. In early February 1807 Peale wrote to Jefferson that he was eager to see Lewis. "I wish to possess his portrait for the museum." Some months later Lewis sat for the artist and the painting soon became an important exhibit in the Peale Museum.*

William Clark, *by Charles Willson Peale. Painted by Peale in 1810 while Clark visited Philadelphia, the portrait reveals a man with a steady gaze and a sure sense of self-confidence. Some observers have noted that this straightforward-looking Clark is quite unlike the averted eyes present in the Lewis portrait.*

National Museum of American Art, Smithsonian Institution, Washington, D.C.; gift of Mrs. Joseph Harrison, Jr.

Black Moccasin, Aged Chief, *by George Catlin. Chief of the Hidatsa village of Meteharta, Black Moccasin was more properly called Ompsehara or "blackens moccasin." Lewis and Clark first met him in October 1804. When George Catlin painted this portrait in 1833, the elderly chief made a point of asking Catlin to remember him to William Clark.*

York, *by Charles M. Russell, 1908. This painting recalls a powerful moment in expedition history when, on March 9, 1805, the Hidatsa chief Le Borgne examined York, thinking his blackness might be merely paint. Russell located this event in one of the Mandan lodges when in fact it happened at Fort Mandan. While not accurate in every detail, the painting does capture the spirit of the event.*

Wolf Calf, 1895. This photograph was taken by the pioneer anthropilogist George Bird Grinnell. He was told that this man was Wolf Calf, one of the Blackfeet men involved in the Two Medicine River confrontation on July 27, 1806. The image gained wide circulation when published in Olin D. Wheeler's popular The Trail of Lewis and Clark *(New York, 1904).*

From Olin Wheeler, *The Trail of Lewis and Clark*

Willard Family Foundation

Alexander and Eleanor Willard, n.d. Alexander Hamilton Willard was recruited for the Corps of Discovery from Captain Amos Stoddart's artillery company. On the journey Willard served as a hunter, gunsmith, and blacksmith. In 1852 the Willard family took the overland trail to California. Willard died there in 1865.

Patrick Gass, n.d. Sergeant Patrick Gass was best known as the expedition's skilled carpenter. Gass's journal, edited by David McKeehan, was published in 1809. There are two surviving images of Gass. The one reproduced here is a woodcut taken from an ambrotype by E.G. Moore, an early method of placing an image on a blackened glass plate. It appears that the Gass ambrotype has not survived, leaving only this second-hand copy. There is also a sketch of Gass in old age taken from what was said to be an old photograph. As in the case of the ambrotype, the "old photograph" evidently is not extant.

From Charles G. Clarke, *Men of the Lewis and Clark Expedition*

Sacagawea, by Leonard Crunelle, 1910. Showing a resolute mother and her infant, this statue of Sacagawea in Bismarck, North Dakota, is one more reminder of the central role native people played in the expedition.

State Historical Society of North Dakota, Bismarck

Great Falls of the Missouri, 1880, photographed by F. Jay Haynes

Part Three

The Journey

UNLIKE SOME OF HIS CONTEMPORARIES, Thomas Jefferson recognized that exploration and discovery were part of two separate yet somehow related pursuits. One of those was the traditional quest, the search for a prized object or place already known or believed to exist. Whether it was the fabled Holy Grail or an elusive Northwest Passage, the desired end was clear. What was in doubt was the path to find the sought-after objective. But as Jefferson's instructions to his explorers made plain, the journey itself was of central importance. The president envisioned a voyage through the West as a means to gather useful knowledge and practical experience. Jefferson did not want Lewis and Clark to stray from their essential search for a water highway across the continent but neither did he charge them to head west wearing blinders. Jefferson's dream passage was at the heart of the journey, giving it energy and direction. But there were many other questions to ask and answer. As the essays and documents in this section point up, those questions ranged from which river bed carried the currents of the true Missouri to measuring the country's length and breadth.

Although later tellers of the Lewis and Clark story emphasized moments of drama and adventure, the explorers themselves knew that their journey was made up of countless decisions—some momentous and others routinely matter-of-fact. There were choices about everything from campsite locations and food preparation to Indian diplomacy and trail directions. As John L. Allen makes clear in his important essay, the decision at the Marias River was reached neither by blind luck nor simple guesswork. Bernard DeVoto once said that "the stars danced for Lewis and Clark." But it was almost always careful planning and measured thinking that carried the day and allowed the journey to proceed on.

While the expedition's journals are filled with recollections of memorable events and detailed descriptions of plants and animals new to European science, few entries so fully represent the complex character of the voyage as Lewis's entry for August 13, 1805. In just a few pages the explorer manages to give a colorful recounting of the meeting with Cameahwait and at the same time provide detailed scientific information about Shoshone tobacco pipes and regional plants. Perhaps more than any other single passage, this one represents the journey in all its drama, adventure, and complexity. Almost without premeditation Lewis portrays exploration as the joining of physical action and intellectual discovery.

Meriwether Lewis
Journal Entry

WE SET OUT VERY EARLY ON THE INDIAN ROAD which still led us through an open broken country in a westerly direction. a deep valley appeared to our left at the base of a high range of mountains which extended from S. E. to N. W. having their sides better clad with pine timber than we had been accustomed to see the mountains and their tops were also partially covered with snow. at the distance of five miles the road after leading us down a long descending valley for 2 Ms. brought us to a large creek about 10 yds. wide; this we passed and on rising the hill beyond it had a view of a handsome little valley to our left of about a mile in width through which from the appearance of the timber I conjectured that a river passed. I saw near the creek some bushes of the white maple, the <small> shumate of the small species with the winged rib, and a species of honeysuckle much in it's growth and leaf like the small honeysuckle of the Missouri only reather larger and bears a globular berry as large as a garden pea and as white as wax. this berry is formed of a thin smooth pellicle which envellopes a soft white musilagenous substance in which there are several small brown seed irregularly scattered or intermixed without any sell or perceptable membranous covering.— we had proceeded about four miles through a wavy plain parallel to the valley or river bottom when at the distance of about a mile we saw two women, a man and some dogs on an eminence immediately before us. they appeared to vew us with attention and two of them after a few minutes set down as if to wait our arrival we continued our usual pace towards them. when we had arrived within half a mile of them I directed the party to halt and leaving my pack and rifle I took the flag which I unfurled and advanced singly towards them the women soon disappeared behind the hill, the man continued untill I arrived within a hundred yards of him and then likewise absconded. tho' I frequently repeated the word *tab-ba-bone* sufficiently loud for him to have heard it. I now haistened to the top of the hill where they had stood but could see nothing of them. the dogs were less shye than their masters they came about me pretty close I therefore thought of tying a handkerchief about one of their necks with some beads and other trinkets and then let them loose to surch their fugitive owners thinking by this means to convince them of our pacific disposition towards them but the dogs would not suffer me to take hold of them; they also soon disappeared. I now made a signal fror the men to come on, they joined me and we pursued the back tarck of these Indians which lead us along the same road which we had been traveling. the road was dusty and appeared to have been much traveled lately both by men and horses. these praries are very poor the soil is of a light yellow clay, intermixed with small smooth gravel, and produces little else but prickly pears, and bearded grass about 3 inches high. the prickley pear are of three species that with a broad leaf common to the missouri; that of a globular form also common to the upper pa[r]t of the Missouri and more especially after it enters the Rocky Mountains, also a 3rd peculiar to this country. it consists of small circular thick leaves with a much greater number of thorns. these thorns are stronger and appear to be barbed. the leaves grow from the margins of each other as in the broad leafed pear of the missouri, but are so slightly attatched that when the thorn touches your mockerson it adhears and brings with it the leaf covered in every direction with many others. this is much the most troublesome plant of the three. we had not continued our rout more than a mile when we were so fortunate as to meet with three female savages. the short and steep ravines which we passed concealed us from each other untill we arrived within 30 paces. a young woman

immediately took to flight, an Elderly woman and a girl of about
12 years old remained. I instantly laid by my gun and advanced
towards them. they appeared much allarmed but saw that we were
to near for them to escape by flight they therefore seated themselves
on the ground, holding down their heads as if reconciled to die
which the expected no doubt would be their fate; I took the elderly
woman by the hand and raised her up repeated the word *tab-babone*
and strip up my shirt sleve to sew her my skin; to prove to her the
truth of the ascertion that I was a white man for my face and hads
which have been constantly exposed to the sun were quite as dark
as their own. they appeared instantly reconciled, and the men
coming up I gave these women some beads a few mockerson awls
some pewter looking-glasses and a little paint. I directed Drewyer
to request the old woman to recall the young woman who had run
off to some distance by this time fearing she might allarm the
camp before we approached and might so exasperate the natives
that they would perhaps attack us without enquiring who we were.
the old woman did as she was requested and the fugitive soon
returned almost out of breath. I bestoed an equvolent portion of
trinket on her with the others. I now painted their tawny cheeks
with some vermillion which with this nation is emblematic of peace.
after they had become composed I informed them by signs that I
wished them to conduct us to their camp that we wer anxious to
become acquainted with the chiefs and warriors of their nation.
they readily obeyed and we set out, still pursuing the road down
the river. we had marched about 2 miles when we met a party of
about 60 warriors mounted on excellent horses who came in nearly
full speed, when they arrived I advanced towards them with the
flag leaving my gun with the party about 50 paces behind me. the
chief and two others who were a little in advance of the main body
spoke to the women, and they informed them who we were and
exultingly shewed the presents which had been given them these
men then advanced and embraced me very affectionately in their
way which is by puting their left arm over you wright sholder
clasping your back, while they apply their left cheek to yours and
frequently vociforate the word *âh-hi'-e, âh-hi'-e* that is, I am much
pleased, I am much rejoiced. bothe parties now advanced and we
wer all carressed and besmeared with their grease and paint till I

was heartily tired of the national hug. I now had the pipe lit and gave them smoke; they seated themselves in a circle around us and pulled of their mockersons before they would receive or smoke the pipe. this is a custom among them as I afterwards learned indicative of a sacred obligation of sincerity in their profession of friendship given by the act of receiving and smoking the pipe of a stranger. or which is as much as to say that they wish they may always go bearfoot if they are not sincere; a pretty heavy penalty if they are to march through the plains of their country. after smoking a few pipes with them I distributed some trifles among them, with which they seemed much pleased particularly with the blue beads and vermillion. I now informed the chief that the object of our visit was a friendly one, that after we should reach his camp I would undertake to explain to him fully those objects, who we wer, from whence we had come and wither we were going; that in the mean time I did not care how soon we were in motion, as the sun was very warm and no water at hand. they now put on their mockersons, and the principal chief Ca-me-âh-wait made a short speach to the warriors. I gave him the flag which I informed him was an emblem of peace among whitemen and now that it had been received by him it was to be respected as the bond of union between us. I desired him to march on, which did and we followed him; the dragoons moved on in squadron in our rear. after we had marched about a mile in this order he halted them ang gave a second harang; after which six or eight of the young men road forward to their encampment and no further regularity was observed in the order of march. I afterwards understood that the Indians we had first seen this morning had returned and allarmed the camp; these men had come out armed cap a pe for action expecting to meet with their enemies the Minnetares of Fort de Prarie whome they Call Pâh'-kees. they were armed with b[o]ws arrow and Shield except three whom I observed with small pieces such as the N. W. Company furnish the natives with which they had obtained from the Rocky Mountain Indians on the yellow stone river with whom they are at peace. on our arrival at their encampmen on the river in a handsome level and fertile bottom at the distance of 4 Ms. from where we had first met them they introduced us to a londge made of willow brush and an old leather lodge which had been prepared for our reception by the young men which the chief had dispatched for that purpose. Here we were seated on green boughs and the skins of Antelopes. one of the warriors then pulled up the grass in the center of the lodge forming a smal circle of about 2 feet in diameter the chief next produced his pipe and native tobacco and began a long cerimony of the pipe when we were requested to take of our mockersons, the Chief having previously taken off his as well as all the warriors present. this we complyed with; the Chief then lit his pipe at the fire kindled in this little magic circle, and standing on the opposite side of the circle uttered a speach of several minutes in length at the conclusion of which he pointed the stem to the four cardinal points of the heavens first begining at the East and ending with the North. he now presented the pipe to me as if desirous that I should smoke, but when I reached my hand to receive it, he drew it back and repeated the same cremony three times, after which he pointed the stem first to the heavens then to the center of the magic circle smoked himself with three whifs and held the pipe untill I took as many as I thought proper; he then held it to each of the white persons and then gave it to be consumed by his warriors. this pipe was made of a dense simitransparent green stone very highly polished about 2½ inches long and of an oval figure, the bowl being in the same direction with the stem. a small piece of birned clay is placed in the bottom of the bowl to seperate the tobacco from the end of the stem and is of an irregularly rounded figure not fitting the tube purfectly close in order that the smoke may pass. this is the form of the pipe. their tobacco is of the same kind of that used by the Minnetares Mandans and Ricares of the Missouri. the Shoshonees do not cultivate this plant, but obtain it from the Rocky mountain Indians and some of the bands of their own nation who live further south. I now explained to them the objects of our journey &c. all the women and children of the camp were shortly collected about the lodge to indulge themselves with looking at us, we being the first white persons they had ever seen. after the cerimony of the pipe was over I distributed the remainder of the small articles I had brought with me among the women and children. by this time it was late in the evening and we had not taisted any food since the evening before. the Chief informed us that they had nothing but berries to eat and gave us some cakes of serviceberries and Choke cherries which had been dryed in the sun; of these I made a hearty meal, and then walked to the river, which I found about 40 yards wide very rapid clear and about 3 feet deep. the banks low and abrupt as those of the upper part of the Missouri, and the bed formed of loose stones and gravel. Cameahwait informed me that this stream discharged itself into another doubly as large at the distance of half a days march which came from the S. W. but he added on further enquiry that there was but little more timber below the junction of those rivers than I saw here, and that the river was confined between inacessable mountains, was very rapid and rocky insomuch that it was impossible for us to pass either by land or water down this river to the great lake where the white men lived as he had been informed. this was unwelcome information but I still hoped that this account had been exagerated with a view to detain us among them. as to timber I could discover not any that would answer the purpose of constructing canoes or in short more than was bearly necessary for fuel consisting of the narrow leafed cottonwood and willow, also the red willow Choke Cherry service berry and a few currant bushes such as were common on the Missouri. these people had been attacked by the Minetares of Fort de prarie this spring and about 20 of them killed and taken prisoners. on this occasion they lost a great part of their horses and all their lodges except that which they had erected for our accomodation; they were now living in lodges of a conic figure made of willow brush. I still observe a great number of horses feeding in every direction around their camp and therefore entertain but little doubt but we shall be enable to furnish ourselves with an adiquate number to transport our stores even if we are compelled to travel by land over these mountains. on my return to my lodge an indian called me in to his bower and gave me a small morsel of the flesh of an antelope boiled, and a peice of a fresh salmon roasted; both which I eat with a very good relish. this was the first salmon I had seen and perfectly convinced me that we were on the waters of the Pacific Ocean. the course of this river is a little to the North of west as far as I can discover it; and is bounded on each side by a range of high Mountains. tho' those on the E. side are lowest and more distant from the river.—

This evening the Indians entertained us with their dancing nearly all night. at 12 O'Ck. I grew sleepy and retired to rest leaving the men to amuse themselves with the Indians. I observe no essential difference between the music and manner of dancing among this nation and those of the Missouri. I was several times awoke in the course of the night by their yells but was too much fortiegued to be deprived of a tolerable sound night's repose.

Confluence of the Marias and Missouri rivers, date and photographer unknown

Lewis and Clark
on the Upper Missouri
Decision at the Marias

John L. Allen

ON APRIL 7, 1805, THE CORPS OF NORTHWESTERN DISCOVERY under the command of Meriwether Lewis and William Clark left winter quarters near the fortified villages of the Mandan nation in present-day North Dakota and, in six canoes and two pirogues, headed up the Missouri River into the unknown—"a country at least two thousand miles in width, on which the foot of civilized man had never trodden."[1]

Like virtually all exploring expeditions, this one had a goal—a goal as old as Europe's realization that the New World was a barrier lying athwart the all-water route to the Orient. For three centuries, the conjectural Northwest Passage or Passage to India had conditioned North American exploration. The experiences of explorers during those centuries had altered the nature of the dream passage and the earliest conceptions of a sea-level strait across the continent gave way to views of inland seas connected to the eastern and western oceans by mighty rivers.

These rivers retreated, in turn, before ideas of great navigable waterways which mingled their waters somewhere in the interior of the continent and provided interconnected water travel from east to west.

But although exploration had changed the nature of the conceptual passage, it had not changed the dream itself. By the time of Lewis and Clark, the Passage to India had been articulated in its final and most realistic form—it was a simple and very short portage between the headwaters of a navigable river which flowed to the Atlantic and the sources of a great river draining toward the setting sun. Guided by Thomas Jefferson's specific instructions to locate the portage between the heads of the Missouri and Columbia rivers and establish thereby the "most direct and practicable water communication across this continent for the purposes of commerce," the men of the Lewis and Clark Expedition turned their faces toward the West and toward the final solution to the centuries-old riddle of the water route across North America.[2]

Preparation for this attempt on the Northwest Passage had been lengthy and careful; among all the planning efforts, none were more painstaking or more important than the accumulation of the then-available geographical knowledge about the western parts of North America. Thomas Jefferson, conceiver and sponsor of the expedition, had spent years gathering and analyzing geographical and cartographic information on the possible connections between the Missouri and the first-mythical-then-actual Great River of the West or Columbia.[3]

Much of this information had been imparted to Meriwether Lewis, Jefferson's personal secretary, prior to the expedition. Before the party left Fort Mandan in the spring of 1805, considerably more lore on western geography had been added.

Lewis and his co-commander, William Clark, had, during the encampment at Wood River near St. Louis in the winter of 1803–4, studied the maps and journals brought from Washington by Lewis or forwarded by Jefferson and others. This material was combined with data obtained from merchants, fur traders, and government officials in the St. Louis area. When the captains started their journey to the Pacific in the spring of 1804, they took with them a set of definite geographical conceptions about the West, gleaned from the materials they had spent months in studying.

Although neither captain wrote a description or drew a map to illustrate their image of the West before leaving Wood River, it is possible to understand the nature of their views on western geography by examining those geographical materials which they considered to be the most important. Among all the items upon

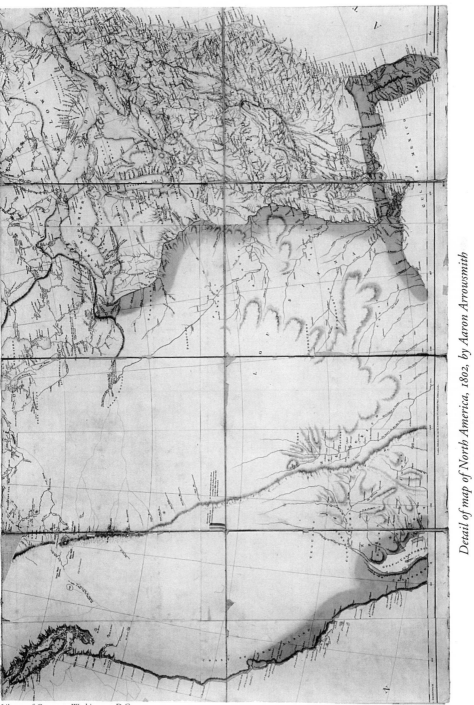

Detail of map of North America, 1802, by Aaron Arrowsmith

which Lewis and Clark relied most heavily in making their plans, none was more representative of the extent and character of their geographical knowledge than the 1802 edition of Aaron Arrowsmith's map of North America.

This map, drawn by a British cartographer and based on the late eighteenth century surveys of Peter Fidler, a Hudson's Bay Company employee, was widely considered by the finest geographical minds of the time to be the best and most accurate representation of the West. As such, it is symbolic of the nature of the image held by Lewis and Clark. From it, and from other materials which supplemented it, the captains derived those elements of their image which bore directly on their central objective of locating the shortest water route across the continent.[4]

In the explorers' mind's eye view of the country through which they were to pass, the significant features were the drainage systems of the Missouri and Columbia rivers, the courses and navigability of those streams, and the Rocky Mountain source region from which they flowed. And in the image held by Lewis and Clark in the spring of 1804, these elements held the promise of the Passage to India.

The drainage system of the Missouri was seen as triangular or fanlike in shape. The base of the triangle lay along the eastern side of a range of mountains where, between the forty-fifth and fiftieth parallels of latitude, a number of small but navigable rivers had their sources. These rivers flowed toward the east and converged to form two major streams which joined at the apex of the triangle near the Mandan villages, recognized by Lewis and Clark as the furthest penetration of explorers and traders into the western interior of the Louisiana territory. From the villages, the river that was now called the Missouri turned toward the southeast to enter the Mississippi at St. Louis.

Of the two main rivers that joined near the Mandan villages, the southern was the true Missouri. It had its source in the mountains near the headwaters of streams which flowed toward the Pacific. From this source it ran a course that was nearly due west-to-east and was navigable throughout. This was the proper route to the Pacific.[5]

The mountain range in which the Missouri had its source

appeared in the captains' image as a narrow, single-ridge structure, extending from south to north and being extensive in neither height nor breadth.[6] On the western slope of this range, opposite the heads of the Missouri and the streams which fed it, were the source waters of the Columbia system. Although the Columbia was more of a geographical unknown than the Missouri, it was assumed that its source rivers were also navigable to their heads.

The assumed navigability of the upper reaches of both the Missouri and the Columbia combined with the captains' notions on the size of the mountain range they knew as the Rocky or Stony Mountains to create the core of misconception upon which their mission was based. The Missouri was navigable to its source in a range of low mountains and only a short and easy portage across that range would be necessary to link the waters of the Atlantic with some navigable branch of the Columbia. With this linking the ancient dream of the Passage to India could become a reality.

The image of western geography that Lewis and Clark carried up the Missouri in the spring of 1804 underwent significant changes during the first summer of exploration and the winter hibernation at Fort Mandan. Acquisition of geographical knowledge did not cease with the expedition's departure from the Wood River camp and inputs of new knowledge from documents and maps, fur traders, and Indians served to restructure the captains' geographical understanding of the West.

Even before leaving Wood River, Lewis and Clark acquired documents from the explorations of John Evans and James Mackay, Spanish-sponsored explorers in the Missouri valley during the late eighteenth century.[7] A journal written by Mackay and a map of the country west of the Mandan villages, drawn by Evans, provided the captains with the most current knowledge available on the West. Although this data was received too late to become assimilated into their image before their departure, Lewis and Clark would find it vital for later modifications of that image.

Even more important was information received during the winter at Fort Mandan. Throughout the long winter there, from November 1804 to April 1805, Lewis and Clark were visited in their winter quarters by Mandan and Hidatsa Indians and by traders in the employ of the British Northwest Company. From these visitors the captains obtained sketches and oral information on the country to the west.[8] This data, in conjunction with the Mackay-Evans material, was responsible for changes in the earlier image. New information had given old ideas new expression and although the central theme in the explorers' image of the West was still the Passage to India, many of the elements within that image had undergone change by the end of the winter at Fort Mandan.

The nature of these changes and the character of the new image can be seen quite clearly in what is, quite possibly, the most important documentary material of the entire expedition. This material, compiled by the captains during the Fort Mandan winter, includes Lewis's lengthy and detailed geographical description of the West and Clark's large map of the country from St. Louis to the Pacific.[9]

One of the major components of the new image was the recognition that neither the straight-line course of the Missouri from the mountains to the Mandan villages nor the fanlike drainage pattern of the Missouri system as shown on the Arrowsmith map were accurate.

From the Mackay-Evans material and from the Indian information, Lewis and Clark had learned that the Missouri did not divide into two major branches above the Mandan villages. Instead, the Missouri proper was the only major river west of the Mandans. It did, it is true, flow a fairly straight course from the mountains. But its sources were far to the south and it flowed northward between several mountain ranges before bending toward the east and passing out of the mountains.

This was a critical restructuring of the view of the West. Lewis and Clark had learned of the long south-to-north passage of the Missouri through the mountains. They had also learned that the Rockies were not a single ridge but were composed of several ranges. And, finally, they had learned of a critical landmark of the Upper Missouri. At the point where the Missouri left the mountains and flowed into the plains there was a great cataract. This was the Missouri's Great Falls and both the Mackay-Evans data and the Indian information agreed on its location near the Missouri's emergence from the Rockies.

Since their sources of data placed the falls near the forty-seventh parallel of latitude, Lewis and Clark concluded that the fanlike drainage system shown on the Arrowsmith map between the forty-fifth and fiftieth parallels was a misrepresentation. Arrowsmith's data provider, Peter Fidler, could not have gone as far south as the forty-fifth parallel without seeing the Missouri or its Great Falls. Therefore, his surveys must have all been made north of the Missouri and the mountains he saw with small streams issuing from them must lie above the forty-seventh parallel.[10]

These corrections in the Arrowsmith map were not the only changes made in the captains' image of the West. Another feature of the new image was an absolute increase in the quantity and quality of knowledge of the country between the Mandan villages and the Pacific. This new knowledge included vital descriptions of the Missouri itself, of the streams tributary to it, of its passage through the Rockies, of the portage between its source and the waters of the Columbia, and, finally, of the course of the Columbia to the Pacific.

Above the Mandan villages, the Missouri ran a direct course to the Great Falls, located near the first or easternmost range of the Rockies. Between the villages and the mountains the Missouri was joined by the Knife, the Little Missouri, the Yellowstone, and the Musselshell, all coming from the south. From the north came the White Earth River and the Missouri's most important northern tributary, a river that the Indians had called "the river which scolds at all others."

From the falls, the Missouri turned to the southwest and was joined from the west by the Medicine River. The southwesterly direction continued through a second and third range of mountains to a point above the third range of mountains where three rivers of nearly equal size joined to form the Missouri proper. Here was knowledge of another critical landmark—the Three Forks.

The westernmost fork of the Missouri above Three Forks was navigable to the foot of the fourth and final range of the Rockies. Across this range to the west, at a distance of a half-day's journey, the waters of a mighty southern branch of the Columbia ran in a south-to-north direction and then, bending westward, flowed through plains to the Columbia proper and thence to the Pacific.[11]

Here was the short portage, the Passage to India. It did exist and therefore it could be located and negotiated and all the commerce of the Orient could be brought to American shores. Full of the hope and expectation and optimism that this image created, the expedition left its winter camp.

The upriver voyage from Fort Mandan, begun on April 7, 1805, proceeded past the mouths of the Little Missouri, White Earth, and Yellowstone rivers, each located approximately where it should have been, according to the available knowledge. This part of the journey was pleasant and without major incident. Although the wind blew violently from the west and northwest, stinging the faces of the men and sometimes obscuring the far shores of the Missouri with clouds of dust and sand, the countryside was rich and beautiful, grass-cloaked and teeming with immense herds of buffalo, deer, elk, and antelope. It was a beautiful spring and if the winds continued to blow and ice formed on the cooking pots during the nights, the days were warm. By May 4, the snow had all but disappeared and the open grasslands and trees along the river were showing the light green of spring in the Great Plains.

On May 8, the expedition reached the mouth of the river that they named the Milk, after the color of its waters. The captains concluded that this river was the one the Indians who had visited Fort Mandan during the winter had called "the river which scolds at all others." The Milk River was the only major tributary entering the Missouri from the north, according to their Indian informants. As such, it was an important landmark and to find it about where they had anticipated meant that the conceptions with which they left Fort Mandan were holding true.[12] Above it lay the Great Falls, the Three Forks, and the short portage to Columbian waters.

For the next ten days the small fleet sailed through the fantastic country of the Missouri Breaks. Although Lewis and Clark believed that the Great Falls were at least two hundred miles from the mouth of the Milk River, both they and the men became extremely anxious to come in sight of the first ranges of the Rockies that their information had represented to them as beginning near the cataracts of the Missouri.[13]

They were temporarily elated when, on May 19, Clark climbed a hill on the northern side of the Missouri and saw to the west and north the first outlying ranges east of the Rocky Mountains. These mountains remained in sight on both sides of the river for several days. They did not match the descriptions given them by the natives, however, and the captains soon realized that they were not viewing the ranges near the falls.[14]

From the first sighting of the scattered ranges east of the Rockies, the progress of the expedition up the Missouri became more tedious. For hours at a time the party was compelled to beach their craft, waiting for the wind to abate. The river became more and more choked with shoals and sandbars and the captains must have begun to wonder about the validity of their assumptions about the navigability of the Missouri. In most places the boats had to be towed by lines from the shore. The rocks of the bluffs, broken here and there by the numerous dry channels through which water from the plains above the Missouri enters the river, closed in on either side and made towing a hazardous and difficult operation. Mountainous country continued to be visible north and south of the river and when, on May 26, the very tips of the Highwood Mountains came into view just above the western horizon, the captains were convinced that they were nearing the first range of the Rockies and, therefore, the Great Falls.[15] Traveling became easier above the unexpected Judith River and the distant mountains remained in sight. Anticipation now ran high. Lewis and Clark knew, from their distance calculations and the proximity of the mountains, that they were close to the falls and to the portage of hope and desire which lay beyond.

But before reaching the Great Falls, the Lewis and Clark Expedition encountered one of the greatest obstacles in the course of their two-year journey, a problem that they would spend more than a week in solving completely. In the late afternoon of June 2, the party came to and camped in a grove of small cottonwoods on the Missouri's left bank, opposite the mouth of a "very considerable river" which entered the Missouri from the north and almost equaled it in size.

This river was the Marias and its presence was puzzling. In the explorers' store of geographical information there was agreement that the Missouri had only one major northern tributary. That was "the river which scolds at all others," and they had passed the river fitting that description more than three weeks before.

What, then, was to be made of this second northern river? Or, if the northern branch were the true Missouri, what was to be made of the southern branch? Their information contained no account of a large southern tributary stream above the mouth of the Yellowstone.[16]

The true Missouri was the river, according to their conceptions of western geography, that had its sources within portaging distance of the navigable waters of the Columbia River. It was, therefore, the river that must be followed to its uppermost reaches if the Passage to India were to be found. But the unexpected division of the Missouri into two streams of near-equal size necessitated a major decision: "which of these rivers was the Missouri, or that river which the Minnetarees call *Amahte Arz-zha* or Missouri, and which they had described to us as approaching very near to the Columbia River?"[17]

For the purpose of answering this question, the party crossed the Missouri below the junction early on the morning of June 3 and "formed a camp on the point formed by the junction of the two large rivers."[18] Here the decision that would determine the success or failure of the entire enterprise would be made:

> to mistake the stream at this period of the season, two months of the traveling season having now elapsed, and to ascent such stream to the rocky Mountain or perhaps much further before we could inform ourselves whether it did approach the Columbia or not, and then be obliged to return and take the other stream would not only loose us the whole of this season but would probably so dishearten the party that it might defeat the expedition altogether. convinced we were that the utmost circumspection and caution was necessary in deciding on the stream to be taken.[19]

The process of making this critical decision was not, as it has often been supposed, a simple one based on field observation alone. Nor was the decision itself just a lucky guess. Instead, the decision-making procedure was a complex and well-calculated series of operations lasting more than a week.

On the first day at the junction, the captains decided to make a preliminary investigation of the width, depth, and speed of flow of the two rivers in order to determine which was the major stream. To this end they sent a light canoe manned by three men up each branch. In an attempt to get some kind of long-range bearing on the direction from which the two forks came, they also sent several small parties by land to travel as far as possible and still return by nightfall.

Meanwhile, Lewis and Clark remained at the camp between the two rivers and made observations in the immediate area. During the morning they strolled to the highest ground between the Missouri and Marias and from this observation point had what Lewis termed an "inchanting view:"

> to the South we saw a range of lofty mountains which we supposed to be a continuation of the S. Mountains. stretching themselves from S.E. to N.W. terminating abbruptly about S.West from us; these were partially covered with snow; behind these Mountains and at a great distance, a second and more lofty range of mountains appeared to stretch across the country in the same direction with the others, reaching from West, to the N. of N.W., where their snowey tops lost themselves beneath the horizon. This last range was perfectly covered with snow.[20]

But although the view was sublime, it was inconclusive. Little could be learned about the courses of the rivers, their channels being obscured by the convolutions of the countryside.

From the high ground the captains wandered down into the lovely little valley of the Teton River, through chokecherry and gooseberry and wild rose, thence back to the junction of the Missouri and Marias. Here they examined the nature of the two main rivers more closely:

> we took the width of the two rivers, found the left hand or S. fork 372 yards and the N. fork 200. The no[r]th fork is deeper than the other but it's currant not so swift; it's waters run in the same boiling and roling manner which was uniformly characterized the Missouri throughout it's whole

course so far; it's waters are of a whitish brown colour very thick and terbid, also characteristic of the Missouri; while the South fork is perfectly transparent runds very rappid but with a smoth unriffled surface it's bottom composed of round and flat smooth stones like most rivers issuing from a mountainous country. the bed of the N. fork composed of some gravel but principally mud.[21]

"In short," wrote Lewis, "the air and character of this river [the Marias] is so precisely that of the Missouri below that the party with very few exceptions have already pronounced the N. fork to be the Missouri."

But at this point, sometime in the afternoon of June 3, Lewis and Clark showed their competence as field observers and analyzers of geographical information and made the initial assessment that further study would prove to be correct.

"If we were to give our opinions I believe we should be in the minority," noted Lewis. It is quite apparent that, in their considered opinion, the southern river was the one the Indians had described to them as approaching the waters of the Columbia. The limited and brief reconnaissance undertaken that morning was responsible for this tentative conclusion. But the conclusion was possible only because the things observed during the mornings' field work were analyzed in the light of what were, to Lewis and Clark, the "known" geographical facts.

When the captains returned from their reconnaissance of the morning of June 3, they returned with a perspective that was crucial for their decision. From the height-of-land separating the Missouri and Marias they had not been able to see the course of either river beyond the junction—but they had seen mountain ranges to the south and southwest. The nearest range of mountains had been in view for over a week and were not, by this time, considered to be the first range of the Rockies that was believed to begin near the Great Falls.

But behind these ranges, to the south and southwest and at a great distance, lofty, snow-covered peaks were visible and these might well have seemed to be the range near the falls. If so, and if the southern branch continued its southwesterly trend above the junction, then it was the river which lay in the proper geographic relationship with the mountains and was, consequently, the river leading to Columbian waters.

Furthermore, their examination of the characteristics of the rivers upon their return to the base camp at the junction had shown the waters of the southern fork to be transparent, running over a bottom of round and flat smooth stones. It was "like most rivers issuing from a mountainous country" and the true Missouri, according to the captains' image, ran through mountains for a considerable distance from its source, all the way to its entrance into the plains at the Great Falls. The northern fork, their examination showed, was a muddy and silty river and although it was very similar to the Missouri below the junction, Lewis and Clark were inclined to view it only as a tributary stream. It might well have been part of the drainage system indicated in their reevaluation of the Arrowsmith map and probably passed through the plains north of the Missouri without penetrating the mountains far enough to interlock with the Columbia.

On the evening of June 3, Lewis wrote: "I am confident that this river rises in and passes a great distance through an open plain country . . . convinced I am that if it penetrated the Rocky Mountains to any great distance it's waters would be clearer unless it should run an immence distance indeed after leaving those mountains through these level plains in order to acquire it's turbid hue."[22] The river whose transparent waters flowed from the southwest, from the mountains, was probably the Missouri and, therefore, the proper route to the Pacific.

But this assumption was only tentative. The parties that had been sent by land and water up both branches had returned with no conclusive information and the captains were still puzzled by the failure of their Indian informants to mention the junction of the Missouri and a large tributary stream.[23] Furthermore, it is apparent from the tone of the captains' journal for June 3, that they were the only members of the party who did not adhere to the belief that the northern fork, because of its similarities with the Missouri below, was the proper river to follow.

Two factors played a role in shaping the events of the week to follow. First, Lewis and Clark were good enough officers to realize the potential deterioration of their command situation should they go against the opinions of their men—some of whom were trained rivermen and wilderness experts—and then be proved wrong. And second, although the captains might have been firm in the belief that the left-hand fork was the Missouri and had the geographical evidence to support this view, they were too competent not to recognize the tactical dangers of a hasty decision without more definite proof of their preliminary assessment. Accordingly, it was concluded that each officer should take a small party and "ascend these rivers untill we could perfectly satisfy ourselves of the one, which it would be most expedient for us to take on our main journey to the Pacific."[24]

On the cool and cloudy morning of June 4, Captains Lewis and Clark departed from the camp at the junction of the Missouri and Marias rivers. Clark and a party of five men set out up the right-hand side of the Missouri, keeping to the higher lands well back from the river in an attempt to get the best views possible. By the end of a rainy afternoon they had traveled nearly thirty miles and made camp in an abandoned Indian shelter somewhere near the later site of Fort Benton. Except for an encounter with a couple of grizzlies, the small party spent an uneventful night alongside the Missouri, the waters of which continued to run rapidly over a gravelly bed.

It rained and snowed intermittently throughout the night and when the party prepared to break camp the morning of the fifth, they noted considerable amounts of snow on the mountains (the Highwood Mountains) southeast of their campsite. By around noon they had come in sight of other snow-covered mountains (the Little Belt and Big Belt ranges) to the southwest and Clark had seen enough to convince him that the river they were following was the true Missouri. From a ridge high above the river Clark could see the waters of the Missouri, still running deep and swift and trending toward the southwest, toward the mountains that he assumed to be those near the falls.

To proceed any further would be useless and Clark and his men struck out overland for the main camp at the junction, reaching the Teton River in the late afternoon and making camp in its valley. At five o'clock on the next afternoon, June 6, the party led by Clark arrived at the junction of the Missouri and Marias where they expected to find Lewis waiting for them.

But Lewis was taking a little bit longer to reach a firm conclusion. He and his party of six men had crossed the Marias from the camp at the junction on the morning of the fourth and had proceeded on foot up that river along its right bank. At a distance of about five miles from the main camp, Lewis climbed a hill from which he viewed the "North Mountains" (the Bears Paws) lying toward the northeast and saw the northwesterly trend of the Marias. To the northwest, along the course of the river he was following, he could see nothing but a range of hills and since this view was inconclusive, he determined to proceed further.

The river continued its course to the north and west and for the remainder of the day, Lewis and his party traveled through the plains behind the river bluffs and, when the ravines grew too steep and numerous, along the bottomlands of the Marias. The evening encampment was made amidst clumps of willows which provided protection against the wind but did little to keep out the rain which continued to fall most of the night.

The men awoke cold and wet on the morning of the fifth and broke camp early, hoping to keep warmer by walking. The river kept to its north by west direction and before noon had led the party to a site from which they could see a high mountain (the main peak of the Sweetgrass Hills) toward the northwest and at a great distance. Late afternoon brought them in sight of still more mountains (the other peaks of the Sweetgrass Hills) in the northwest and here they made camp in a grove of cottonwoods and the ever-inquisitive Lewis experimented by roasting some prairie dogs for supper and found them "well flavored and tender."[25]

Had it not been for his systematic method of observation and analysis, the view of the mountains to the northwest could have led Lewis to the conclusion that this range was the one represented as starting near the Great Falls and that this northern river, therefore, was the Missouri. But the mountains were, Lewis believed, at least eighty or one hundred miles away. This was too distant to have been the ranges near the falls, according to the captains' mileage calculations not a very great distance above the junction on whichever river was the true Missouri. Moreover, the course of the river that Lewis was following ran so far north that it, in his thinking, must have drained a vast plains area and be part of the northern waters of the Missouri as shown on his and Clark's reinterpretations of the data from the Arrowsmith map. By the morning of the sixth Lewis had become "well convinced that this branch of the Missouri had its direction too much to the North for our rout to the Pacific" and decided to return to the main camp.[26]

While Lewis and four of his men engaged themselves in constructing rafts to descend the Marias, two others traveled farther up the river in order to get a more precise bearing on its course. They returned around noon with the report that the river did continue its northerly course as far as they could see and, after lunching on elk killed the night before, the small force embarked on their two hastily constructed rafts to the mouth of the Marias. But attempted navigation of the Marias was unsuccessful and the rafts were soon abandoned for a less comfortable but more secure land route. This took them along the river bottoms where possible and across the exposed plains that offered little protection from the wind and rain which began soon after they left the rafts and continued through the afternoon and evening.

After a night spent in an unsheltered spot, Lewis and his cold, exhausted men broke camp early and resumed their trek across plains grown slippery and treacherous from the prolonged rains. On the evening of the seventh they bivouaced comfortably in an old Indian shelter. They resumed the return journey to the main camp on the cloudy and cool morning of June 8. By ten o'clock that morning the clouds had broken under a warming spring sun. As the weather improved so did Lewis's spirits as the party passed through "one of the most beautifully picturesque countries I ever beheld."[27]

But the captain had little else to be enthusiastic about. For although he had fully concluded that this river was "neither the main stream, nor that which it would be advisable for us to take" and gave it the name "Maria's River," the whole of his party was "fully persuaded that this river was the Missouri."[28] This was a potentially serious problem and one that he and Clark would have to work out when, at five o'clock on the afternoon of the eighth, the two captains were reunited at the junction of the Missouri and the river that was now officially the Marias.

While Lewis and his men relaxed with a "drink of grog" during the evening of the eighth, Clark began plotting the courses of the two rivers as far as he and Lewis had ascended them. Looking at the crude charts, both captains were more convinced than ever that their initial supposition about which stream was the Missouri was correct. They also came to the conclusion that they had been justified in making corrections in the Arrowsmith map during the winter at Fort Mandan. In his journal for June 8, Lewis wrote:

> I now began more than ever to suspect the varacity of Mr. Fidler or the correctness of his instruments . . . we are now within a hundred miles of the Rocky Mountains, and I find from my observations of the 3rd. Inst [June 3] that the latitude of this place is 47°.24′12″.8. the river must therefore turn much to the South between this place and the rocky Mountains to have permitted Mr. Fidler to have passed along the Eastern border of these mountains as far S. as nearly 45° without even seeing it. but from hence as far as Capt. C. had ascended the S. fork or Missouri being the distance of 55 (45 miles in straight line) Miles it's course is S. 29°W. and it still appeared to bear considerably to the W. of South as far as he could see it. I think therefore that we shall find that the Missouri enters the rocky mountains to the North of 45°.[29]

Analysis of the geographical data derived from all sources, including the captains' own separate field reconnaissances, continued on the ninth and further settled in the minds of Lewis and Clark "the propryety of addopting the South fork for the Missouri, as that which it would be expedient for us to take."[30] The captains determined that the Arrowsmith map, incorrect as it was, provided a strong argument against the north branch or Marias as the true Missouri. Even if Arrowsmith's informant, Fidler, had penetrated as far south as forty-seven degrees and had seen only small streams running east, then the presumption was that "those little streams do not penetrate the rocky mountains to such distance as would afford rational grownds for a conjecture that they had their sources near any navigable branch of the Columbia."[31] This eliminated the Marias from consideration as the true Missouri or route to the Pacific.

On the other hand, the Indian information obtained during the previous winter, combined with the Mackay journal and Evans map, argued strongly in favor of the southern branch:

> they [the Indians] informed us that the water of the Missouri was nearly transparent at the great falls, this is the case with the water of the South fork; that the falls lay a little to the South of sunset from them; this is also probable as we are only a few minutes [of latitude] North of Fort Mandan and the South fork bears considerably South from hence to the Mountains; that the falls are below the rocky mountains and near the No[r]thern termination of one range of those Mountains. a range of mountains [the Little Belts] which apear behind the S. mountains [the Highwoods] which appear to terminate S.W. from this place and on this side of the unbroken chain of the Rocky Mountains [the Big Belts] gives us hope that this part of their information is also correct, and there is sufficient distance between this and the mountains for many and I fear for us much too many falls. another impression on my mind is that if the Indians had passed any stream as large as the South fork on their way to the Missouri that they would not have omitted mentioning it; and the South fork from it's size and complexion of it's waters must enter the Ry. Mountains and in my opinion penetrates them to a great distance, or els whence such an immence body of water as it discharges; it cannot proceed from the dry plains to the N.W. of the Yellow Stone river on the East side of the Rocky Mountains for those numerous large dry channels which we witnessed on that side as we ascended the Missouri forbid such a conjecture; and that it should take it's sources to the N.W. under those mountains and travels of Mr. Fidler fo[r]bid us to belive.[32]

This was a brilliant piece of deduction from a fuzzy set of facts and illustrates, as well as any other event during the course of the expedition, the competence and intelligence of the two officers.

Investigation had borne out the tentative conclusion made by Lewis and Clark on the very first day at the junction. But as before, the men remained obdurate in their belief that the northern branch was the true Missouri. The captains tried to impress their geographical concepts and reasoning on the men but Peter Cruzatte, an old Missouri hand and the party's most expert riverman, "had acquired the confidence of every individual of the party [and] declared it as his opinion that the N. fork was the true genuine Missouri and could be no other."[33]

Discipline had been remarkably good on the trek from the Mandan villages to the Missouri-Marias junction. Nevertheless, this was a delicate situation. Although Lewis noted that the men "were ready to follow us any wher we thought proper to direct," the seeds of a possible breakdown must have existed.[34] "Finding them so determined in this belief," wrote Lewis, "and wishing that if we were in error to be able to detect it and rectify it as soon as possible it was agreed between Capt. C. and myself that one of us should set out with a small party by land up the South fork and continue our rout up it untill we found the falls or reached the snowy Mountains by which means we should be enabled to determine this question prety accurately."[35] This decision to split the party again does not indicate the captains' lack of assurance in their conclusions nearly as much as it indicates the necessity to maintain the confidence of their men.

The afternoon of the ninth was spent in making preparations for caching equipment prior to a departure from the junction and, in the evening, the party enjoyed a ration of grog distributed by the officers and danced and sang to the rhythms of Cruzatte's fiddle. June 10 was a fair, dry day and work on the cache continued.

Although Lewis was down with dysentery, it was decided that he and four men would depart the camp early the following morning, leaving Clark and the remainder of the party to complete the cache and the repair of the canoes and then to follow Lewis by water up the left-hand fork. Hopefully, before Clark and the main body could proceed too far up the south fork, Lewis would have found the proof they all desired.

At 8:00 A.M. on the morning of June 11, Lewis and his men swung their packs onto their shoulders and proceeded along the right bank of the Missouri, following Clark's earlier route. The march of the eleventh was a short one and camp was made early as Lewis's illness grew more severe and he was unable to proceed. But he healed himself with a concoction made from the bark of chokecherry bushes and by morning, feeling quite revived, resumed the ascent of the Missouri.

Their route on the twelveth carried them through level and open plains above the river and, after a side trip to the river for rest and refreshment during the morning, the party reached a ridge of land considerably higher than the rest of the plains. From here they saw the "august spectacle" of the Little Belt and Big Belt ranges to the south and southwest and Lewis's suspicions that they were nearing the Great Falls were confirmed. They did not reach that vital landmark on the twelfth, however, and camp was made before sunset in a clump of cottonwoods along the Missouri.

After breakfasting on venison and fish, Lewis and his small band again ascended the hills beyond the river and continued their travel across the open plains. The river took a sharp bend to the south and, fearing that he would miss the falls if he continued through the plains, Lewis altered his southwesterly course near Square and Crown buttes and headed directly for the river.

About noon on June 13, Captain Meriwether Lewis found the proof he sought. After moving through a beautiful meadow above the river, his ears were met with the sound of falling water and his eyes with a column of spray that rose like smoke above the plains. The roaring noise increased and became too great "to be mistaken for any cause short of the great falls of the Missouri."[36]

Lewis hurried down the hills "to gaze on this sublimely grand specticle" and, from a position atop some rocks, he came in sight of one of the great unknowns of the West.

Here at the Great Falls of the Missouri all the information he and Clark had collected, all the assumptions they had made, must have seemed correct. The presence of the falls fulfilled Lewis's dreams and ambitions and, unwilling to leave before having a look at what lay beyond the cataracts, he determined to make camp in the vicinity for the remainder of the afternoon and evening. His hunters killed buffalo during the afternoon while one of the men fished in the Missouri and that evening they feasted sumptuously on buffalo hump and fine trout.

The next morning Lewis dispatched a courier to Clark with a message dated "from the Great falls of the Missouri," and set out himself up the river to find the extent of the break in navigation created by the falls. Cascade after cascade met his eyes and, apparently not worrying about the difficulties the long and extensive rapids would place in the way of their navigation toward the Passage to India, Lewis wrote glowingly of the views that presented themselves. He passed an eagle's nest which the Indians had told him lay near the upper end of the falls and once beyond he climbed to the top of a hill and toward the south saw the Missouri running a meandering course toward the southwest.

From the west came the Medicine River (now the Sun River) the Indians had described to him and, on the horizon, was the second snow-clad range of the Rockies. All the components of the image and the Passage to India were there, and Lewis turned back to rejoin Clark and prepare for the glory that must be beyond.

The Great Falls, the mountains, the Medicine River—all were as the captains had expected to find them. And when, on June 16, Lewis and Clark met at the camp Clark had made at the base of the falls in preparation for the portage around them, they must have been convinced that the easy Passage to India would also be fulfilled. Their geographical knowledge had proved accurate thus far. It should prove accurate in the future and they could expect to reach the Three Forks, the half-day portage across the final range of mountains, and then the Columbia and the Pacific—the ultimate goal of American exploration.

But disappointment and failure lay ahead. The Pacific would be reached—but not via the short portage. The Passage to India was not there. All their seeking would not reveal it and, with very few exceptions, they were the last who looked.

The dream of the passage would end above Great Falls and the quality of the explorers' information and the acuracy of their images would begin to fade. They would learn these things in the months ahead and after their hungry and tortuous struggle through mountains that were supposed to be easy and through mountains that were not supposed to be there at all, after the constant drought and bad food of the dusty Columbian plains, after their sodden and dreary winter on the Oregon coast, they would turn their backs on the dream—on the promise of the Golden Chersonese and the breezes from the Spice Islands and the golden sands of Cathay.

But when these intrepid men turned their backs on the dream and on the Pacific, they would begin to fill in the map of the West. The Passage to India would be no more—for when man fills his maps there is little room left for his dreams.

Notes

1. Reuben Gold Thwaites, ed., *Original Journals of the Lewis and Clark Expedition, 1804–1806* (New York, 1904–5), 1:284 (hereafter Thw).

2. Jefferson's instructions to Lewis, June 19, 1803, Jefferson Papers, vol. 132, folios 22884-87, Manuscripts Division, Library of Congress, Washington, D.C. (hereafter Jefferson Papers), reprinted in this volume, 31-38.

3. A full treatment of the efforts of Jefferson and others in gathering geographical data on the West prior to the expedition may be found in the author's doctoral dissertation: J. L. Allen, "Geographical Images of the American Northwest, 1673 to 1806" (doctoral diss., Clark University, 1969), 273-416.

4. The Arrowsmith map compiled nearly all of the available information on the West. But as supplementary material, the captains possessed a detailed map of the vicinity of the Mandan villages, several maps of the Missouri River between St. Louis and the Mandans, charts of the Pacific coastal area near the mouth of the Columbia, journals of several British and French explorers in the West, and a considerable volume of less formal data in the form of letters, reports, and governmental documents. None of this material was in substantial disagreement with the view of the West presented on the Arrowsmith map.

5. The northern branch of the Missouri above the villages was not given a name and was of little importance to the expedition's objective. It supposedly headed near the Saskatchewan River in what is now southern Alberta. Lewis and Clark had already been warned away from this northern branch by Jefferson who wrote: "These northern waters have been ascertained to a considerable degree, and are still in a course of ascertainment by English traders and travellers." Jefferson's instructions to Lewis, Jefferson Papers.

6. This was the common American view of the Rockies during the opening years of the nineteenth century. See J. L. Allen, "Geographical Knowledge and American Images of the Louisiana Territory at the Time

of the Purchase," *Western Historical Quarterly*, 2 (April 1971), 151-70, reprinted in this volume, 39-58.

7. The best source of information on the Evans-Mackay travels (including a large number of pertinent documents) is: A. P. Nasatir, ed., *Before Lewis and Clark: Documents Illustrating the History of the Missouri, 1785–1804*, 2 vols. (St. Louis, 1952).

8. Refer to the footnotes from the captains' entries in their daily journals for December 17-19, 1804, in Thw, 1:238-39; January 5, 1805, in ibid., 244-45; January 7, 1805, in ibid., 245-46; January 16, 1805, in ibid., 249; February 18, 1805, in ibid., 263; and February 27, 1805, in ibid., 266.

9. These documents were sent down the Missouri in the spring of 1805, along with many other materials gathered during the first summer and winter of the expedition. Lewis's description of western geography is reproduced in Thw, 6:29-55.

10. The northern tributaries of the Missouri, wrote Lewis in his description, were the channels "through which, those small streams, on the E side of the Rocky mountains laid down by Mr. Fidler, pas to the Missouri." Thw, 6:53.

11. See Thw, 6:55. The western fork of the Missouri, was, of course, the Jefferson. The southern branch of the Columbia probably represented misinterpreted information about the Lemhi-Salmon system and the Bitterroot–Clark's Fork drainage.

12. A set of distance estimates between key points along the Missouri made by Clark during the winter at Fort Mandan gave the distance from the Mandan villages to the "river which scolds . . ." as 370 miles in a straight line. The captains' mileage figures taken during the expedition, with corrections for the Missouri's meandering course, corresponded closely with this estimate. Thw, 6:60-61.

13. Thw, 6:60.

14. "Those mountains [the Little Rocky Mountains to the north and the Moccasin and Judith ranges on the south] appear to be detached, and not ranges as laid down by the Minetarrees." Clark's Journal Entry, May 25, 1805, in Thw, 2:77.

15. In his magnificently edited condensation of the journals, Bernard DeVoto, *The Journals of Lewis and Clark* (Boston, 1953), identifies the range seen on May 26 as the Little Rocky Mountains. This is a rare error in DeVoto's identifications and results from a misinterpretation of the compass readings given by Lewis and Clark. Clark, the first to see the range, clearly indicates they lay to the south and west. But Lewis (from whose journal DeVoto made his identification) noted that they bore sixty-five degrees west of north. This does not mean that the mountains were northwest of the observer but that their direction of alignment was from

southeast to northwest. Lewis frequently gave compass readings like this, a fact that has resulted in considerable confusion in trying to identify landmarks along the expedition's course. Furthermore, the Little Rocky Mountains are northeast of the point of observation on May 26 and therefore could not have been the mountains whose peaks were visible to the west.

16. Thw, 2:109. The Marias is, of course, nowhere near as big a river as the Missouri under normal conditions. But Lewis and Clark had the misfortune of viewing it during peak runoff conditions and considered it to be a greater and more important river than it actually is. Had they seen the Marias later in the season, the probability of confusion would have been greatly reduced.

17. Thw, 2:112-13.

18. Ibid., 2:112.

19. Ibid., 2:113.

20. Ibid., 2:113-14. The first range of mountains mentioned by Lewis was the Highwood range. The rugged country behind this first range included the Little Belt and Big Belt ranges. Note that Lewis is again giving compass directions according to the directional alignment of the mountains rather than the bearing from the observer to the ranges.

21. Thw, 2:114.

22. Ibid., 2:114-15.

23. "What astonishes us a little is that the Indians who appeared to be so well acquainted with the geography of this country should not have mentioned this river on [the] wright hand." Lewis's Journal Entry, June 3, 1805, in Thw, 2:115.

24. Thw, 2:116.

25. Ibid., 2:124.

26. Ibid., 2:125.

27. Ibid., 2:131.

28. Ibid., 2:130.

29. Ibid., 2:131-32.

30. Ibid., 2:134.

31. Ibid.

32. Ibid., 2:136.

33. Ibid.

34. Ibid.

35. Ibid.

36. Ibid., 2:147.

The Scientific Instruments of the Lewis and Clark Expedition

Silvio A. Bedini

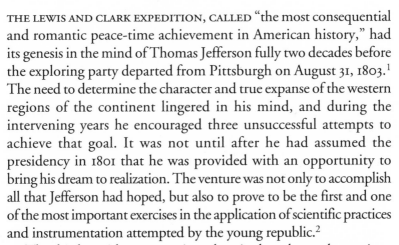

THE LEWIS AND CLARK EXPEDITION, CALLED "the most consequential and romantic peace-time achievement in American history," had its genesis in the mind of Thomas Jefferson fully two decades before the exploring party departed from Pittsburgh on August 31, 1803.[1] The need to determine the character and true expanse of the western regions of the continent lingered in his mind, and during the intervening years he encouraged three unsuccessful attempts to achieve that goal. It was not until after he had assumed the presidency in 1801 that he was provided with an opportunity to bring his dream to realization. The venture was not only to accomplish all that Jefferson had hoped, but also to prove to be the first and one of the most important exercises in the application of scientific practices and instrumentation attempted by the young republic.[2]

The third president was eminently suited to plan such a project, for he was unquestionably the best informed individual in the United States on national geography. Not only had he spent many years collecting and studying all that had been written and published about the subject, but the public offices he had held had also provided ample opportunity for him to meet Indians and others who had traveled in the West, and he recorded all that he could learn from them. Furthermore, he was knowledgeable about scientific practices and instruments in general and was personally experienced in surveying and mapping and making astronomical observations, all of which would be required to record the regions to be explored. As president also of the American Philosophical Society, he could call upon the most eminent men of science for advice on all the subjects with which the proposed expedition would be concerned.[3]

Having selected his personal secretary, Meriwether Lewis, to lead the exploring party, Jefferson gave him the task of compiling lists of the needs and estimates of costs of such an undertaking even before submitting the proposal to Congress. Lewis was to prove to be an excellent choice, for he was self-taught in the natural sciences and a lover of the outdoors, and his previous army career had made him experienced in the handling of men. He also had the advantage of being familiar with the lands beyond the Allegheny Mountains.[4]

Jefferson made available his own instruments and scientific library to Lewis and personally instructed Lewis in the use of the instruments required for surveying and determining latitude. By his own admission, Jefferson was not a practicing astronomer and unfamiliar with the use of the octant, but he nonetheless had a firm understanding of the principles involved. Lewis practiced particularly with the octant, an instrument designed primarily for use at sea but applicable also on land to observe altitudes of the sun or a star for determining latitude.[5]

Octants were made in a triangular shape from a dark, close-grained tropical wood, preferably ebony. A moveable arm, or index, was pivoted from the apex of the triangle and pointed to a scale of degrees on the arc opposite the apex. A mirror attached to the apex moved with the index arm. A sight, with two sets of colored glass shades for observing the sun, was attached to the right limb of the triangle. A horizon glass, half-mirrored and half-clear, was situated on the left limb.

With the octant, the observer looked through the sight to observe simultaneously the horizon, visible through the unsilvered portion of the horizon glass, and the object, the sun or a star, reflected by the mirror at the apex of the index arm to the silvered portion of the horizon glass and then to his eye. To achieve this alignment the angle between the two mirrors had to be one-half the altitude of the object being sighted. The angle through which the index mirror moved from the position of parallelism was determined by the movement of the index arm; double this angle was read on the arc, which was calibrated to ninety degrees.[6]

The sextant closely resembled the octant in appearance and function and was based on the same principles of optics. However, it was made entirely of cast brass instead of wood and was provided with an arc of 120 degrees, which enabled it to measure lunar distances.[7]

Although Lewis apparently became reasonably competent in the use of the octant, it was obvious that more professional training was required. Jefferson thereupon enlisted the cooperation of fellow members of the American Philosophical Society. As consultants on scientific instrumentation he selected Robert Patterson, professor of mathematics at the University of Pennsylvania, and Major Andrew Ellicott, secretary of the Pennsylvania Land Commission at Lancaster. Patterson was an authority on scientific principles and instruments, and Ellicott, as the nation's foremost surveyor, had considerable field experience in their use.[8]

For advice and instruction in the scientific data to be collected by the exploring party, the president sought out the botanist Benjamin Smith Barton; Caspar Wistar, anatomist with a wide knowledge of zoology; and Dr. Benjamin Rush of the Pennsylvania Hospital, who advised on medical practices and supplies.[9]

In anticipation of Lewis's visit, Patterson immediately began to prepare astronomical formulas for field use, including one for computing the longitude from observations of lunar distances, and another for calculating the time, altitudes, etc., expressed in the same manner by algebraic signs, which, he assured Jefferson, would make it "easy enough for boys or sailors to use."[10]

In response to the president's request for his cooperation with Lewis's instruction in the use of surveying and astronomical instruments, Ellicott stressed the necessity for Lewis to "acquire a facility, and dexterity, in making the observations, which can only be attained by practice." He also cautioned that the final calculations of latitude and longitude could not be made in the field, but would have to be computed after the expedition's return because of the considerable quantity of astronomical tables and other reference material that was needed.[11] He noted further that the instrumentation required by the exploring party was identified in his published account of the survey of the southern boundary with the Spanish territory, a copy of which he had given to the president. In this work he had specified that all that was required for determining both latitude and longitude was "a good sextant, a well made watch with seconds, and the artificial horizon, the whole of which may be packed up in a box 12 inches in length, 8 in width, and 4 in depth."[12]

Ellicott went on to provide specific instructions for determining the meridian altitude of the sun by means of a method of taking equal altitudes that he had used successfully for years, although it was generally not practiced by other American surveyors of his time.[13]

Ellicott also enclosed detailed instructions for making an artificial horizon of his own preference, using water instead of the other liquids commonly used, and with the trough made separate from the cover to avoid possible disturbance of the liquid by the wind.

In order to take altitudes with the octant, a clear and distinct horizon was essential, but such was not always available because of fog, mist, or inclement weather. The artificial horizon served as a substitute and enabled the observer using the instrument to dispense with the visible horizon when taking sights of the sun or a star. It featured a trough of mercury, the surface of which served as a reflector, with two sheets of glass attached gablewise over the trough to prevent movement of the mercury by the wind. With the artificial horizon, the instrument measured the angle between the sun and its image on the mercury's surface, this angle being equal to twice the sun's apparent altitude.[14]

On March 14, 1803, Lewis began his journey of instruction, departing from Washington en route to Harpers Ferry, Lancaster, and Philadelphia to meet and work with the various advisers. William Irvine and Israel Whelen, the purveyor of public stores, had been notified by the War Office that Lewis was to be provided with such items as he requested from military supplies. Whelen was to purchase whatever Lewis needed that could not be obtained from that source, inasmuch as all preparations for the expedition were to be vested in the War Office.[15]

At Harpers Ferry, Lewis arranged to obtain weapons and supervised the construction of an iron-framed folding boat to be used on the Upper Missouri River.[16] These duties kept him there for almost a month before he could move on to Lancaster. At Lancaster he spent part of each day with Ellicott, who drew from his own field experience, particularly of the difficulties and hazards to be anticipated in uninhabited and unknown country. During his many years surveying the wilderness, Ellicott had frequently experienced every type of privation and unexpected danger and had learned how to deal with them. His wise counsel was to prove of immeasurable value to Lewis and his companions in the next several years. Lewis remained at Lancaster for two weeks and practiced using Ellicott's field instruments, including the octant and sextant, profiting greatly from Ellicott's instruction and the experience with the instruments. In retrospect, however, it became apparent that the training period allowed was much too brief to achieve the competence required for the level of scientific responsibility imposed by Jefferson.[17]

In Philadelphia, Lewis lost no time consulting with the other advisers, in accordance with Jefferson's arrangements, and collecting and purchasing supplies for the expedition. Most of them were readily available from military stores or could be purchased, but acquisition of the instruments presented difficulties because some of them, such as thermometers, sextants, and chronometers, were not yet being made in the United States. They had to be imported from England, and high-quality ones were not always available.[18]

Jefferson had definite opinions not only about the scientific data to be collected, but also concerning the instrumentation to be used for the purpose. He had concluded that the best means of determining the longitude in the field was by the measurement of lunar distances, to be accomplished with a theodolite or possibly a portable equatorial instrument. The establishment of latitude was relatively simple, requiring only an octant, but the determination of the longitude was considerably more difficult.

At that time there were two common methods used for determining longitude. One required observation of the times that one of Jupiter's major satellites entered or exited from the shadow of the planet. Inasmuch as four major satellites were readily visible, observations could be made with relative frequency, except when the planet was not favorably situated for observation. The difficulty in using this method resulted from the uncertainty of the times of the satellites's appearances, and because for long periods the planet was not easily observed.

The second method consisted of measurement of the lunar distances—determining the local time of the moon's transit and comparing it with its time of transit at a prime meridian. Basically, this method used the moon's movement around the earth as a clock, with the moon functioning as the hand or index and the sun, planets, and stars serving as the markers or indicators. The method using the Jovian satellites was easier to calculate, but their appearances were infrequent and uncertain, whereas the moon was visible quite often. Considering the advantages and disadvantages of both methods, Jefferson selected lunar observation for the expedition.[19]

In addition to a sextant or other astronomical instrument to observe lunar distances, a precise timekeeper was required to establish the times of observation. Jefferson opposed taking the usual timepiece, an astronomical regulator in the form of a tall case clock or a pocket chronometer, into the field, noting that being "fearful that the loss or derangement of his watch on which these lunar observations were to depend, might lose us this great object of his journey, I endeavored to devise some method of ascertaining the longitude by the moon's motion without a timepiece."[20]

Jefferson proposed employing a theodolite or a universal equatorial instrument. He owned examples of both instruments and was inordinately fond of them. Like the octant and sextant, they were used to measure angles and were most accurate for measuring horizontal angles such as those between a celestial body and a fixed point on the earth. The universal equatorial instrument was made portable, with an elaborate mounting which could be set by clockwork to follow the course of an observed celestial body across the sky to provide a continuous record, and it was the most sophisticated astronomical instrument of the time. He later noted that his proposal for observing lunar distances "was founded too in the use of the Equatorial the only instrument with which I have any familiarity. I never used the Quadrant at all; and had thought of importing three or four Equatorials for the use of those parties. They get over all difficulty in finding a meridian." It was true, he admitted, that Jesse Ramsden, the maker of the theodolite, specified that it was necessary to use a timekeeper with it, but it was

Jefferson's opinion that "this cannot be necessary, for the margin of the equatorial circle of this instrument being divided into time by hours, minutes, and seconds, supplies the main function of the timekeeper, and for measuring merely the interval of the observations, is such as not to be neglected. A portable pendulum for counting, by an assistant, would fully answer the purpose."[21]

Equatorial instruments were extremely expensive, however, while theodolites were more readily available. The latter consists of a telescopic sight and two circles, mounted at right angles to each other, each divided into degrees and readable in minutes. The pedestal stand supporting the apparatus could be leveled and adjusted.

In Jefferson's opinion, both the equatorial and the theodolite had distinct advantages over the sextant and the Borda reflecting circle because their telescopes were more flexible and their apparatus for correcting refraction and parallax rendered the notations of altitude unnecessary, and even dispensed with the need for the timekeeper or portable pendulum.[22]

So convinced was Jefferson that these instruments of his selection could satisfactorily eliminate the need for a timekeeper for observing lunar distances, that he communicated his proposal not only to Ellicott and Patterson, but to others as well. Among them were William Dunbar, John Garnett, William Lambert, Isaac Briggs, Joshua Moore, and possibly others to whom he had written concerning the expedition.[23] In response, Ellicott and Patterson suggested alternative methods for determining longitude, each requiring timekeepers, but diplomatically did not comment on the use of the equatorial or theodolite.[24]

Jefferson now began to have some doubts of his own, for in a letter to Lewis he commented, "I would wish that nothing that passed between us here should prevent your following his [Ellicott's] advice, which is certainly the best. Should a time-piece be requisite, it is possible Mr. Arnold could furnish you one. Neither Ellicott not Garnet [sic] have given me their opinion on the substituting the meridian at land instead of observations of time, for ascertaining longitude by lunar motions. I presume, therefore, it will not answer."[25]

Lewis reported that both Ellicott and Patterson disagreed with the use of the equatorial or theodolite in the field. They believed that such instruments were too delicate for the rough use they would be given, difficult to transport, and easily put out of order. In short, Lewis went on, referring to the theodolite, "in its application to my observations for obtaining the longitude, it would be liable to many objections, and to much more inaccuracy than the sextant." Instead, both Patterson and Ellicott recommended that Lewis be equipped with two sextants; one or two artificial horizons; a good "Arnald's watch" (chronometer); a plain surveying compass, with ball-and-socket joint; a two-pole chain; and a set of drafting instruments. "As a perfect knowledge of the time will be of the first importance in all my Astronomical Observations," Lewis went on to explain to the president, "it is necessary that the time-keeper intended for this expedition should be put in the best possible order, if therefore Sir, one has been procured for me and you are not perfectly assured of her being in good order, it would be best perhaps to send her to me by safe hand." He explained that the Philadelphia clockmaker Henry Voigt had offered to clean it and Ellicott would regulate it.[26]

With all the advice that Jefferson had sought from members of the American Philosophical Society and others, there was inevitably some overlap. John Vaughan, librarian of the society, had also been consulted by someone to whom Jefferson had written, and he in turn sought advice from Ellicott. The latter informed him that for use in the field a brass sextant was infinitely superior to a wooden octant, and that one of the best quality might be purchased for between eighty and one hundred dollars. Ellicott himself planned to make an artificial horizon for the expedition, a project that required a slice of talc he wished to obtain from a block in the philosophical society's museum.[27] Ellicott's use of talc for the reflecting surface of the instrument was an innovation evidently not used by others. Soon after his arrival in Philadelphia, Lewis visited Vaughan, bringing an artificial horizon made by Ellicott and a letter from him. Lewis also called upon Patterson with a letter from Ellicott asking him to provide Lewis with his own formulas for longitude.[28]

Lewis had done his homework well, for the list he had compiled with Jefferson's cooperation while he was still in Washington included most of the instruments later recommended by Ellicott and Patterson, as well as others they did not consider necessary.

Each instrument listed would fulfill a particular aspect of the expedition's mission. On Lewis's earlier list, but not included on the surviving record of instruments acquired for the expedition, were a microscope for study of plant life and minerals; a theodolite, originally intended for astronomical observation but useful also for surveying; hydrometers for determining the amount of water vapor in the atmosphere; a brass rule; magnetic needles; and a measuring tape. Some of these items were probably deleted by Ellicott and Patterson as impractical, and others may have been eliminated simply because they were not available in Philadelphia at that time. Or some of them could have been purchased from other makers or dealers, from whom no records of purchase have survived.[29]

Additions made to the list included a spirit level for surveying, one plated and three brass pocket compasses, a magnet for "touching" the compass needles when they lost their magnetism, a sextant, spare talc for the artificial horizon, a plain surveying compass for surveying through dense woodland and underbrush, a circular protractor with index arm for map-making, a six-inch pocket telescope, a log line and reel, and a log-ship.

Particularly interesting on Lewis's original list is an:

> Instrument for measuring made of tape with feet & inches marked on it, confined within a circular lethern [sic] box of sufficient thickness to admit the width of the tape which has one of its ends confined to an axis of metal passing through the center of the box, around which and within the box it is readily wound by means of a small crank on the other side of the box which forms a part of the axis, its tape when necessary is drawn out with the same facility & ease with which it is wound up.[30]

This instrument described is the common surveyor's measuring tape. Such tapes were not commercially produced until almost the mid-nineteenth century. Among the earliest examples of a commercial tape measure known is one manufactured in England in about 1846.[31] The unusually detailed nature of the description suggests that a commercial tape measure did not then exist. Jefferson may have proposed that such an item would be useful and should be ordered to be made by one of the Philadelphia instrument makers. Expedition records mention a "tape line" used to measure the size of fishes, indicating that some form of the tape measure had been obtained.

In 1800, Philadelphia was a major American shipping center, with many makers and dealers of mathematical instruments. Some specialized in the production of navigational and surveying instruments, while others imported and sold optical and meteorological instruments from England and France.[32] With the assistance of Patterson and Whelen, Lewis was able to obtain most of the instruments he required, the majority purchased from Thomas Whitney's shop on Water Street. In addition to making and selling instruments, Whitney also modified them as required by his clients. For example, he attached a small high-powered reading lens, which he called a "microscope," to the index arm of the sextant that Lewis purchased.[33] The vernier scale was so minute that it required magnification to be read, and at that time sextants were equipped with separate hand-held magnifiers that fitted into the field case. It was not until a decade or more later that a lens attached directly to the index arm of the sextant became a standard feature.

Whitney provided a total of fifteen instruments to the expedition, at a cost of $162.20. From him Lewis purchased a late-model octant with tangent screw, probably English, for $22.00. It had a fourteen-inch radius and a vernier scale, and it was capable of making back observations. For $90.00 Lewis also obtained a sextant of a ten-inch radius and equipped with a vernier scale and three eyepieces: a hollow tube and two telescopes, one of which reversed the image. A cased set of plotting, or drafting, instruments was needed for map-making; the spirit level and two-pole chain were standard surveying equipment. The log line, reel, and log-ship were used with a timekeeper to determine the speed of a ship or boat or the distance it had run in a given period of time. A brass boat or marine compass was a basic necessity for navigating. Lewis purchased one silver-plated pocket compass, probably for his own use, and three others of brass. Since a compass was an item that was frequently damaged or lost, he made certain that he would have replacements. From Whitney he also obtained a spare parallel glass and a slab of talc as replacements for the artificial horizon prepared for the expedition by Ellicott.[34]

One of Lewis's most important purchases was a gold-cased

chronometer from the Philadelphia watch and clockmaker Thomas Parker.[35] The chronometer, or "Arnald's watch" as Jefferson had called it, cost $250.00, with an additional seventy-five cents for the winding key. As yet no chronometers were being manufactured in the United States, and the expedition's schedule did not allow time to order one from England, as Jefferson had suggested. The only alternative was to purchase such an English-made timepiece that was already available in Philadelphia. As Lewis described it, the chronometer he purchased had a balance wheel and escapement of "the most improved construction."[36]

For cleaning and adjustment, Lewis brought the chronometer to the shop of Henry Voigt, the foremost clockmaker of the time. Voigt also constructed a protective mahogany case, in which he suspended the chronometer by means of "an universal joint," by which Lewis may have meant gimbals. Voigt also cleaned and adjusted Lewis's own silver pair-case watch with second hand, which Lewis planned to take on the expedition. Voigt's total bill for the work was $7.37.[37] Lewis sent the chronometer by Dr. Barton to Ellicott to be regulated and rated. Ellicott checked the chronometer's rate for two weeks until he felt assured that it was properly adjusted.

Meanwhile Patterson had begun work on a "Statistical Table," on which Lewis was to record each astronomical observation as he made it. Patterson originally had planned to furnish Lewis with just a sketch from which he could develop such a table, but not having completed the sketch in time, Patterson compiled the table and sent it on to Lewis after his departure. As he assured Jefferson, it was "an expedient that would save a great deal of time, and be productive of many advantages."[38]

Jefferson's final instructions to Lewis, submitted on June 30, specified, in addition to a multitude of other requirements, the instrumentation to be used "for ascertaining by celestial observations the geography of the country thro' which you will pass." Lewis was instructed to make observations, beginning at the mouth of the Missouri, of latitude and longitude at all notable points of the river, and especially at distinguishable points, such as mouths of rivers, rapids, islands, and natural landmarks that would be recognizable again later. He was asked to determine the river courses between such points by means of the compass, the log line, and observations of time that were to be corrected by the celestial observations themselves. Variations of the compass at various places also were to be noted. Points of interest on the portage between the heads of the Missouri and water offering the best communication with the Pacific were also to be fixed by means of observations.

Jefferson was particularly insistent that all "observations are to be taken with great pains & accuracy" and that they were to be recorded distinctly and in such a manner that they would be comprehensible to others as well as the observers, who would be able to establish the latitude and longitude for the locations at which they had been taken by using the requisite tables. These records were to be submitted to the War Office so that final calculations could be made later by several qualified individuals working at the same time. To ensure against possible loss of records, Jefferson directed the explorers to make several copies of their notes during their leisure and give them into the safekeeping of their most trustworthy men. "A further guard," he wrote, "would be that one of these copies be on the paper of birch, as less liable to injury than common paper."[39] Jefferson also required the explorers to record climatological data similar to the records he personally had maintained daily since he was a law student at Williamsburg.[40]

Realizing the need for a second leader if an accident or illness should befall Lewis, Jefferson left the selection to Lewis, who chose William Clark, one of his former army friends and a younger brother of the explorer George Rogers Clark. Clark's considerable military experience and familiarity with the region where the Ohio and Mississippi rivers met later proved him to have been an excellent choice. Clark had no role in planning the expedition, for there was little time between his selection and Lewis's departure on July 5 for Pittsburgh. After further unexpected delays in procuring equipment, the exploring party finally departed from Pittsburgh at the end of August 1803. Clark would join the party later.[41]

The scientific entries in the surviving journals for the early part of the expedition proper apparently were kept only by Clark. He carefully compiled tables of courses, times, and distances during which the party followed the river, noting such landmarks as islands, sandbars, towns, river openings, unusual items observed along the riverbanks, weather, and observations made with the octant.

Lewis began making his scientific entries in the spring of 1805, after the party left the Mandan villages, and continued consistently for the remainder of the expedition. From the time that the exploring party wintered with the Mandans, the explorers adopted the procedure of having Clark make a copy of all of Lewis's scientific entries in his own journal. The decision to undertake this duplication may have resulted from the accident on May 14 when "some of the papers and nearly all of the books got wet, but not altogether spoiled" when their white pirogue capsized. Lewis's entries were copied by Clark, frequently without alteration but often dated earlier for no apparent reason.[42]

The earliest temperature records were kept by Lewis as the party progressed down the Ohio River in autumn 1803, and Clark continued the practice at the Wood River camp in early 1804. The last of their thermometers was accidentally struck against a tree and broken in September 1805, however, and no temperatures could be recorded thereafter. The thermometers were probably of a type similar to those described by Jefferson to Isaac Briggs. "The kind preferred," he wrote, "is that on a lackered plate slid into a mahogany case with a glass sliding cover, these being best weather."[43]

Although Lewis is usually considered the scientific specialist of the expedition, Clark made many more significant scientific contributions than are generally realized, particularly relating to natural history. Lewis may have been given more credit because his journal entries reflected superior qualities of writing and expression. Because Lewis had been trained to use the octant and Clark had not, Lewis probably instructed him in its use in the field, for Clark practiced with it constantly at the Wood River camp and may even have become more proficient in its use than Lewis. His previous experience as a surveyor served him well, and he kept a notebook in which he had written problems of celestial navigation with their solutions. Clark was responsible for recording navigational data as well, and he also prepared sketches and observational notes. His maps proved to be remarkable for their fine quality and accuracy.[44]

In an entry for July 22, 1804, of the journal recording astronomical observations, Lewis provided a detailed description of the instruments he used for this purpose: a sextant, an octant, three artificial horizons, a chronometer, and a surveying compass. Lewis preferred the reversing telescope and used it in all his observations. He found the octant particularly useful for making back observations when the sun's altitude at noon proved too great to be observed with the sextant.

Of the three artificial horizons with which the exploring party was equipped, the one prepared by Ellicott utilizing water as the reflecting surface turned out to be useful "when the object observed was sufficiently bright to reflect a distinct immage." The one provided by Patterson, consisting of a glass pane cemented to the side of a wooden ball and adjusted by a spirit level and platform, was more adaptable for taking altitudes of the moon and stars and of the sun under dull conditions. The third horizon, utilizing the index mirror of a sextant attached to a flat board and adjusted also by a spirit level and platform, was the most adaptable with bright objects such as the stars.

The chronometer, protected in the field case made for it by Voigt, was, according to Lewis's account, wound up each day at noon and its "rate of going" confirmed by observations made by Lewis. He found it to be fifteen and five-tenths seconds too slow within a twenty-four hour period on mean solar time, which was very close to the rate established for it by Ellicott. For taking the magnetic azimuth of the sun and the pole star, Lewis used the surveying compass, and he found it useful also for taking a traverse of the river. From these compass bearings, combined with the distances from point to point that he estimated, he was able to chart the Missouri River. From the onset of the expedition to the winter of 1805, Lewis made as many as seven or eight observations for each attempt to determine longitude, the number dependent on the degree of visibility of the object or objects observed.[45]

A careful study of the astronomical data in the expedition's journals suggests that any deficiencies in the observations made by Lewis and Clark probably resulted as much from their lack of skill and experience with instruments as from the difficult conditions under which the observations had to be made. It is doubtful whether even an expert astronomer or surveyor such as Major Ellicott would have been able to make a set of lunar observations without the help of several assistants. Single-handedly, an observer would have to take several altitudes of the moon and of the planet or star in rapid succession, then proceed to observe several lunar distances and, finally, take several altitudes of the moon and planet or star once more.

A less experienced observer, however, such as Lewis or Clark, probably required as many as three assistants. As the principal observer measured the angle between the moon's limb and a star or planet, one assistant measured the moon's altitude, another the altitude of the star or planet being observed, and the third assistant recorded the times of observations with the chronometer. The three required angles had to be measured simultaneously and the observations repeated four or five times; then the mean of each group of observations had to be calculated. Finally, the sums of the lunar distances, each of the two sets of altitudes, and the times were to be divided by the number of sets to eliminate or reduce minor errors of observation.[46]

The explorers' relative inexperience with sophisticated scientific instrumentation was compounded not only by the difficult field conditions under which they had to make their observations but also by the vagaries of their chronometer. Although the timepiece had been carefully regulated first at Philadelphia and later at Lancaster, and its "rate of going" established, Lewis and Clark neglected it occasionally and permitted it to run down. Consequently, the original "rate of going" established in Pennsylvania no longer applied, and local time had to be obtained by observing equal altitudes of the sun to establish the moment of noon. Lewis faithfully recorded longitude by celestial observation as well as by dead reckoning, but the observations rarely proved to be correct, and the most useful data were the records made by dead reckoning, especially those showing their westering, combined with the observations for latitude. Lacking the time, convenience, and expertise to make the necessary calculations of longitude in the field, the task was left for later, as Ellicott had urged.[47]

Lewis had been instructed to submit his records of observations to the War Office after the exploring party's return so that the necessary calculations for longitude and latitude could be made from his data. Ferdinand Rudolph Hassler, instructor in mathematics at West Point, was selected for the task, and he attempted to correct the longitudes by making additional calculations. After considerable trial and error, he reported that he could make nothing of the observations. Errors made by the explorers may have been partly to blame, but it is also likely that Hassler did not have clear knowledge of the procedures that had been used in the field. For example, he could not have known that although Lewis regulated the chronometer on mean solar time, he entered the observations on local time. Writing to Patterson in 1810 after having received a chart of Lewis's calculations from Vaughan, Hassler stated that he had compared these with results he had obtained before, but continued to find discrepancies. Although he had been promised all the journals to study, he complained that he had received "only one, in a fair copy, which I see has many faults in writing."[48]

The problem was undoubtedly compounded by the fact that Lewis and Clark had compiled the journals after their return from rough notes made in the field, notes which were later discarded or lost, except for a few pages, so that comparisons could not be made. Although for the most part the explorers were careful to date their observations in the journals according to the original drafts, occasionally they inserted data wherever space permitted, and not necessarily related to the dates on which they had occurred.

More than a decade after the expedition's return, Jefferson commented on Lewis's observations for longitude and latitude in a letter to José Corrèa da Serra, newly appointed Spanish minister to the United States, with whom he shared scientific interests. He wrote, "altho', having with him the Nautical almanacs [for the three years during which they were in the field], he could and did calculate some of his latitudes, yet the longitudes were taken merely from estimates by the log-line, time, and course. So that it is only as to latitudes that his map may be considered as tolerably correct; not as to its longitudes."[49]

The many kinds of observations of the country that the explorers were required to record, their camp duties, and the rigors of survival under difficult conditions left Lewis and Clark insufficient time for difficult scientific observations. Despite the shortcomings of their astronomical records, the explorers returned with a remarkable corpus of information on flora, fauna, ethnology, and the geography of the regions they had traversed. Unfortunately, neither Jefferson nor Congress had made any special provisions to preserve the appurtenances of the expedition, the collections, or the records kept by the explorers on the nation's first scientific endeavor. Jefferson's lack of foresight is surprising in view of the considerable concern for the preservation of records he had always demonstrated since his student days at Williamsburg.[50]

When the exploring party returned to St. Louis, preserved materials were stored temporarily, but some botanical specimens were shipped to Jefferson, and some were permanently lost. No arrangement was made for the classification and preservation of the scientific collections, notes, and reports sent or brought back by Lewis and Clark; consequently, the materials were dispersed to various repositories, with inadequate record keeping and inevitable loss.

Jefferson allowed Lewis and Clark to keep their original journals so that they could benefit financially from their publications. Many of the journals were subsequently dispersed and lost. It was not until 1904 that presumably all the written records of the expedition were finally located and brought together for publication, a full century after Lewis and Clark had arrived at their preliminary camp.[51].

Particularly regrettable is the dispersal of the scientific instruments used on the nation's first organized scientific exploration. All that survive are a handful of unimportant personally owned items, few of which can be satisfactorily documented as having been used on the expedition.[52] The appurtenances of the trip—knives, tomahawks, fishing gear, weapons, scientific instruments, keelboat and canoes, handmade clothing, and many other items used and collected by the exploring party—would have been of enormous interest and value to the public at that time and in future generations. In the absence of a request for Congress to appropriate funds to preserve the items, they were sold at public auction at St. Louis in the autumn of 1806 for $408.62.[53]

In retrospect, in addition to the important specific information the explorers brought back about the new lands in the West, the Lewis and Clark Expedition had two important results. It had provided Jefferson with an opportunity to enlist government support of science for the first time, and it served as a precedent for future exploring expeditions to support the American position in the West. As Jefferson wrote to William Dunbar in 1805, while the expedition was still in progress, "The work we are now doing, is, I trust, done for posterity, in such a way that they need not repeat it. . . . We shall delineate with correctness the great arteries of this great country: those who come after us will extend the ramifications as they become acquainted with them, and fill up the canvas we begin."[54]

Notes

1. Seymour Adelman, "Equipping the Lewis and Clark Expedition," *American Philosophical Society Bulletin for 1945* (Philadelphia, 1946), 39.

2. Paul Russell Cutright, *A History of the Lewis and Clark Journals* (Norman, Okla., 1976), 3; Reuben Gold Thwaites, ed., *Original Journals of the Lewis and Clark Expedition, 1804–1806* (1904–5; reprint, New York, 1969), 7:193-205 (hereafter Thw).

3. Donald Jackson, *Thomas Jefferson and the Stony Mountains* (Urbana, Ill., 1981), 86-97; Silvio A. Bedini, "Jefferson: Man of Science," *Frontiers* (Annual of the American Academy of Natural Sciences of Philadelphia), 3 (1981–82), 10-23.

4. John E. Bakeless, "Lewis and Clark's Background for Exploration," *Journal of the Washington Academy of Sciences,* 44 (November 1954), 334-38; Dumas Malone, *Jefferson the President: First Term, 1801–1805* (Boston, 1970), 43-44, 275-76; Jackson, *Thomas Jefferson,* 117-21.

5. Jefferson to Robert Patterson, March 2, 1803, in *Letters of the Lewis and Clark Expedition with Related Documents, 1783–1854,* ed. Donald Jackson, 2d ed. (Urbana, Ill., 1978), 1:21; Herman R. Friis, "Cartographic and Geographic Activities of the Lewis and Clark Expedition," *Journal of the Washington Academy of Sciences,* 44 (November 1954), 343-46.

6. The octant, or Hadley Reflecting Quadrant, as it was originally known, was simultaneously invented about 1730 in Philadelphia by a plumber and self-taught man of science named Thomas Godfrey and in England by John Hadley, a mathematician and mechanician employed by the admiralty. The instrument incorporated two principles of optics: first, that the angle of coincidence equaled the angle of reflection in a plane containing the normal to the reflecting surface at the point of reflection, and second, that if a ray of light suffered two successive reflections in the same plane by two mirrors, the angle between the first and last direction of the ray was twice the angle between the mirrors. Because the angle of the mirrors was one-half the altitude of the object observed, double the angle would be read on the arc

when the mirror on the index arm moved from parallel through the angle. In this manner the arc would read to ninety degrees, although it was in itself one-eighth of a circle, or forty-five degrees.

Within a short period after its invention, the octant was improved by the addition of a vernier scale, a small sliding scale for making more accurate fractional readings, and a small telescope that replaced the earlier pinnule sight, or that was offered as an alternative. After 1750 the wooden arm, or index, was replaced with brass, and by 1775 the instrument was substantially reduced in size so that it was easier to use. See H. O. Paget-Hill and E. W. Tomlinson, *Instruments of Navigation* (London, 1958), 13-14; Silvio A. Bedini, *Thinkers and Tinkers: Early American Men of Science* (1975; reprint, Rancho Cordova, Calif., 1983), 118-23; "The Description of a New Instrument for Taking Angles. By John Hadley, Esq., Vice-Pr. R. S. Communicated to the Society on May 13, 1731," *Philosophical Transactions of the Royal Society for August and September 1731*, 37 (no. 420, 1733–34), 147-57, pl. 13.

7. The invention of the sextant in about 1757 is attributed to Captain John Campbell, a British naval officer, and resulted from his experiments to find a more accurate means of measuring lunar distances. See E. G. R. Taylor, *The Mathematical Practitioners of Hanoverian England, 1714–1840* (Cambridge, U.K., 1965), 32, 45, 199; Charles H. Cotter, *A History of Nautical Astronomy* (New York, 1968), 87-91.

8. Cotter, *Nautical Astronomy*, 91-96; E. G. R. Taylor and M. W. Richey, *The Geometrical Seaman* (London, 1962), 79-81.

9. Dumas Malone, ed., "Robert Patterson," in *Dictionary of American Biography* (New York, 1934), 7:305-6; Silvio A. Bedini, "Andrew Ellicott, Surveyor of the Wilderness," *Surveying and Mapping*, 36 (June 1976), 113-35; Catherine Van Cortlandt Mathews, *Andrew Ellicott: His Life and Letters* (New York, 1908), 50-79; Bedini, *Thinkers and Tinkers*, 160-61.

10. Paul Russell Cutright, "Contributions of Philadelphia to Lewis and Clark History," *We Proceeded On*, supplement no. 6 (July 1982), 1-18, previously published as "Meriwether Lewis Prepares for a Trip West," *Bulletin of the Missouri Historical Society*, 23 (October 1966), 3-20; Jackson, *Letters*, 1:16-19.

11. Robert Patterson to Jefferson, March 15, 1803, in Jackson, *Letters*, 1:28-31.

12. Andrew Ellicott to Jefferson, March 6, 1803, in Jackson, *Letters*, 1:23-25. Jefferson's letter to Ellicott of February 28, 1803, has not survived.

13. [Andrew Ellicott], *The Journal of Andrew Ellicott, Late Commissioner on Behalf of the United States . . . for Determining the Boundary between the United States and the Possessions of his Catholic Majesty in America* (1803; reprint, Chicago, 1962), app., 42.

14. Silvio A. Bedini, *The Life of Benjamin Banneker* (1972; reprint, Rancho Cordova, Calif., 1984), 113-14; Bedini, "Andrew Ellicott," 121, 124.

15. Thw, 6:231-37; Adelman, "Equipping the Expedition," 40-41; Jackson, *Letters*, 1:7577.

16. Jackson, *Letters*, 1:37-40, 75-76; Thw, 7:217; Donald W. Rose, "Captain Lewis's Iron Boat: 'The Experiment,'" *We Proceeded On*, 7 (May 1981), 4-7.

17. Lewis to Jefferson, April 9, 1803, in Jackson, *Letters*, 1:48-49.

18. Jackson, *Letters*, 1:48-55, 69-97.

19. Cotter, *Nautical Astronomy*, 180-267; Bedini, *Thinkers and Tinkers*, 346-52. Longitude is measured in an east-west direction from an arbitrary point. To calculate the difference in time and of the meridian of longitude, the observer must know the time at the arbitrary point at the moment of the sun's meridian at his position. See A. Pannekoek, *A History of Astronomy* (New York, 1961), 276-81; Cotter, *Nautical Astronomy*, 189-92.

20. Jefferson to Robert Patterson, November 16, 1805, in Jackson, *Letters*, 1:270.

21. Jefferson to Robert Patterson, December 29, 1805, microfilm, series 1, reel 35, Jefferson Papers, Manuscripts Division, Library of Congress, Washington, D.C. (hereafter Jefferson Papers). Jefferson owned a theodolite and a universal equatorial instrument, both made by the noted Jesse Ramsden of London, and the latter described in pamphlets by Ramsden entitled *Description of a New Universal Equatorial Instrument* (1771) and *Description of the Universal Equatorial, and of the New Refraction Apparatus, Much Improved by Mr. Ramsden* (London, 1791).

22. The Borda reflecting circle was considered to be one of the most accurate instruments for measuring lunar distances as well as for taking altitudes. Invented in 1752 as a replacement for the octant by Tobias Mayer, a German astronomer, the reflecting circle was constructed on the same basic principle as the octant but was circular in shape, with two mirrors that could be moved alternately so that altitudes could be taken successively. To establish a mean, the altitudes totaled by the instrument were divided by the number of observations made. The instrument was named for Chevalier de Borda, a French inventor who greatly improved the instrument and published a description of it in 1787. The instrument was produced by various English and French makers. Cotter, *Nautical Astronomy*, 83-87.

23. All were Jefferson's correspondents on scientific matters over a period of years. William Dunbar (1749–1810) was a Scottish planter and man of science who settled near Natchez in 1792 and was surveyor of the district. He served as representative of the Spanish Government in the establishment of the boundary between the United States and Spanish

possessions. John Garnett (ca. 1751–1820) of New Brunswick, New Jersey, was a publisher of astronomical tables and nautical almanacs and also imported and sold navigational instruments. William Lambert (fl. 1790–1820) of Washington, D.C., was a clerk in the War Department and an amateur astronomer with his own observatory. He corresponded with Jefferson on astronomical subjects and later avidly supported the establishment of a national observatory in Washington. Isaac Briggs (1763–1825), a Quaker from Sandy Spring, Maryland, was one of Ellicott's assistant surveyors in the survey of the Federal Territory (District of Columbia). In 1803 he undertook the survey of the Mississippi Territory for the federal government. See particularly Jefferson to Dunbar, May 25, 1805, in Jackson, *Letters*, 1:55-56; Dunbar to Jefferson, July 9, 1805, in ibid., 244-46; Jefferson to William Lambert, December 22, 1804, in ibid., 250-51; and Jefferson to Dunbar, January 12, 1806, in ibid., 290.

24. Ellicott to Jefferson, March 6, 1803, in Jackson, *Letters*, 1:23-25; and Patterson to Jefferson, March 15, 1803, in ibid., 28-31.

25. Jefferson to Lewis, April 30, 1803, in Jackson, *Letters*, 1:44-45.

26. Lewis to Jefferson, May 14, 1803, in Jackson, *Letters*, 1:48-49. An "Arnald's watch," or chronometer, was designed to keep time with considerable precision, having a compensated balance to overcome irregularity because of temperature changes. It was invented in the third quarter of the eighteenth century by John Harrison, an English carpenter turned clockmaker. It was modified and improved by several other English clockmakers: Larcum Kendal, Thomas Earnshaw, and John Arnold. Arnold's improvements included a bimetallic compensation balance, an improved pivoted detent escapement, and a helical balance spring. See Rupert T. Gould, *John Harrison and His Timekeepers* (London, 1958); and R. Good, "John Harrison's Last Timekeeper of 1770," *Pioneers of Precision Timekeeping*, monograph no. 3 (London, n.d.), 7-8, 19-29.

27. Ellicott to John Vaughan, April 16, 1803, vol. 5, imprint 1193, Andrew Ellicott Papers, Manuscripts Division, Library of Congress, Washington, D.C.; Ellicott to Jefferson, April 18, 1803, in Jackson, *Letters*, 1:36-37. John Vaughan (1756–1841), a Philadelphia merchant, was treasurer and librarian of the American Philosophical Society.

28. Ellicott to John Vaughan, May 7, 1803, and Ellicott to Robert Patterson, May 7, 1803, in Jackson, *Letters*, 1:45-46.

29. See Jackson, *Letters*, 1:69-97, for records relating to the acquisition of supplies by Lewis.

30. Jackson, *Letters*, 1:69-97.

31. In the collections of the Science Museum, South Kensington, London.

32. Silvio A. Bedini, *Early American Scientific Instruments and Their*

Makers (Washington, D.C., 1964), 30-33, 58-64; Bedini, *Thinkers and Tinkers*, 354-56.

33. Invoice of Thomas Whitney, May 13, 1803, in Jackson, *Letters*, 1:82. Thomas Whitney (?–1823) was an English-born maker of mathematical instruments who established himself in Philadelphia about 1797. He specialized in surveying instruments of all types; an 1819 advertisement claimed he had made more than five hundred surveying compasses. See Bedini, *Early Scientific Instruments*, 30.

34. Jackson, *Letters*, 1:82; Cutright, "Contributions," 14-16; Thw, 6:231-46.

35. Invoice of Thomas Parker, May 19, 1803, in Jackson, *Letters*, 1:88. Thomas Parker (1761–1833), trained as a clockmaker by David Rittenhouse and John Wood, established his own shop in 1783 at 13 South Third Street, Philadelphia, and produced tall-case and shelf clocks.

36. Lewis to Jefferson, May 14, 1803, in Jackson, *Letters*, 1:48-49; and Lewis to Ellicott, May 27, 1803, in ibid., 1:51.

37. Invoice from Henry Voigt, June 19, 1803, in Jackson, *Letters*, 1:91. Henry Voigt (1738–1814) was a German-born clockmaker and mechanician who operated a wire mill in Reading, Pennsylvania. From about 1780 he worked as a clockmaker and mathematical instrument maker. He was well known to Jefferson, for whom he repaired clocks and watches over a period of years. He moved to Philadelphia about 1791. Sebastian Voight, who was also a clockmaker in Philadelphia in the same period, may have been a brother. Henry Voigt's son, Thomas Voight, also worked as a clockmaker in Philadelphia from 1811 to about 1835. See Bedini, *Thinkers and Tinkers*, 326-27.

38. Patterson to Jefferson, March 15, 1803, and June 18, 1803, in Jackson, *Letters*, 1:2831, 51.

39. Jefferson's instructions to Lewis, June 20, 1803, in Jackson, *Letters*, 1:61-66 (reprinted in this volume, pp. 31-38); Paul Cutright, "Jefferson's Instructions to Lewis and Clark," *Bulletin of the Missouri Historical Society*, 22 (April 1966), 302-20.

40. Fred J. Randolph and Fred L. Francis, "Thomas Jefferson as Meteorologist," *Monthly Weather Review* (December 1895), 456-58; Alexander McAdie, "A Colonial Weather Service," *Popular Science Monthly*, July 7, 1894, 39-45.

41. Lewis to William Clark, June 19, 1803, in Jackson, *Letters*, 1:57-58; John Louis Loos, "William Clark's Part in the Preparation of the Lewis and Clark Expedition," *Bulletin of the Missouri Historical Society*, 10 (July 1954), 490-511; Jerome O. Steffen, *William Clark, Jeffersonian Man on the Frontier* (Norman, Okla., 1977), 44-46.

42. Jackson, *Letters*, 1:173-76; Friis, "Cartographic Activities," 349-50;

Reuben Gold Thwaites, "The Story of Lewis and Clark's Journals," *Annual Report of the American Historical Association for the Year 1903*, 1 (1904), 107-29; Cutright, *History of the Journals*, 8-15.

43. Jefferson to Isaac Briggs, June 5, 1804, microfilm, series 1, reel 30, Jefferson Papers. Jefferson purchased some of his thermometers from a Philadelphia stationer named Sparhawk. An example of the type of thermometer he described to Briggs and which he once owned is in the collections of the Historical Society of Pennsylvania.

44. Cutright, *History of the Journals*, 3-15; Friis, "Cartographic Activities," 349-51; Thw, 2:131-32.

45. Thw, 6:230-65.

46. Cotter, *Nautical Astronomy*, 189-92.

47. Jefferson to José Corrèa da Serra, April 26, 1816, in Jackson, *Letters*, 1:611-12.

48. Clark to Ferdinand Rudolph Hassler, January 26, 1810, in Jackson, *Letters*, 1:491-92; and Hassler to Patterson, August 12, 1810, in ibid., 1:556-59.

49. Jefferson to Corrèa da Serra, April 26, 1816, in Jackson, *Letters*, 1:611-12.

50. Jefferson to the Hon. St. George Tucker, May 9, 1798, and Jefferson to George Wythe, January 16, 1796, microfilm, series 1, reel 21, Jefferson Papers; Helen Bullock, "The Papers of Thomas Jefferson," *American Archivist*, 4 (January–October 1941), 243-44.

51. E. G. Chuinard, "Thomas Jefferson and the Corps of Discovery: Could He Have Done More?" *American West*, 12 (November–December 1975), 4-13; Dumas Malone, *Jefferson, the President: Second Term, 1805–1809* (Boston, 1974), 208-12.

52. Jan Snow, "Lewis and Clark in the Museum Collections of the Missouri Historical Society," *Gateway Heritage*, 2 (Fall 1981), 36-41. The watch discussed in the *Gateway Heritage* article does not bear a maker's signature or other identification, but is believed to be the silver paircase watch owned by Lewis and carried on the expedition. A pocket compass made by Thomas Whitney with a leather case, claimed by family tradition as having been owned by Clark and carried on the expedition, with some documentation, is in the collections of the National Museum of American History of the Smithsonian Institution, Accession No. 122,864.

53. Roy E. Appleman, *Lewis and Clark: Historic Places Associated with Their Transcontinental Exploration (1804–6)* (Washington, D.C., 1975), 235, 375 n. 150.

54. Jefferson to William Dunbar, May 25, 1805, in Jackson, *Letters*, 1:245.

Pass near Hole in the Wall, on the Missouri River, 1880,
photographed by F. Jay Haynes

Part Four

Mutual Discovery

THE "WHAT IF" HISTORY GAME HAS ALWAYS had an enthusiastic following among Lewis and Clark scholars and aficionados. What if the Spanish and their Pawnee allies had captured the American party? What if the Teton Sioux had attacked the expedition at the mouth of the Bad River? What if Cameahwait and his warriors had killed Lewis instead of welcoming him with open arms and greasy hugs? What if the Chinooks and Clatsops had laid siege to Fort Clatsop and destroyed it? In each case these "what ifs" did not happen, but the questions, centered as they are on the active presence of native people, bring us closer to a question about the fundamental reality of the Lewis and Clark Expedition.

There is one "what if" question that can illuminate what is perhaps the central expedition story—the encounter between the Corps of Discovery and native peoples. What if Lewis and Clark had made their way through a country where they were the only human beings? What if there had been no Mandans offering corn or Clatsops bargaining fish for favors? What if there had been no Hidatsas or Shoshones sharing vital geographic information? What if there had been no Atsina hospitality or Nez Perce friendship? Of course all of that did happen. The food, shelter, knowledge, and friendship offered by native people sustained the expedition and on many days ensured its very survival. The Corps of Discovery was not alone in the country between the Missouri and the Pacific. For every Lewis and Clark there was a Le Borgne and a Coboway; for every John Ordway and York there was an Old Toby and a Twisted Hair; and for little Jean Baptiste Charbonneau there were countless Indian children.

The essays and documents in this section remind us that the encounters between Lewis and Clark and native people were times of mutual discovery. Dr. Benjamin Rush's list of questions suggests some of what educated white Americans wanted from such mutual encounters. In those moments of discovery each group of explorers—whether native or newcomer—had strategies for learning about the other, and ways to cope with strangers and potential friends. No part of the Lewis and Clark story brings modern readers more quickly into the presence of larger and more consequential American narratives than those moments when men, women, and children reached across the cultural divide.

Benjamin Rush to Lewis

Questions to Merryweather Lewis
before he went up the Missouri.

I. PHYSICAL HISTORY & MEDICINE?

What are the *acute* diseases of the Indians? Is the bilious fever ever attended with a black vomit.

Is Goiture, apoplexy, palsy, Epilepsy, madness [. . .] ven. Disease known among them?

What is their state of life as to longevity?

At what age do the women *begin & cease* to menstruate?

At what age do they marry? How long do they suckle the Children?

What is the provision of their Childrn. after being weaned?

The state of the pulse as to *frequency* in the morning, at noon & at night—before & after eating? What is its state in childhood. Adult life, & old age? The number of strokes counted by the quarter of a minute by glass, and multiplied by four will give its frequency in a minute.

What are their Remidies?

Are artificial discharges of blood ever used among them?

In what manner do they induce sweating?

Do they ever used voluntary fasting?

At what *time* do they rise—their Baths?

What is the diet—manner of cooking—& times of eating among the Indians? How do they preserve their food?

II. MORALS

1. What are their vices?

2. Is Suicide common among them?—ever from love?

3. Do they employ any substitute for ardent spirits to promote intoxication?

4. Is murder common among them, & do they punish it with death?

III. RELIGION

1. What Affinity between their religious Ceremonies & those of the Jews?

2. Do they use animal Sacrifices in their worship?

3. What are the principal Objects of their worship?

4. How do they dispose of their dead, and with what Ceremonies do they inter them?

May 17. 1803.   *B. Rush*

Plains Indian Reactions to the Lewis and Clark Expedition

John C. Ewers

ON THEIR HISTORIC OVERLAND JOURNEY during the years 1804–6 the men of the "Corps of Volunteers for North-Western Discovery," led by Captains Meriwether Lewis and William Clark, explored the valley of the Missouri to its headwaters, crossed the Rocky Mountains, descended the Columbia River to the shores of the Pacific Ocean, and returned safely to St. Louis on the Mississippi. They traveled more than nine thousand miles in roughly twenty-eight months. They logged some seven thousand of those miles and spent eighteen of those months *east* of the Rockies in the valley of the Missouri and its most important upper tributary, the Yellowstone. They met Indians from eleven of the fourteen tribes who then inhabited the Upper Missouri region from the mouth of the Platte to the Rockies, and they initiated the first official relations between the United States and these Indian tribes. They conferred with the chiefs of the three largest farming tribes on the Missouri—the Arikara, Mandan, and Hidatsa. And they encountered men of the two strongest military powers on the northern plains—the nomadic Teton Dakota (Western Sioux) and the Piegan Blackfoot. The reactions of these Indians to their meeting with Lewis and Clark were important to the future relations of United States citizens with the native peoples of an area larger than that of the original thirteen United States.

Although the men of the Lewis and Clark Expedition were the first from the United States to meet the Indians of the Upper Missouri, it would be a mistake to think of those Indians at that time as unsophisticated aborigines whose lives had been untouched by influences from the white man's world. Nor were they ignorant of the interests white men had in them and in the resources of their country.

Radical changes had taken place in the lives of the Indians of the northern plains since Henry Kelsey, a Hudson's Bay Company employee, first met some of them in their own country in 1691.[1] Then the Indians hunted buffalo and made war on foot, using weapons of their own manufacture. The farming tribes, living in sedentary villages and combining hunting with the growth of crops, enjoyed greater economic security than did the nomads who depended largely upon buffalo hunting for their subsistence. But the acquisition of the European horse by tribes of this region during the eighteenth century greatly increased the mobility of the nomads and decreased the feast or famine character of the hunter's life. Some tribes of farmers left their villages to become wandering nomads. Those who persisted in their horticultural practices found themselves surrounded by and largely at the mercy of the mounted nomads. Penned up in their compact villages, they suffered heavy losses from smallpox plagues, so that by the time of Lewis and Clark the numbers of villages as well as the populations of the farming tribes were greatly reduced.[2]

Horses were wealth among all the Upper Missouri tribes in Lewis and Clark's time. Poor but ambitious young men found that the simplest way to acquire horses was to steal them from alien people—whether Indians or whites. There was no stigma attached to this action. Rather, the theft of a horse was recognized as a minor war honor. Consequently horse raiding was, by 1804, a common action in the warfare of the region.[3]

Intertribal trade was almost as typical of northern plains Indian life as was intertribal warfare. When Pierre La Vérendrye first visited the Mandan villages on the Missouri in present North Dakota in 1738, he found a flourishing native trade center to which nomadic tribesmen brought products of the chase to exchange for the agricultural produce of the villagers. He observed that some articles of European manufacture, introduced by Indian intermediaries who traded directly with whites farther northeast, had already appeared in the trade at the Mandan villages. The Mandan as well as the warlike nomads farther south and west with whom the Mandan traded were eager to obtain firearms, ammunition, metal arrowheads, knives, and axes.[4] Although the trade in these items increased in volume by the time of Lewis and Clark, the supply still fell far short of the Indians' demands.

Before the end of the eighteenth century, direct trade between whites, involving the exchange of European-made goods for furs and peltries, developed on a rather modest scale. British traders built fixed posts on the Assiniboine River and the upper waters of the Saskatchewan and traded with the nomadic tribes of the plains south of the Saskatchewan. Several French Canadians established residences in the villages of the Mandan and of their neighbors, the Hidatsa, learned the Indian languages, married Indian women, and exerted considerable influence in behalf of either the Hudson's Bay Company or rival North West Company traders who made periodic trading expeditions some one hundred fifty miles southwestward from their posts in the valley of the Assiniboine River.[5]

Employing similar methods, operating through white residents in Indian villages, businessmen from St. Louis extended their trade up the Missouri to the Arikara villages, less than two hundred miles south of the Mandan. In 1796 John Evans, a Welshman acting in the interest of the St. Louis traders, pushed upriver as far as the Mandan villages where he distributed flags, medals, and other presents to the chiefs, and urged them to recognize "Their Great White Father the Spaniard." He ordered the British traders to return to Canada, but since the Spaniards failed to establish a more permanent contact with the Mandan, British traders continued to do business at the Mandan trading center.[6]

It is significant that before the time of Lewis and Clark not only the Mandan and Arikara but all other tribes of the Upper Missouri had gained some knowledge of white men. Furthermore, most if not all of these tribes knew from experience that white men were in competition for their trade. And they had no reason to believe that there were *any* whites who were not closely associated with the fur trade.

For many years traders visiting the Upper Missouri tribes had been accustomed to making liberal gifts to prominent Indian chiefs in order to win their loyalty and obtain a share of their tribe's trade. Three articles—flags, medals, and ornate, semi-military coats (known to the trade as "chiefs' coats")—had become standard traders' gifts to Indian chiefs. Presented in formal councils, these gifts appealed to a chief's vanity. Furthermore, possession of these articles became concrete evidence to a chief's followers that he was recognized as a tribal leader by important whites, and this in turn strengthened his position in the eyes of his fellow tribesmen.

In a series of formal councils with the leaders of the Oto and Missouri, Yankton Dakota, Arikara, Mandan, and Hidatsa on their way up the Missouri, Lewis and Clark presented flags, medals, and chiefs' coats to the principal chiefs. They also gave smaller medals to lesser Indian leaders.[7] These gifts must have confirmed the Indians' beliefs that all whites were traders.

Sixteen hundred and nine miles up the Missouri, and seven miles below the mouth of Knife River, the explorers spent the winter of 1804–5 near the Mandan and Hidatsa villages. This was the only neighborhood *on* the Missouri where British traders did business with the Indians. Because this was a critical location for the establishment of American prestige, and because these Indians, over a period of five and a half months, had better opportunities to get to know the explorers than did any other tribes of the Great Plains (who met the Lewis and Clark party only briefly), let us examine in some detail the reactions of the Mandan and Hidatsa to the expedition.

The two villages of the Hidatsa on the Knife River and the two Mandan villages on the Missouri were less than five miles apart. Yet moving up the Missouri the Lewis and Clark party was met and welcomed by Mandan Indians on October 24, 1804, three days before they met any Hidatsa Indians. The Mandan proceeded to take advantage of their initial friendship with the explorers to the disadvantage of their Hidatsa neighbors. At the grand council with the two tribes on October 29, Lewis and Clark recognized a greater number of Mandan than Hidatsa chiefs.[8] After the explorers built their winter quarters—Fort Mandan, three miles downstream from the lower Mandan village—the ranking Mandan chiefs, Black Cat and Big White, paid them frequent visits, even in the dead of winter when the thermometer registered twenty degrees or more below zero. The chiefs enjoyed spending the night at the white men's fort. They entertained the whites in their own villages and invited some of them to take the parts of old men in their buffalo-calling ceremony, during which the wives of younger men gave themselves to the elders.[9] That Mandan women were more than friendly toward these whites is attested by their leaders' repeated comments in their journals upon the prevalence of "venereal complaints" among the enlisted men that winter.[10]

As the winter wore on and meat became scarce at the fort, the Mandan brought corn to exchange for the services of the expedition's smiths in mending tools and utensils and making iron battle axes. More significant as an indication of the friendship that developed between the Americans and the Mandan Indians was the captains' offer to assist these Indians in case of a Sioux attack upon their villages, and the later Mandan aid to Captain Lewis in the pursuit of his horses stolen by the Sioux.[11]

In marked contrast to the warm friendship of the Mandan was the aloofness and suspicion of Hidatsa relations with the explorers. Nearly a month passed following the initial council with the chiefs before a Hidatsa visited Lewis and Clark. During the entire winter One Eye, the principal Hidatsa chief, made a single visit to Fort Mandan, and Captain Lewis visited the Hidatsa but once.[12]

Undoubtedly the Hidatsa coolness toward the Americans was influenced by the agents of the Hudson's Bay Company and the North West Company, who spent considerable time in the Hidatsa villages that winter. These British traders not only wanted to maintain their foothold among the farming tribes of the Mandan region, but they were eager to expand their trade southwestward into the Crow Indian territory of the Yellowstone Valley where "beaver were as rich in their rivers as buffalo and other large animals were in their plains."[13] They feared that the expansion of trade into that region by men from the United States would deny golden opportunities. When Antoine Larocque of the North West Company visited Fort Mandan in late November, the American captains forbade him to give medals or flags to the Indians of the newly acquired United States territory in which he was trading. Word reached Lewis and Clark in January through their Hidatsa interpreter, Toussaint Charbonneau, that the North West Company's clerk had been speaking unfavorably of the Americans to the Hidatsa.[14]

Perhaps this explains why Alexander Henry of the North West Company, on his visit to the Hidatsa in the summer of 1806, reported that those Indians believed the medals and flags Lewis and Clark had given their chiefs "conveyed bad medicine to them and their children" and "supposed they could not better dispose of those articles than by giving them to the natives with whom they frequently warred, in hope the ill-luck would be conveyed to them."[15]

Henry also claimed that the Hidatsa "are disgusted at the high-sounding language the American captains bestowed upon themselves and their own nation, wishing to impress the Indians with an idea that they were great warriors, and a powerful people, who if exasperated, could crush all the nations of the earth. This manner of proceeding did not agree with these haughty savages, who had too high an opinion of themselves to entertain the least idea of acknowledging any race to be their superiors."[16]

Nevertheless, Alexander Henry acknowledged that "the Mandan are more tractable, and appear well inclined toward the United States."[17]

Perhaps one prominent Hidatsa chief, whom Lewis and Clark recognized as the first chief of their smaller village, Black Moccasin, did not share the opinion of the American leaders that Henry claimed prevailed in that tribe. At least we know that a quarter of a century later this aged chief told George Catlin of his fond memories and high regard for "Red Hair" (Clark) and "Long Knife" (Lewis) and insisted that Catlin convey his best wishes to General Clark in St. Louis.[18]

Of the other members of the exploring party, York, Captain Clark's African American servant, attracted the most attention from both the Hidatsa and Mandan Indians. They had never before seen an African American and did not know quite what to make of him. York himself, a dark, corpulent man, tried to make the

Indians believe he had been wild like a bear and tamed. One Eye, the principal Hidatsa chief, examined York closely, spit on his hand and rubbed York's skin, believing that he might be a painted white man. Possibly this Indian reaction to York survives in the name for Negro in the languages of some of the Upper Missouri tribes, which may be translated as "black white man."[19]

The smiths of the Lewis and Clark party were highly regarded by the Indians of both tribes. The Mandan believed their bellows were strong medicine. A Hidatsa chief, appraising the Lewis and Clark Expedition to Charles Mackenzie, a North West Company trader, in 1805, said: "Had I these white warriors in the upper plains, my young men would do for them as they would for so many wolves, for there are only two sensible men amongst them, the worker in iron and the mender of guns."[20]

The explorers' brief contacts with the most powerful nomadic tribes of the Upper Missouri were hostile ones. The Teton Dakota at that time were the scourge of the Missouri valley in the present region of North and South Dakota. They were the aggressive enemies of the Mandan and Hidatsa. At that time the Teton secured guns and ammunition in trade with more easterly Dakota tribes at a rendezvous on the James River. And they tried to prevent Missouri River traders from taking arms upriver to strengthen their enemies. Only by a show of force and determination to fight if need be were the explorers able to prevent the Teton from stopping them at the mouth of the Teton River on their way upstream, and they narrowly averted open conflict with these Sioux while descending the river in 1806. Lewis and Clark's initial encouragement of the Arikara, Mandan, and Hidatsa to make peace with their enemies was of little avail without the cooperation of the most powerful enemies of those tribes—the Teton Dakota. So the bitter intertribal warfare of the Upper Missouri continued unabated, little affected by the peace talks of the well-meaning American captains.[21]

On their journey westward in the spring of 1805, the explorers traveled from the mouth of the Little Missouri to the Rocky Mountains (a distance of nearly one thousand miles) without sighting an Indian. The country through which they passed was a marginal area between the warring Assiniboine, Gros Ventres, and Blackfoot on the north, and the Crow on the south. The travelers saw numerous timbered lodges that had been built as overnight shelters by Indian war parties among the trees on the banks of the Missouri. Some of these "war lodges" appeared to have been occupied recently. But the explorers deemed themselves lucky *not* to encounter any Indian warriors.[22]

They were much less fortunate on their return journey across the plains of present Montana. The expedition was then divided into two parties. One, under Lewis's command, descended the Missouri. In July 1806, Lewis and three picked enlisted men explored the upper waters of the Marias River in order to ascertain the northwestern boundary of Louisiana. Lewis knew he was in the country of the aggressive Blackfoot and Gros Ventres. But he had no desire to meet any of these Indians when he was confronted by a party of red men who outnumbered his little force two to one. Mutually suspicious, the groups exchanged untruths through sign language. Lewis claimed he was happy to meet the Indians and had come in search of them. The Indians signed that they were Gros Ventres and that there were three chiefs among them. Although dubious of their chiefly claims, Lewis gave a medal, a flag, and a handkerchief to those three. Forced to spend the night with the Indians, the whites were roused at dawn by the red men's attempt to steal their guns and horses. In the ensuing melee one Indian was stabbed to death and another shot in the belly.[23]

This small-scale skirmish with the Piegan (not Gros Ventres) on July 27, 1806, in the valley of the Two Medicine River on the present Blackfeet Reservation, Montana, was the only mortal combat between the explorers and any Indians.[24] It was probably the most unfortunate incident in the entire expedition. The whites could not have been blamed for protecting their lives and property. Nevertheless, this action was the *first* cause of the prolonged Blackfoot Indian hostility towards Americans. In the next year David Thompson, a British trader on the Saskatchewan, noted that "the murder of two Peeagan Indians by Captain Lewis of the U. S. drew the Peeagans to the Missouri."[25] It was a full quarter-century before peaceful trade was established between Americans and the Piegan. In the interval the aggressive Blackfoot killed numerous American trappers and twice forced the Americans to abandon their efforts to take beaver from the streams of the Montana region.[26]

William Clark, with ten men and some forty-eight horses, descended the Yellowstone Valley to that river's junction with the Missouri. On the Upper Yellowstone his party began to see smoke signals on the high points in the distance. They met no Indians, but awoke one morning to find half their horses missing. A diligent search of the vicinity revealed no tracks—only a moccasin and robe left by Indians. This was the first, but by no means the last, theft of American horses by the Crow Indians, who became renowned as the cleverest horse thieves of the American West.[27]

In his instructions to Meriwether Lewis, penned nearly a year before the explorers started up the Missouri, President Jefferson specifically stated: "If a few of the[ir] influential chiefs, within a practicable distance, wish to visit us, arrange such a visit with them."[28] Surely Lewis and Clark placed a very liberal interpretation upon Jefferson's phrase "practicable distance." More than three thousand miles above St. Louis on his return journey, Clark carefully prepared a speech for delivery to the Crow Indians (whom he never met) inviting them to send chiefs to Washington.[29] Farther downstream, at the Mandan and Hidatsa villages, sixteen hundred miles from the mouth of the Missouri, he offered similar invitations to the chiefs of both tribes. They declined, fearing that their enemies, the Sioux, would kill them en route. A young Mandan of poor reputation volunteered to make the hazardous journey, but Clark refused him. Only after the captain agreed to take the interpreter, René Jusseaume, and his wife along did that canny Frenchman persuade Big White, principal chief of the Lower Mandan village, to risk the long journey to a strange land to meet his new Great White Father. And before he returned Big White had good reason to regret his decision, for intertribal warfare on the Missouri prevented his reaching home until 1809.[30]

At the Arikara villages Clark was even less successful in soliciting chiefly delegates to Washington. The chiefs flatly refused to consider making the trip until their chief "who went down" the previous year returned home. Lewis and Clark had arranged for that chief's journey during their trip up the Missouri. They were very fortunate that at the time of their meeting with the Arikara on their return journey those Indians had not yet learned of the death of their beloved leader in the nation's capital. When word of this chief's death reached them shortly thereafter, the Arikara abused the interpreter who brought them this news along with President Jefferson's personal message of condolence and liberal presents for the family of the deceased. There was a strong suspicion among the Arikara that the Americans had killed their leader.[31]

Prior to that time the Arikara had been friendly to traders from St. Louis. But thereafter these Indians repeatedly demonstrated their hostility toward Americans, preventing the passage of trading parties up river, and killing numerous whites. In 1823, a battle between William Ashley's traders and the Arikara led to the first campaign of the United States Army against any Plains Indian tribe. A quarter century after the Lewis and Clark Expedition American traders still referred to the Arikara as "the horrid tribe."[32]

IN RETROSPECT . . .

Looking back upon the Lewis and Clark Expedition after the passage of 160 years, it appears that this pioneer American venture into the wilds of the Upper Missouri was much less successful in the field of Indian diplomacy than in the fields of geographical exploration and scientific discovery. Lewis and Clark were handicapped from the start by the fact that the Indians of the region had never known any white men who were not fur traders. They did score a noteworthy success in winning and holding the friendship of the Mandan. Yet it seems most probable that even those Indians whom they came to know best regarded the explorers as the advance party of a great trading company, "the United States," in whose name and interests Lewis and Clark spoke to them, and which was not much different from the Hudson's Bay Company or the North West Company, whose agents were well known to the northern tribes.

The explorers could not have been expected to have made any great progress in weaning the Indian tribes away from their allegiance to the entrenched British traders. It required a quarter-century of courageous and ingenious activity on the part of American traders before they could compete favorably with the experienced Hudson's Bay Company for the fur trade of the nomadic tribes north of the Missouri.

Two persistent impediments to the progress of the American

fur trade on the Upper Missouri were in part a heritage from the Lewis and Clark contacts with the Indians. I refer to the prolonged Arikara and Blackfoot hostility toward Americans. In both cases the hostile feelings on the part of the Indians were the results of accident rather than of design. But in the minds of the proud members of those primitive tribes, the causes were very real.

Notes

1. *The Kelsey Papers*, ed. A. G. Doughty and Chester Martin, Public Record Office of Northern Ireland, Public Archives of Canada (Ottawa, 1929).

2. John C. Ewers, *The Horse in Blackfoot Indian Culture*, Bureau of American Ethnology, Bulletin 159 (Washington, D.C., 1955), 332-36.

3. Ibid., 176-91.

4. P. G. V. La Vérendrye, *Journals of Letters of Pierre Gaultier de Varennes de la Vérendrye and his Sons*, ed. Laurence J. Burpee (Toronto, 1927), 153-60, 332-38.

5. John C. Ewers, "The Indian Trade of the Upper Missouri Before Lewis and Clark: An Interpretation," *Bulletin of the Missouri Historical Society*, 10 (July 1954), 429-46.

6. A. P. Nasatir, ed., *Before Lewis and Clark: Documents Illustrating the History of the Missouri, 1785–1804* (St. Louis, Mo., 1952), 2:495-98.

7. Ernest S. Osgood, ed., *The Field Notes of Captain William Clark, 1803–1805* (New Haven, Conn., 1964), 109-10, 121-26, 158, 169-72.

8. Ibid., 164-72.

9. Reuben Gold Thwaites, ed., *Original Journals of the Lewis and Clark Expedition, 1804–1806* (New York, 1904–5), 1:218-47 (hereafter Thw).

10. Thw, 1:248, 250, 279.

11. Ibid., 1:243-72. On March 13, 1805, the explorers noted that so great was the Indian demand for battle axes that "the Smiths have not an hour of idle time to Spare."

12. Thw, 1:226-80. Apparently the Mandan, jealous of their inside track with the Americans, also tried to keep Hidatsa from visiting Fort Mandan by starting a rumor that the white men would kill them if they came to the fort. Ibid., 1:249.

13. Charles Mackenzie, "The Missouri Indians, 1804–1805," in *Les Bourgeois de la Compagnie du Nordouest*, ed. L. R. Masson (Quebec, 1889–90), 1:341.

14. Thw, 1:228, 248-49.

15. Alexander Henry and David Thompson, *New Light on the Early History of the Greater Northwest*, ed. Elliott Coues (New York, 1907), 1:350.

16. Ibid.

17. Ibid.

18. George Catlin, *Letters and Notes on the Manners, Customs, and Condition of the North American Indians* (London, 1841), 1:186-87.

19. Osgood, *Field Notes*, 119; Donald Jackson, ed., *Letters of the Lewis and Clark Expedition with Related Documents, 1783–1854* (Urbana, Ill., 1962), 539.

20. Mackenzie, "Missouri Indians," 1:330.

21. Thw, 1:162-70, 5:361-68.

22. Ibid., 2:80-249; Olin D. Wheeler, *The Trail of Lewis and Clark* (New York, 1926), 1:279.

23. Thw, 5:218-28. More than a half-century later Piegan Indians identified their tribesman killed in this action as He-that-looks-at-the-Calf. See James H. Bradley, "The Bradley Manuscript," *Contributions to the Historical Society of Montana* (1910; reprint, Boston, 1966), 8:135.

24. Mrs. Helen B. West of Cut Bank, Montana, published a detailed, illustrated study in which she identifies the site of this historic skirmish, entitled *Meriwether Lewis in Blackfeet Country*, Museum of the Plains Indian (Browning, Montana, 1964).

25. David Thompson, *David Thompson's Narrative of his Explorations in Western America, 1784–1812* (Toronto, 1916), 375.

26. John C. Ewers, *The Blackfeet: Raiders on the Northwestern Plains* (Norman, Okla., 1958), 48-71.

27. Thw, 5:276, 279-81.

28. "Jefferson's Instructions to Lewis," in Jackson, *Letters*, 64, reprinted in this volume, 31-38.

29. Thw, 5:299-300.

30. Ibid., 5:338-45; Jackson, *Letters*, 382-83, 411-12, 414, 432-38, 445-50, 456-58, 460-61, 479-84.

31. Thw, 5:350-55, 383; Jackson, *Letters*, 306, 437.

32. Edwin Thompson Denig, *Five Indian Tribes of the Upper Missouri*, ed. John C. Ewers (Norman, Okla., 1961), 54-59.

Exploring the Explorers
Great Plains Peoples and
the Lewis and Clark Expedition

James P. Ronda

THERE ARE FEW STORIES THAT SEEM MORE COMMONPLACE than the narrative of the exploration of the American West. It is the stock-in-trade of countless textbooks, classroom lectures, and popular novels. In the traditional telling, European and American adventurers are the actors at center stage while Native Americans stand silently in the wings or have bit parts.

Much of exploration history labors under two burdens. First, we still see exploration events through the eyes of the European explorers themselves. Their stories become the only stories, their visions the only vision. For the most part exploration scholarship has not taken into account the ways native and nonnative peoples worked together to probe a shared world. And scholars have not paid sufficient attention to native voices as they give balance and meaning to the exploration encounter. Second, many recent accounts continue to envision exploration as simply a physical journey across a material landscape. Generations of artists and writers have sought to reveal exploration as a venture aimed at understanding self, place, and the other. Exploration was, and remains in the Space Age, an interior pilgrimage, a passage that Joseph Conrad dared call a journey into "the heart of darkness."[1]

These observations carry special force when applied to the Lewis and Clark Expedition. The Lewis and Clark story is an emblematic tale, one that transcends the particular events to represent larger cultural truths. Lewis and Clark's odyssey has become a touchstone event in the history of the American West, a part of something that might be called the tale of the tribe. But the telling of that tale has often been narrow in range and focus. Like the rest of exploration history, the Lewis and Clark narrative has been repeated as the exclusive adventures of white American males. We need to reimagine the Lewis and Clark voyage, not as a trip through empty space but as a mutual encounter between diverse peoples and cultures.[2]

The expedition was as much the object of exploration as it was the agent for exploring. Lewis and Clark were both explorers and the explored. Native people looked at the American expedition and saw a new world. Travelers on both sides of the cultural divide struggled to fit new faces, new words, new objects, and new ways of being into familiar patterns of meaning. What happened along the Missouri River was mutual discovery. When we say the word "explorer" we should see a native face as quickly as we see the face of a bearded stranger. So I propose that we turn the familiar Lewis and Clark story upside down, that we see it through native eyes. What we need to do is make Lewis and Clark the uncharted territory and native people the explorers. Then perhaps we can grasp the complexity of this American discovery.

Long before Lewis and Clark left St. Louis, they had a set of images and preconceptions about the land and peoples they would meet along the way. Those images, drawn from many sources, informed and directed the expedition throughout its journey. We might begin by asking what images, what previous experiences Great Plains native people had about Europeans before 1804.

For native people who called the northern plains home, white travelers were no novelty. By the time Lewis and Clark made their way upriver, there was already half a century of contact between plains peoples and the outsiders. Beginning in the 1730s, first a trickle and then a steady stream of European visitors came to call. It was commerce, the traffic in furs, that brought men like David Thompson, James Slater, and René Jusseaume to the Mandan and Hidatsa villages. Those merchants simply became part of a vast and complex native trade system in place long before any French *coureurs de bois* or Hudson's Bay Company men came to the northern plains.

From these contacts plains people fashioned a set of expectations about white outsiders. These men, always men, came in small numbers. The typical trading party counted perhaps five or seven men. In the fifty years before Lewis and Clark, the largest recorded European trading expedition had ten men.[3] By the 1780s those visits fell into an almost predictable seasonal cycle. The traders, especially those from Canada, arrived in late fall or early winter and stayed several weeks. Native people expected those weeks to be filled with business, the exchange of pelts and skins for ironware, textiles, guns, and luxury goods.

The business they neither expected nor welcomed was politics and diplomacy. European empire builders rightly understood that fur traders were agents of imperial expansion. Along with the usual goods to sell, the traders brought flags, medals, and other symbols of national sovereignty. While Indians often accepted such objects out of curiosity, respect, or hospitality, they did not think that those things in any way diminished native sovereignty or bound them to a distant great father. While most of the traders left once the exchanges were concluded, the villagers came to expect that a few might take wives and enter the native social world. These men, known as resident or tenant traders, became important intermediaries bridging the cultural divide. Two of them—René Jusseaume and Toussaint Charbonneau—played significant roles in the Lewis and Clark experience.

To these expectations about outsiders, we need to add one additional element. Early in the history of contact between native people and European traders, the goods that passed into native hands took on a special meaning. Meriwether Lewis grasped something of this when he wrote that Indians believed the first white traders "were the most powerful persons in the nation."[4] The apparent power of the whites—their technologies, seeming resistance to certain diseases, and exotic customs—could be shared with others by wearing or using things connected to the outsiders. A button, an awl, a gun, or an old tobacco box might have both utility in this world and a special force in the invisible but ever-present other world.

When the Lewis and Clark Expedition came up the Missouri in 1804 the Corps of Discovery presented native people with a spectacle at once familiar and yet strangely unexpected and unsettling. First there was the matter of size. What came up the river was by any standard a very large party, perhaps the largest yet seen on the Missouri. While the precise number remains elusive, there were at least forty men in the expedition company. And even a cursory look revealed a second unmistakable fact. These men were exceptionally well armed. Trading parties always carried guns but no Indian could have confused this traveling infantry company for a traders' brigade. Weapons of all shapes and sizes—small cannons, pistols, rifles, muskets, and knives— were displayed for all to see. How this large, well-armed party sailed upriver was also a source of wonder. St. Louis traders had used rafts, canoes, and pirogues for river traffic. In the 1790s Spanish officials briefly experimented with small galleys but nothing could quite compare with the impressive keelboat captained by Lewis and Clark. Here was a river craft unique in design and impressive in size.

Once the American expedition settled into winter quarters at Fort Mandan, near present-day Bismarck, North Dakota, the sense of the new and the strange continued. The fort itself was an architectural curiosity. Mandan and Hidatsa villagers knew all about constructing very large earth lodges, and they had seen an occasional trading party put up a crude post, but the American fort was something altogether different. Walls, barracks, guards, and a locked gate—here was a new way to define space under Dakota skies. What happened in and around the fort was equally new and bewildering. Native people reasonably assumed that trade was the principal reason any party came to the Missouri. At first glance Lewis and Clark certainly looked like traders. Their bales of goods held a virtual country store—everything from knives and fish hooks to mirrors and calico shirts. And Lewis and Clark talked about trade, trade with St. Louis merchants who were part of an expanding American commercial empire. But commerce did not follow the words. While the soldiers at Fort Mandan were always ready to buy meat and corn, they showed no interest in pelts. These men were traders who did not trade.

*Mandan earth lodge, Lewis and Clark Trail, west bank of the
Missouri River, circa 1900, photographed by L. A. Huffman*

The mystery of their intentions deepened as winter closed in. Earth lodge people always assumed that some of the resident traders would take village wives and become part of the family world. But the fort men were somehow different. They certainly sought the comforts of sex but made no moves to fulfill family obligations. For native women sex was bound up in family duties and, in the case of the buffalo-calling ritual, the quest for spirit power. Expedition men plainly saw intimate relations in a wholly different light. The bodies and some of the desires were the same; it was the meaning that did not translate across the divide.

What the captains said and did in their daily routine also did not square with previous plains experience. Squinting at the stars, recording temperatures, and collecting plant and animal specimens were strange things that demanded some explanation. Just as disturbing was all the American talk about the Great Father in Washington and the obedience owed to his wishes. During the Mandan winter, Lewis and Clark pursued an ambitious and ultimately unsuccessful diplomatic agenda. They sought to establish American sovereignty, to discredit Canadian rivals, and to forge an alliance with village peoples against the Sioux. A new political order had evidently come to the northern plains, one that chiefs and elders now struggled to understand.

And there was one final part of the Lewis and Clark territory that demanded exploration. Most of the objects carried by the American explorers were now quite familiar to native people. European clothing, guns, all sorts of trade items—none of this was new. But there were some things, "curriossities" the captains called them, that were striking in form and function. When the Mandan chief Black Cat visited the fort in late November 1804 he asked to see those objects. Out from their boxes came the latest wonders of western scientific technology. Surveying compasses, a precision chronometer, a sextant, and several telescopes—these things represented a reality as remote and mysterious as anything from NASA.[5]

To native eyes the space in and around the expedition was a new world. Here were people, objects, and ways of behaving that challenged previous assumptions. All exploration involves measuring images and preconceptions against what is immediately seen. Along the Missouri, plains people began to explore the shadowy Lewis and Clark country just as other natives had done elsewhere since the 1490s. Even before the Mandan winter and its longer time for mutual discovery, river folk had tried to chart the expedition world. In early September 1804 Black Buffalo's band of Brulé Sioux had an angry face-off with the Americans at the confluence of the Bad and Missouri rivers. That confrontation revealed Lewis and Clark as unwelcome intruders, commercial rivals bent on both political and economic dominion.[6]

Further upriver the American party spent five days at the Grand River Arikara villages. Like other river people, the Arikaras had seen white traders and their goods. But the intentions and behavior of the captains, their fascinating technology, and the presence of the black slave York sparked intense interest. What came out of that encounter was a vivid set of stories, a kind of exploration folklore. Arikaras asked: who were these strangers, where did they come from, and what was the meaning of their journey? Pierre-Antoine Tabeau, a French trader well acquainted with the Arikaras, recorded many of those stories. Kakawita, Tabeau's leading informant, reported that Arikaras thought the Americans were on a special vision quest and had encountered terrible monsters along the way. A sextant, a magnet, and phosphorous were pointed to as evidence of spirit powers. And there was York. He was the clearest sign of the supernatural, "a large fine man, black as a bear who spoke and acted as one."[7]

Those plains and river folk—Sioux and Arikaras—had only a brief moment to explore the mysterious strangers. Genuine exploration takes time; it is the work of larger views and longer talks. The winter of 1804–5 at Fort Mandan was such a time. Here the American expedition was at rest, no longer defined by the traveling routines of up and out and on the way. For the Americans, exploration meant moving, measuring, observing, and recording. This was an abstract, almost detached process well suited to the scientific spirit of the age. Landscape meant exploitable resources; people were objects to be studied and classified.

Native explorers pursued a different strategy. As hitherto unknown people, goods, and experiences entered the traditional circles of life, native people sought to maintain a harmonious balance between the old and the new. Exploration meant finding a suitable place for each new thing or person within the familiar framework. Indian explorers sought to domesticate the unknown, to name what seemed nameless. The native question was not so much "who are you" as "where do you fit?" To find the "fit" was to fix the meaning and keep all in balance. Indian explorers, and that means all native peoples of whatever age or gender, used simple but effective methods to probe the strangers. They looked at them, visited them, traded with them, shared all sorts of information, and on occasion made love with them. Lewis and Clark sought the new and gloried in it. Native explorers confronted the new, tried to soften its edges, and make it like the old and the familiar.

Looking out from Fort Mandan, Lewis and Clark imagined a wilderness, a crowded wilderness but a wilderness nonetheless.

From their earth lodges, Mandan and Hidatsa folk held a very different view of the landscape. When they surveyed the northern plains they saw a great community of life. Fort Mandan, that odd one-house town, and its strange inhabitants were a challenge to the settled order of things. Here was something that needed to be folded into the everyday routines of life, made commonplace, and therefore comprehensible. Like European adventurers on their various travels, native discoverers undertook a journey to Fort Mandan, a journey of exploration and explanation. That voyage began by simply watching the strangers. For many plains people the American expedition was an almost irresistible tourist attraction. As the Lewis and Clark navy nosed its way upriver into what is now North Dakota the banks were lined with curious onlookers. Sergeant John Ordway noticed that on many days the riverside galleries were packed with children.[8]

Once construction began on the fort there was even more to see. Native sidewalk superintendents observed everything from building the various quarters and rooms to setting the palisades and digging the latrines. As William Clark put it in one journal entry, Indian neighbors were "verry Curious in examining our works."[9] Little wonder, since the fort looked like no other piece of plains architecture. Its angular lines, vertical walls, heavy gate, and windows must have fascinated Indians more accustomed to the rounded lines of domed earth lodges.

For all the pleasures of seeing, looking was not enough for native explorers. Exploration demanded participation. It was not a spectator sport. Visiting was an essential part of any frontier culture, whether in tidewater Virginia or on the northern plains. Fort Mandan was no isolated outpost, caught in the grip of a Dakota winter and cut off from the simple joys of human companionship. Long before Lewis and Clark came into the country, Mandan and Hidatsa villagers had brightened their winters with a steady round of visits to the lodges of friends and neighbors. Life in the winter camps could be harsh and hungry, but there also were times for storytelling and gossip. Once Fort Mandan was built, the Americans became part of the social web that bound the villagers together. Indians were drawn not only to the fort itself but to the many "curriossities" they found inside.

It had long been expedition policy to display all sorts of weapons and scientific instruments in an effort to impress Indians with American power. When Hidatsa chief Le Borgne came to visit in early March 1805, he was shown everything from Lewis's airgun to spyglass. The Hidatsa promptly proclaimed these devices to be "Great Medicines." Whether impressed or not, many visitors found the objects both mysterious and compelling. Thermometers, quadrants, writing paper, and metal goods of all sorts were worth a special visit to the fort. It was as if Fort Mandan had become a living museum of white American life, familiar in some ways but novel in so many others.[10]

During most of the winter, Indians found an unfailing welcome at Fort Mandan. And on most days, despite snow and falling temperatures, Indians came to explore the fort. Only once during the entire season were native people asked not to come calling. On Christmas day 1804 the expedition evidently wanted to do its own celebrating. Native neighbors were told that the festivities were part of a special "medicine day" for whites only.[11] On every other day the gates were open. Indian visitors brought a sense of friendship and good company. Visits usually meant sharing food and enjoying a dance or some fiddle music by Pierre Cruzatte. There must have been time to appreciate a fine bow, a good gun, or a skillfully decorated pair of moccasins. Visiting put names to faces and words to things. It humanized the unknown, softened its rough edges, and civilized the pale savages.

Plains people expected that strangers coming from afar made the journey to trade. Villagers used trade not only to enhance individual status but as a means to make and cement personal friendships. Indians who traded at the Mandan and Hidatsa villages were for the most part potential enemies or relatives of those killed in combat. Some means had to be found to stop possible violence and allow peaceful relations. Reflecting the fundamental native social reality that defined relatives as friends and outsiders as enemies, villagers and their trading partners created a ceremony in which strangers were made temporary, fictional relatives. Men who might later fight each other could for a brief time exchange goods, swap stories, and even share ritual practices as friends. Perhaps the bearded strangers could be made trading "relatives."

Lewis and Clark surely fit the image of traders. They came with all sorts of goods. And the Americans talked a trading game. A large part of the expedition's diplomacy was aimed at redirecting the Indian trade away from Canadian markets and toward a St. Louis–based commercial system. Not only did the Americans look like traders and talk like traders, they sometimes acted like traders. Fort Mandan became a busy marketplace where skilled native merchants brought corn and meat in exchange for metal and textile items. At one point during the winter the American expedition was so desperate for corn that Indians were offered war axes in exchange for food. Lewis and Clark diplomacy preached intertribal peace but the power of necessity put weapons in the hands of those same warriors.

It seemed to make sense that the American explorers were in fact a large group of traders. But somehow for Indians exploring Lewis and Clark, that answer did not quite make sense. For all the goods and all the talk, the Americans did not behave like visitors from Canada. Fort Mandan had no fur warehouse. And these outsiders showed no inclination to become even temporary "relatives." By January 1805 some Mandan villagers were beginning to doubt that the label "trader" fit their fort neighbors. Earth lodge gossip had it that the Americans were stingy bargainers, unable or unwilling to compete with their Canadian rivals. When William Clark bitterly complained about all this loose talk, two Mandan elders quickly reassured him that the words were only in "jest and lafture."[12]

But this explanation barely covered what an increasing number of Indians had come to believe. Lewis and Clark were not traders. And if they were not traders, who were they? Exploring the American explorers, village people had come up against an almost unanswerable question. The concept, the linguistic category employed to describe a large-scale expedition not for war, not for trade, not for hunting, simply did not exist. Warriors plotted war trails; merchants sought trade routes; hunters scouted game lands. Exploration apart from these activities was a pursuit utterly foreign to native peoples. Eventually Lewis and Clark hit upon an identity explanation that more completely fit the native universe of experience. Indians were told that the party was in search of distant, long-lost relatives.

Thomas Jefferson expected that his explorers would not so much march across the continent as question their way west. Deeply influenced by Enlightenment strategies, the president understood exploration as inquiry, not grand romantic adventure. Lewis and Clark went up the Missouri armed with a comprehensive set of questions on everything from botany and climatology to diplomacy and ethnography. Native explorers did not have such detailed question lists but they were inquirers nonetheless. One example here can stand for many. Few Indians were more regular visitors at Fort Mandan than Black Cat, chief of the Mandan village called Ruptáre. Lewis respected the quality of Black Cat's mind, calling him a man of "integrety, firmness, inteligence, and perspicuety."[13]

On a cold windy morning in November, Black Cat worked his way along the riverbank to Fort Mandan. As Clark later recalled it, Black Cat "made Great inquiries respecting our fashions." We need to be sensitive to the many meanings of the word "fashion" as used by Clark. Black Cat was not especially interested in frontier *haute couteur*, the latest stylings from a nineteenth-century Bill Blass or Christian Dior. Fashion meant customs, habits, and ways of being. Black Cat had already seen the "curriossities." Now he wanted to understand something about the fabric of ordinary American life. What kind of a world produced and used such objects? Clark's journal is silent on the particulars. We don't know if Black Cat's questions headed toward the shape of American houses or the domestic relations between husbands and wives. But whatever the questions, Black Cat must have found the process satisfying. Within a few days he was eagerly sharing what Clark called "little Indian aneckdts."[14] The questions of exploration had sparked the dialogue of encounter.

Looking, visiting, questioning—this was exploring the new and the other on a personal level. But the American expedition posed a challenge on a much larger scale. That challenge was all about diplomacy—the complex web of relations between the native nations and their new neighbors. Lewis and Clark came to the Missouri with a diplomatic scheme that if implemented would have revolutionized the politics of the northern plains. Were Lewis and Clark to have had their way, it would have indeed been a new world order. As agents of a young and ambitious imperial republic, the captains sought to proclaim American sovereignty and fashion an alliance of village peoples against the Sioux. Diplomacy was no new game for village chiefs and elders, but the American demands were so stiff that they called for another kind of exploring.

In hurried meetings and formal councils throughout the winter of 1804–5, native diplomats probed the territory that would come to be if Lewis and Clark prevailed. Typical of such gatherings were the exchanges at the end of October 1804. In a speech that was now a stock part of his repertory, Lewis sketched the outlines of a new political landscape on the plains. There were the familiar themes—federal sovereignty, American trade, and intertribal peace. Such proposals did not seem extraordinary to the captains, but they did amount to substantial changes to the traditional ways the five Mandan and Hidatsa villages did business with both native and nonnative outsiders.

At the end of the speech, Lewis introduced the most controversial feature in his plan. The assembled Indians must have known that the Arikara chief sitting in the council was more than a chance visitor. Now was the time to open the touchy issue of peace between the Arikaras and their Mandan and Hidatsa neighbors. That peace, so Lewis and Clark believed, was a necessary preliminary to a general village coalition against the Sioux. The captains did not record the words they used to propose the peace treaty but what does survive is evidence of a culturally significant gesture. Clark, by now familiar with the protocol of plains diplomacy, took a pipe, smoked it, and passed it to the Arikara chief. That pipe was in turn handed around to the Mandan and Hidatsa representative. Clark noted later, "They all smoked with eagerness."[15]

That eagerness did not mean assent. At most it meant that men like Black Cat were ready to begin a diplomatic exploration of what must have seemed suspect terrain. Black Cat, adept at probing other parts of that terrain, was equally skilled at feeling his way in the murk of diplomacy. Because the American explorers thought Black Cat was the most powerful Mandan chief, they were anxious to know his thoughts. At midday on October 31, Clark and interpreter René Jusseaume walked down to Black Cat's village. At Ruptáre Clark was welcomed "and with great ceremoney was Seeted on a roabe by the Side of the Chief." Black Cat placed a fine buffalo robe over Clark's shoulders "and after smoking the pipe with several old men around" began to speak.[16]

Black Cat's speech was a carefully worded reply to the American proposals. It was a response designed to reassure Lewis and Clark without tying the villages too closely to an uncertain policy and a chancy future. He went directly to the heart of the matter. Intertribal peace made sense, at least to elders and chiefs. Black Cat graphically illustrated what he saw as the benefits of such a peace, saying it would mean "they now could hunt without fear, and their womin could work in the fields without looking every moment for the enemy." But this bright vision of a promising future did not mean that Black Cat was ready to become an American client. In his mind there were many unanswered questions. Earlier trader-diplomats, men like John Evans, had made extravagant promises about goods, markets, and protection against hostile outsiders. Those proved empty offers. Would the American ones be any better? The Great Father in Washington was only the most recent in a long line of distant sovereigns who handed out medals and flags. Each father asked much but in the end proved powerless and faithless. Would the chief of the American fires be any better? Later in November, Black Cat accepted a peace medal and an American flag. And there was his promise—made under considerable duress—to keep Union Jacks and King George medals out of his village.[17] Lewis and Clark imagined a plains diplomatic landscape filled with treaties, alliances, and the fixed bureaucracies of nation-states. Black Cat and his successors now had to explore that country. Such a journey would prove a perilous voyage, far more dangerous than any trek across the windswept plains.

T. S. Eliot once wrote that all exploring begins with an outward journey and ends with an interior passage back to one's inner self. Exploration is a kind of self-knowledge. When native people explored Lewis and Clark they may have come to know themselves with more clarity. Whether that happened or not, Indian explorers pursued the obvious strategies as they faced the new country.

Looking, visiting, questioning, and counseling—all these were visible voyages made before the public gaze. But there was a final kind of discovery and exploration, one that was intensely personal and profoundly private. It was the exploration of the body, the intimate territory of another self.

Lewis and Clark knew that there would be liaisons between members of the expedition and Native American women. The captains accepted such relations as inevitable and thought about them in largely medical terms. For the practical captains, sex meant venereal disease. It was a clinical issue, something to be dealt with by doses of mercury from penis syringes. The American exploration strategy never considered sex as anything other than a physical problem or a momentary dalliance.

For Native American women on the northern plains sexual relations with men other than their husbands took place within rigidly prescribed limits. In the buffalo-calling ceremony, wives of younger men courted and had intercourse with older men. Those intimate relations were like a conduit that transferred spiritual power and hunting skill from an older man to a younger one. When nonnatives, both black and white, appeared on the scene, Indian women, and sometimes their spouses, sought them out. As Clark noted, "the Indians say all white flesh is medisan." In one especially revealing incident, an Arikara husband stood guard at the door of his lodge lest anyone interrupt the tryst between his wife and York.[18] Sex could appropriate power and place it in native hands. Here Indian women explored the intimate unknown, expecting to find great strength and a different kind of knowledge.

No nineteenth-century American exploring party made a fuller and more intimate record of its daily doings than the Lewis and Clark Expedition. When expedition journal keepers encountered native women, the accounts they wrote revealed some things while concealing others. Journal entries made it plain that women were defined in terms of sexual identity, reproductive history, and domestic labor. Euro-American explorers were bound by those definitions and blinded to the other ways that native women explorers might behave. What is either missing in or concealed by the journals are the ways native women explored the worlds beyond the sexual. Like native men, women must have studied the ways and means, the sights and sounds of the bearded strangers. That the strangers took no notice of that exploring activity diminishes both the written record and our appreciation of the larger exploration encounter.

It is not easy to judge how well native explorers came to know their strange neighbors. What did all the looking, visiting, questioning, talking, and lovemaking finally produce? Did native explorers succeed in "civilizing" the strangers? Did they give them new names or influence their behavior? There are no certain answers to these questions. There is no scholarly edition of documents and maps called *The Journals of Black Cat*. What survives are evocative fragments hinting at a major effort of mind and spirit, the struggle to know the other. Two unrelated events at the end of the winter of 1804–5 can tell us something about the Indian enterprise to understand what had quite suddenly become a new world.

In early March 1805 the Hidatsa chief Le Borgne came to Fort Mandan for a meeting with Lewis. As the two men talked through an interpreter, there was a buzz of commotion in the Hidatsa delegation. Finally the chief explained what was going on. "Some foolish young men had informed him that there was a black man in the party." Le Borgne doubted that any man was wholly black. Perhaps the man in question was simply wearing black paint in mourning for a lost relative. With that, Lewis produced Clark's slave York. In that moment Le Borgne the explorer had to confront what seemed the unthinkable, the unimaginable. Was York a man, was he really black? Clark heard later that Le Borgne was "astonished" by the sight of York. The chief examined York closely and then "spit on his hand and rubbed in order to rub off the paint." York quickly grasped what was going on, pulled off the bandanna from his head, and showed Le Borgne his hair. Amazed by black skin and curly hair, the Indian was convinced that York was "of a different species from the whites."[19]

If Le Borgne was bewildered by his foray into the unknown, Black Cat's more extensive exploration of the Lewis and Clark world produced a larger measure of understanding. On a warm day in early April 1805, just before the American explorers left for the Pacific, Black Cat had a final visit with the captains. They smoked together and then the Indian gave Clark "a par of excellent Mockersons."[20] Smoking and a gift—perhaps gestures that acknowledged an exploration enterprise at least partially fulfilled. Clark now had a place in Black Cat's world. The pipe and the moccasins said as much. What happened along the Missouri was a continuation of a process that began in 1492. Two very different worlds collided and out of that collision came something new and unsettling. Black Cat, Le Borgne, Lewis, and Clark—all were new world explorers bound together in the common cause of discovery.

Notes

1. Exploration historiography is discussed at length in James P. Ronda, *The Exploration of North America* (Washington, D.C., 1992).

2. The full range of Lewis and Clark scholarship is discussed in James P. Ronda, "The Writingest Explorers: The Lewis and Clark Expedition in American Historical Literature," *Pennsylvania Magazine of History and Biography*, 112 (October 1988), 607-30, reprinted in this volume, 299-326.

3. W. Raymond Wood and Thomas D. Thiessen, eds., *Early Fur Trade on the Northern Plains: Canadian Traders among the Mandan and Hidatsa Indians, 1738–1818* (Norman, Okla., 1985), table 1.

4. Lewis, "Observations and Reflections, August, 1807," in *Letters of the Lewis and Clark Expedition with Related Documents, 1783–1854*, ed. Donald Jackson, 2d ed. (Urbana, Ill., 1978), 2:698.

5. Gary E. Moulton, ed., *The Journals of the Lewis and Clark Expedition* (Lincoln, Nebr., 1983–97), 3:242 (hereafter JLCE).

6. James P. Ronda, *Lewis and Clark among the Indians* (Lincoln, Nebr., 1984), 27-41.

7. Annie H. Abel, ed., *Tabeau's Narrative of Loisel's Expedition to the Upper Missouri* (Norman, Okla., 1939), 200-201.

8. Milo M. Quaife, ed., *The Journals of Captain Meriwether Lewis and Sergeant John Ordway* (Madison, Wis., 1916), 159.

9. JLCE, 3:238.

10. Ibid., 3:310-11; Quaife, *Journals of Lewis and Ordway*, 186.

11. Quaife, *Journals of Lewis and Ordway*, 174.

12. JLCE, 3:267.

13. Ibid., 3:289.

14. Ibid., 3:237, 238, 240, 311, quotations on 237 and 311.

15. Ibid., 3:208-11, quotation on 209.

16. Ibid., 3:218.

17. Ibid., 3:218-19, 242.

18. "Biddle Notes," in Jackson, *Letters*, 2:503, 538; JLCE, 3:209, 268.

19. "Biddle Notes," in Jackson, *Letters*, 2:539.

20. JLCE, 4:13-14.

Cloud studies over the Missouri River, Dakota Territory, 1883,
photographed by F. Jay Haynes

Part Five

Homecoming

IT HAS ALWAYS BEEN EASIER TO TELL THE EXCITING STORY of the expedition journey than to consider the results of the enterprise. Who can resist recounting yet again the struggles up the Missouri, the wonders of the Great Falls, or the roar of the Columbia through The Dalles. And this is a cast of characters that makes for a memorable tale. The journey seems so impressive that its consequences must have been equally important. But when pressed for specifics, historians often fall back on familiar phrases about Lewis and Clark "advancing the American empire" or "expanding the fur trade" or at the very least "blazing the trail" for generations of westering pioneers. But such clichés do the explorers no favors. In fact, the real and enduring consequences of the journey are often cheapened or obscured by empty praise.

When the expedition returned to St. Louis in 1806, friends and well-wishers were quick to celebrate the journey and hail the travelers. But the results of the "tour to the Pacific" seemed hard to define. The dinner toasts recorded in the Frankfort, Kentucky, *Western World* were long on good cheer and predictably short on thoughtful consideration of larger meanings. Was the voyage about the rising American empire or the expanding fur trade or just plain American courage and good luck? Enthusiastic Americans claimed one or all of those as expedition outcomes. But Jefferson knew better. In the months and years after September 1806 he had to face the Corps of Discovery's ambiguous record. And perhaps beyond ambiguity, there was a knawing sense of failure on a grand scale. The expedition had failed to find what the president was sure the geography of the West must contain—a passage from Atlantic to Pacific waters. Did that geographic failure doom Jefferson's larger western dreams as well? And compounding the lack of discovery of a water route to the Pacific were the publication delays, Lewis's suicide, and the loss of key scientific data.

Despite all those accidents and disappointments, the journey did have tangible and immediate results. There were scientific specimens, even if their study was a long time coming. The Clark map of the West, included in Nicholas Biddle's 1814 narrative of the expedition, proved a landmark in the cartographic understanding of the West. And the very fact of the journey sparked literary imagination. Albert Furtwangler's essay takes us into the world of polished literature and rough politics, depicting the ways the expedition fueled a political and intellectual controversy between John Quincy Adams and Joel Barlow. And the fevered imagination of one Anthony G. Bettay appropriated the Lewis and Clark story to make it his own personal and improbable adventure. Bettay's letter reminds us that the expedition story had many immediate and unpredictable results, including individual fantasy as well as national ambition.

St. Louis Welcomes Lewis and Clark

James P. Ronda

WHEN THE LEWIS AND CLARK EXPEDITION RETURNED TO ST. LOUIS on September 23, 1806, William Clark recorded that the explorers were "met by all the village and received a harty welcom from it's inhabitants."[1] Just how "harty" that welcome was became clear when two days later prominent St. Louis citizens celebrated the expedition's return with a grand dinner and ball. The event was held at the inn operated by William Christy, a noted city businessman, politician, and someone Clark described as "my old acquaintance."

Because St. Louis did not have a newspaper until 1808, the only report of the festivities appeared in the Frankfort, Kentucky, *Western World* for October 11, 1806. I would like to thank my good friend James Holmberg, Curator of Manuscripts at The Filson Club, Louisville, Kentucky, for helping me obtain a copy of this very rare issue of *The Western World*.

Arrival of Captains Lewis and Clark at St. Louis

This desirable and unexpected event, took place on Tuesday, the 23d of this instant, about the hour of 10 o'clock in the morning. On Monday evening the news reached this place, that Captains Lewis and Clark had arrived at the cantonment; near the mouth of the Missouri; and the great concourse of people that lined the bank of the river at the time of their landing at this place the next day, must be considered as a strong evidence of the respect entertained of those gentlemen for the danger and difficulties they must have encountered in their expedition of discovery. But the citizens of St. Louis, anxious to evince fully their joy at this event, (which cannot but be considered as very interesting to every American) united in celebrating their arrival by a splendid dinner at Christy's Inn, on the 25th, which was succeeded by a Ball in the evening. The respectable number of persons who attended both the dinner and ball, given on the occasion, together with the unanimity which prevailed throughout the company, cannot but be esteemed an honorable testimony of the respect entertained for those characters who are willing to encounter, fatigue and hunger for the benefit of their fellow citizens: but what is not due to those who penetrate the gloom of unexplored regions, to expel the mists of ignorance which envelope science, and overshadow their country?

The following were the Toasts drank at the Dinner:

1. The president of the United States—The friend of science, the polar star of *discovery*, the philosopher and the patriot.

2. The Heads of Department—The pillars that support the world's *best* hope.

3. The Missouri expedition—May the knowledge of the newly explored regions of the West, be the least benefit that we may derive from this painful and perilous expedition.

4. The hardy followers of Captains Lewis and Clark— May they be rewarded by the esteem of their fellow citizens.

5. The United States—Whilst they tolerate a spirit of enquiry, may never forget, that *united they stand—but divided they fall.*

6. The Territory of Louisiana—Freedom without bloodshed, may her actions duly appreciate the blessing.

7. The memory of Christopher Columbus—May those who imitate his hardihood, perseverence and merit, never have, like him, to encounter public ingratitude.

8. The Federal Constitution—May the Eagle of America convey it to the remotest regions of the globe; and whilst

they read they cannot but admire.

9. The memory of the illustrious Washington, the father of America— May his guardian spirit still watch over us, and prove a terror to the engines of despotism.

10. The Capitol of the United States—May the goddess of liberty, never cease to preside there.

11. Peace with all nations; but submission to none.

12. The Commerce of the United States—The basis for the political elevation of America.

13. Agriculture and Industry—The farmer is the best support of government.

14. Our fathers who shed their blood and laid down their lives to purchase our independence—May we emulate their actions, and inherit their virtues.

15. The Missouri—Under the auspices of America, may it prove a vehicle of wealth to all the nations of the world.

16. Our National Council—May the baneful influence of private ambition and political intrigue, be ever expelled thence by the genuine spirit of republicanism.

17. The fair daughters of Louisiana—May they ever bestow their smiles on hardihood and virtuous valor.

AFTER CAPTS. LEWIS AND CLARK RETIRED:

18. Captains Lewis and Clark—Their perilous services endear them to every American heart.

Notes

1. Reuben Gold Thwaites, ed., *Original Journals of the Lewis and Clark Expedition, 1804–1806*, (New York, 1904–5), 5:394.

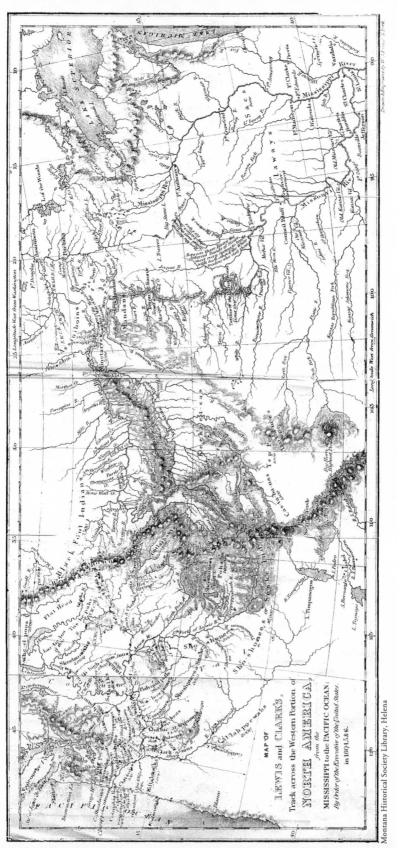

Printed in 1814, this map of Lewis and Clark's trek reflects the corps' experience as well as information Clark gathered from travelers who visited the Northwest after the expedition's return.

Anthony G. Bettay
to Thomas Jefferson

FAYETTE COUNTY *State of pennsylvania*
Jany the 27th 1808

HONOURABLE SIR. Having lately Returnd from the interior parts
of Louisiana Where I Have Spent the last three years during that
time I made Some discoveries of the most interesting nature to the
united States and feel it my duty as citizen of the united States to
communicate the Same to you as Chief Magistrate, I was on my
way from Louisiana to Washington, and would have been in
Washington Before this date had not Several causes combind to
have prevented it. therefore I think proper to address you by way
of a letter, and hasten to inform you that I have found an immence
bed of Rich Silver ore or at least it has the appearance of being
immence I feel Restless to See the United States in the possession
and injoying the benefits that may arise from it, if it may be thought
So, which is unquestionable with me, therefore if a knowledge of
the Spot where this treasure lies is desirable to the united States I
am willing to conduct any party that may be appointed to make a
further examination of its extent, and value, for one hundredth
part of the proceds of the mine for Seventy five years to be paid to
me or my heirs or assigns or for a Suitable Sum paid to me of the
first proceds of the mine   this mine lies on the River Platte or at
Least on one of its Branches about 1700 computed miles from St
Louis I have been at the trouble to mark the way and to commit
it to paper So that if I should never Live to reach that Spot again

the papers will direct the inquirer to the place. I have likewise discovered an eligible passage across that chain of mountains dividing the waters of the atlantick from those of the Passifick by way of the River platte and Cashecatrongo River a learge navigable River of the Passifick on the waters of which I found a plant that I suppose hitherto unknown to the world and one that promises to be highly beneficial to the world this plant I have given the name of the Silk nettle from its inflicting severe pain to whoever touches it when growing it grows to about eight feet high, produces a thick strong bark that after being exposᵈ to the weather for a few month the bark of which assooms the appearance of Silk the fibers of which are inconceivably fine, of a transparent white and Somewhat elastick its Strength Surpassing anything of the kind hitherto known to me this bark is properly calculated for the manufactury of the finest wares and may be cultivated to great advantage for cordage of every discription if your Excellency wishes to have any further information on those Subjects you can signify the Same to me by way of a letter directed to me at Union Town Penn Where I will wait on you to explain any question that may arise or if it Should be desirable for me to come to washington you may calculate on my attendance when ever it may be desirable by the government, or his Excellency, with respect I conclude by Ascribing myself your Verry Obedient Servᵗ.

Anthony G. Bettay

The Race to Publish Lewis and Clark

Donald Jackson

WHEN MERIWETHER LEWIS WENT TO PHILADELPHIA in the spring of 1807 to arrange for the publication of his journals, he went with a sense of urgency. Two enlisted members of his exploring party already had announced plans to publish their own narratives of the recent expedition to the Pacific.

Other journals might be in preparation, Lewis feared, including "some spurious publications," and he had just voiced in print his disapproval of such accounts. His attempt to dissuade the public from patronizing the writings of his fellows was coupled with a promise to bring his own story of the expedition off the press soon. It was a promise that he proved unable to keep.

Lewis and his partner William Clark had brought the expedition safely back to St. Louis on September 23, 1806, and had immediately begun the task of giving to the world some accounting of the more than two years they had spent beyond the Mississippi. On the day after their arrival, Lewis turned ghost writer by penning a long letter for Clark to sign and send to one of his brothers, probably George Rogers Clark, near Louisville. Knowing that this letter would inevitably reach the newspapers, and that it would be the first published news of the expedition's success, both Lewis and Clark must have realized that it could best be phrased by the more literate member of the team.[1] The letter was published first in the

Frankfort (Kentucky) *Palladium* of October 9, and was copied by many other newspapers as soon as the editors could obtain it. The Pittsburgh *Gazette* ran the letter on October 28, and it reached the Philadelphia papers about a week later.

Even before this letter was made public, a prospectus was circulating in St. Louis for the publication of Robert Frazer's journal. Lewis had read the prospectus and had warned Frazer to avoid discussing the scientific aspects of the expedition. Frazer was promising his subscribers "an accurate description of the Missouri and its several branches; of the mountains separating the Eastern from the Western waters; of the Columbia river and the Bay it forms on the Pacific Ocean; of the face of the Country in general; of the several Tribes of Indians on the Missouri and Columbia rivers; of the vegetable, animal and [mineral] productions discovered in those Extensive regions."[2]

There is no evidence that Frazer ever published such a book, nor has any manuscript journal of his been located. A manuscript map has survived, with a legend reading: "A Map of the discoveries of Capt. Lewis & Clark from the Rockey mountain and the River Lewis to the Cap of Disappointment Or the Coloumbia River at the North Pacific Ocean By observation Of Robert Frazer."[3]

With Frazer's intentions known, there still remained a question about the future of the journals—at least four of them—kept by other men on the expedition. Lewis and Clark bought Sergeant John Ordway's journal outright for $150, splitting the cost between them, and it became a useful reference in the later preparation of their own manuscript.[4] The journal of the late Sergeant Charles Floyd, who had died en route, was too fragmentary to be significant. Private Joseph Whitehouse had kept a journal, aided in the early stages by two other men, and Sergeant Patrick Gass had kept still another. It was perhaps a report that Gass had sold his journal to a publisher that caused Lewis to issue his warning to the public. The following notice, dated March 14, 1807, ran in the Washington, D.C., *National Intelligencer* of March 18:

> Having been informed that there were several unauthorised
> and probably some spurious publications now preparing
> for the press, on the subject of my late tour to the Pacific

Ocean by individuals entirely unknown to me, I have considered it a duty which I owe the public, as well as myself to put them on their guard with respect to such publications, lest from the practice of such impositions they may be taught to depreciate the worth of the work which I am myself preparing for publication before it can possibly appear, as much time, labor, and expense are absolutely necessary in order to do justice to the several subjects which it will embrace: With a view therefore to prevent the practice of those deceptions the public are informed that the lists for subscriptions which have been promulgated by myself are headed with the subjoined Prospectus, and that those who wish to possess the genuine work, may obtain it by entering their names on those lists. The Prospectus will serve to shew the distribution and contents of the work.

The map will most probably be published by the latter end of October next, and the first volume of the work about the 1st of January 1808; the two remaining volumes will follow in succession as early as they can possibly be prepared for publication.

As early as a just estimate of the price of the several parts of this work can be formed, public notice will be given of the same through the medium of the Press.

To Robert Frazier only has permission been given either by Gen. William Clark or myself, to publish any thing in relation to our late voyage. When the proposals were first drawn in October last for the publication of the journal of that man, they were submitted to me for correction; I then expunged the promise which had been made, that the work should contain certain information in relation to the natural history of the country through which we had passed and cautioned the persons concerned in the publication not to promise the world any thing with which they had not the means of complying; but as the hope of gain seems to have outstripped their good faith to the public in this respect; I think it my duty to declare that Robert Frazier, who was only a private on this expedition, is entirely unacquainted with celestial observations, mineralogy, botany, or zoology, and therefore cannot possibly give any accurate information on those subjects, nor on that of geography, and that the whole which can be expected from his Journal is merely a limited detail of our daily transactions. With respect to all unauthorised publications relative to this voyage, I presume that they cannot have stronger pretensions to accuracy of information than that of Robert Frazier.

Meriwether Lewis.

The man who had bought the Gass journal was David McKeehan, a Pittsburgh bookseller who kept a "Book and Stationary Store, in front of the Court House," and whose name also appeared under notices of the Pittsburgh land office which ran in the Pittsburgh *Gazette* of the period. Perhaps he is the David McKeehan who was graduated from Dickinson College in 1787 and was admitted to the Pennsylvania bar in 1792. It is unlikely that he had seen Lewis's public statement when, in the *Gazette* of March 24, he announced plans to publish "a Journal of the Voyages & Travels of a Corps of Discovery, under the command of Captain Lewis and Captain Clarke of the Army of the United States . . . with geographical & explanatory notes, by the Publisher."

He proposed to issue a work of about three hundred pages, "handsomely bound in boards," priced at one dollar. To assure the subscriber of the authenticity of the work, he declared that "at different resting places during the expedition, the several journals were brought together, compared, corrected, and the blanks, which had been unavoidably left, filled up; and that, since he [McKeehan] became the proprietor, in order to render it more useful and acceptable, he has undertaken and completed the laborious task of arranging and transcribing the whole of it."

The caveat by Lewis must have struck hard at McKeehan's hopes, for Lewis and Clark were now the objects of national acclaim. Lewis had arrived in Washington in late December accompanied by a picturesque Mandan chief,[5] had been lionized at public functions, had heard a public reading of a eulogistic poem written by Joel Barlow, and then had been appointed governor of the Territory of Louisiana.[6] His criticism of unauthorized journals could have been ruinous for McKeehan.

With his investment at stake, McKeehan wrote an excoriating letter—obviously intended more for the public eye than for

Lewis's—and handed it to the editor of the Pittsburgh *Gazette*. It occupied the whole of page two in the issue of April 14, 1807, and seems to have been overlooked by the biographers of Lewis and Clark and the subsequent editors of their journals. The complete text follows:

> *To his Excellency Meriwether Lewis, Esquire, Governor of Upper Louisiana.*
>
> Sir,
>
> Your publication in the National Intelligencer, dated the 14th of last month, has forced into notice an obscure individual, who, of course, has had the misfortune of being "entirely unknown to you," to defend his character and his rights. However unpleasant it may be to his feelings to appear before the public in his own defence; and however he may regret the necessity of drawing their attention to the remarks he may offer, it is some consolation that the conduct of his antagonist claims of him no scrupulous adherence to the rules of formality, or of punctilious delicacy; and that to meet Your Excellency on the subject of your publication requires to *you* no apology. Your rapid advancement to power and wealth seems to have changed the polite, humble and respectful language of a *Sir Clement* into that of him who commands and dispenses favours; even your subscription lists, when you offer your learned works for publication must be *"promulgated."*
>
> As your notice may not be favored with a general insertion in the newspapers, it may be an act of candour towards Your Excellency, before I proceed in my principal remarks relative to it, to give, as far as necessary, a statement of its contents.
>
> Your Excellency is pleased to observe,—"Having been informed that there *were* several unauthorized and probably some spurious publications *now* preparing for the press, on the subject of *my* late tour to the Pacific Ocean, by individuals entirely unknown to me, I have considered it a duty which I owe to the public, as well as myself to put them on their guard against such impositions, lest from the practice of such impositions they may be taught to depreciate the worth of the work which I am myself

preparing for publication before it can possibly appear, as much time, labour and expense are absolutely necessary in order to do justice to the several subjects which it will embrace."—The public are then referred to the lists for subscriptions which have been *promulgated* by yourself, and the prospectus with which they are headed; and obligingly informed, "that those who wish to possess the genuine work, may obtain it by entering their names on those lists." But, as an inducement perhaps to make the entries, we are told that the price of this "genuine work" is to be fixed at a future day; that the map *will most probably* be published the latter end of October next; the first volume of the work *about* the first of January, 1808; and that the two remaining volumes will follow in succession as early *as they possibly can be prepared for publication*; or (as it stated in the proposals) *at as early periods as the avocations of the author will permit.* Next you tell the public that to Robert Frazer only permission has been given to publish any thing relative to your late voyage. But even the *proposals* of Frazer must feel the effect of your expunging fingers: what amputations and mutilations his journal itself has suffered, you do not think proper to communicate; but it is reasonable to suppose that all those parts were *expunged* which might *depreciate the worth of the work,* which you are preparing for publication. Do you yet stop here? No, but in order to defeat the ostensible object of your own permission, and to deprive poor Frazer, or those who may have purchased from him, of all benefit arising from his publication, you attack his capacity, and "declare that Robert Frazer, *who was only a private on this expedition,* is entirely unacquainted with *celestial observations, mineralogy, botany,* or *zoology,* and therefore cannot possibly give any accurate information on *those subjects,* nor on that of geography, and that the whole which can be expected from his journal is merely *a limited detail* of our daily transactions." Limited perhaps in proportion to your expunging operations! Having thus attempted to expose Frazer and his work, you conclude your notice with the following sweeping clause intended to affect all other persons interested in any of the journals; "With respect to all unauthorised publications relative to this voyage, I presume that they cannot have stronger pretensions to accuracy or information than that of Robert Frazer."

Having given this exposition of your note, it may perhaps be agreeable to Your Excellency to know the reasons of my intefereing in this affair of the journals of what you very modestly call *your* late tour. You will therefore please to understand, that, without soliciting either your permission or authority, I have purchased the journal of one of the persons engaged in the late expedition from the mouth of the Missouri to the Pacific ocean "performed by order of the government;" that I have arranged and transcribed it for the press, supplying such geographical notes and other observations, as I supposed would render it more useful and satisfactory to the reader; that a large edition of it is now printing in this place, and will be published and ready for delivery (unless some unforeseen circumstances occur to prevent it) the latter end of next month; according to the proposals inserted in this paper.

After having furnished Your Excellency with this information, I must be permitted to make some short observations, which I think necessary, on a few points in order to render the subject in discussion between us fairly understood.

With respect to the hazardous nature of the enterprize and the courage necessary for undertaking it, candour compels me to say, that public opinion has placed them on too high ground. Mr. M'Kenzie[7] with a party consisting of about one fourth part of the number under your command, with means which will not bear a comparison with those furnished you, and without the *authority*, the *flags*, or *medals* of his government, crossed the Rocky mountains several degrees north of your rout, and for the *first time* penetrated to the Pacific Ocean. You had the advantage of the information contained in his journal, and could in some degree estimate and guard against the dangers and difficulties you were to meet; and I have no doubt that, had government given an invitation, hundreds as daring, enterprising and capable as your Excellency, would have offered to engage in the expedition, and for compensations much smaller than were received by yourself and the other persons composing the corps actually engaged in it.

Having mentioned compensations; with your Excellency's leave, I will next notice that received by you. What compensations did your Excellency receive? By an act of congress passed the 3d of last month, double pay was allowed you as captain of infantry, during the expedition, and also a grant of 1600 acres of land; to these may be added the value of your rations and your pay as private secretary or master of ceremonies to the president, the latter of which it is alledged and believed you pocketed though you could perform no part of the duties or ceremonies attached to the office.[8] Have we got through the items of the account? No. To these perquisites the executive adds the honorable and lucrative office of Governor of Upper Louisiana! Why, sir, these grants and rewards savour more of the splendid munificence of a Prince than the economy of a republican government. It ought not to escape notice that the land is to be located within your own government, where your influence and means of information may render the value of the grant incalculable. There is besides a good deal of tinsel thrown into the scale with these solid considerations; such as the praises of the president (for a hobby horse as well as another will sometimes run away with his rider); the honor of leading such an expedition; of knighting or making chiefs (an act perhaps not strictly constitutional) of the poor savages of the west; of immortalizing your name and those of your friends by giving them to the mighty streams which flow from the Rocky mountains; and what I had almost forgot, the warblings of the Muses, who have been celebrating the "*Young Hero's name.*" Who could have thought that after so much liberality shewn by the country, your Excellency would have been found contending with the poor fellows, who for their small pittance were equally exposed with yourself to the toils and dangers attending the expedition, about the publication of their journals, which cost them so much trouble and anxiety to keep and preserve! I am afraid Captain Clarke, who appears to have acted during the whole of the tour with the greatest prudence, firmness and courage, will be forced to blush for the man he has called his friend.

Solomon says, "There are three things which are never satisfied, yea, four things say not, *It is enough*." Had your Excellency lived in the days of Solomon, and been as near his court, as you have lately been to that of the United States, the wise and discerning monarch would easily have found a *fifth thing* which would say not, *It is enough*.

By way of interlude in this exhibition of curious things, let me put a question to Your Excellency. Where was your journal during the session of Congress? Snug, eh! No notice is given in the government paper of an intention to publish it;—No warnings against impositions;—only a few proposals circulated among booksellers at a distance! Some of the members begin to wince, complain that they are called upon to legislate in the dark, that no journal of the expedition was laid before them; others boldly assert that the grants they are asked for are extravagant—that double pay is a sufficient compensation; and that to get rid of importunate applicants, and to be allowed to attend to the important business of the session, they are obliged to consent to grants which they know to be unreasonable and unjust. This was the time to keep the journal out of view; and to be silent about the fortune to be made out of the *three* volumes and a map. "I'll squeeze, (says His Excellency in embrio) "I'll squeeze the nation first, and then raise a heavy contribution on the citizens individually: I'll cry down these *one*-volume journals, and frighten the publishers; and no man, woman, or child shall read a word about *my* tour, unless they enter their names on *my* lists, and pay what price I shall afterwards fix on my *three* volumes and map." Without thinking it worth while to ask by what right you call this tour, which you acknowledge was "performed by order of the government," *your* tour, let me enquire by what high grant or privilege you claim the right of authorizing, licensing or suppressing journals or other publications concerning it? Every man of sense must agree that these journals are either *private* property of the individuals who took them, or *public* property; for none but an ideot could for a moment suppose, that any officer upon the expedition could have a property in any but his own. If therefore they are the private property of the individuals severally who kept them, there is an end to the question. Are they public property and has the government done any act either to manifest or relinquish its claim? In my opinion there may be cases where the journals, maps, surveys, and all other documents taken during a military expedition, especially where policy and the interest of the country requires secrecy, ought to be considered the property of the public and delivered up to the government; but where no such policy, interest or secrecy exist; and where it is for the public advantage that the information collected shall be diffused as widely as possible; where the government never calls for any documents for their inspection but those taken by the commanding officers; where other persons belonging to the expedition, who had taken journals or other documents, were discharged from public service with these journals and documents in their hands, and no claim made of them as public property when other public property in their possession was delivered up; where the commanding officers have been allowed by the government to publish their journals, maps and other documents for their private emolument; will it be said that in a country governed by equal laws, and where equal rights and privileges are secured to all the citizens, these persons who have been so discharged from public service and become private citizens, have not also a right to publish the documents they have taken and preserved? Why, sir, scorn itself would hardly deign to point its finger at the administration, which would attempt to suppress them and prevent their publication; and despotism would blush at the deed, even to advance its favorites and sycophants. The fact is, sir, that these journals were considered as unnecessary (those of the commanding officers being preserved) for the information of the government, and all claim relinquished to them by the act of discharge, without a demand, when the persons who had taken them were retiring from public service, to private life. These journals, when first ordered to be taken were intended to be made use of only conditionally, and therefore more of the nature of private property than the others. The object of multiplying journals of the tour was that, in case of defeat or other misfortune affecting the safety of those taken by the commanding officers, the chances of preserving information with respect to the country through which the expedition was to pass might also be multiplied. Connected with this part of the investigation, is another point (and a material one) on which I must ask a question or two, and say a few words: this respects the credit due to these journals and their claim to correctness. Was it not a part of your duty to see that these journals were regularly kept, and, if necessary, to supply from your journal, any defects or omissions? Were not all the journals belonging to the corps brought together at certain resting places, examined, compared and corrected? If Mr. Gass (from whom I purchased) "is unacquainted with celestial observations" (which I will grant) was it not your duty, and did you not supply him with the result of those made by yourself? How else did Mr. Gass find out the latitude of certain places where your observations were taken to the exactness of minutes, seconds and tenths of seconds? Without information from Captain Clarke or yourself, how did he ascertain the distances of places, the breadth of rivers and bays, height of falls and length of portages? But it is unnecessary to multiply questions: you know that these journals will furnish the necessary information relative to the tour; and that the publication of them will "*depreciate the worth of the work you are preparing for publication.*" This is what alarms your insatiable avarice. If there were not some consequence connected with these journals, why all this uneasiness about them? Why purchase them at high prices in order to have them supressed? Did you not lately purchase the journal of sergeant Prior or Sergeant Ordway, for that purpose? I will next grant that Mr. Gass is not acquainted with mineralogy, botany or zoology, that his geographical knowledge is neither extensive nor correct, "and (to use your own words) that the whole which can be expected from his journal is merely a limited detail of your daily transactions," and yet strange as it may appear to such a phenomenon in literature as Your Excellency, I am of opinion it will be more interesting and useful to readers generally than the volume of your work, which is to be "confined exclusively to scientific research." He may in some respects be considered as having the advantage; for while your Excellency was star-gazing, and taking celestial observations, he was taking observations in the world below. If Mr. Gass and the publisher of his journal can lead their readers along the rout of the expedition and make them acquainted with those things which were the objects of the external senses, and as they appeared to those senses, the greater number will willingly dispense with "scientific research." Of what consequence is it to the generality of readers to know how a plant has been classed, to what order, genus or species it has been confined by Botanists? And as to zoology and mineralogy similar questions might be asked with equal propriety. Who is not pleased with M'Kenzie's journal? And what does he say of himself? Does he pretend to be either a mineralogist, a botanist or zoologist? "I do not possess," says he, "the science of the naturalist; and even if the qualifications of that character had been attained by me, its curious spirit had not be gratified. I could not stop to dig into the earth, over whose surface I was compelled to pass with rapid steps; nor could I turn aside to collect the plants which nature might have scattered on the way, when my thoughts were anxiously imployed in making provision for the day that was passing over me." Yet he "flatters himself" that his "work will be found to excite an interest, and conciliate a regard, in the minds of those who peruse it." What! without "scientific research!" Unacquainted with "mineralogy, botany and zoology!" What a presumptuous fellow!

To shew the public that Mr. Gass has some talents and merit, I will introduce the following extract from a paper delivered to him under your own signature.

"As a tribute justly due the merits of the said Patrick Gass, I with cheerfulness declare that the ample support, which he gave me under every difficulty; the manly firmness, which he evinced on every necessary occasion; and the fortitude with which he bore (*boar*, in the original) the fatigues and painful sufferings incident to that long voyage, entitles him to my highest confidence and sincere thanks, while it eminently recommends him to the consideration and respect of his fellow citizens."[9]

This certificate does you honor, and it is to be regretted that the wealth and honours heaped upon you so soon rendered your heart callous towards the companions of your "fatigues and painful sufferings." Perhaps I ought to beg pardon for using the word *companions*, as it has been thought proper at the seat of government to degrade them to mere "*Followers.*"

The publication of the journal of Mr. Gass I expect will have the following good effects; first, It may save many the trouble of purchasing your *three volumes* and map, by affording them at a cheap rate, a plain and satisfactory account of the tour; in the second place, it will so *depreciate the worth of your work* that there may be a chance of getting it at a reasonable price; and in the third place, as it will contain plain matter of fact, it may deter you from swelling your work with such *tales of wonder* as have sometimes issued from the *Ten-mile-square.*

But, by the bye, did your Excellency never attend to the advice given to those who have glass houses? Were you not afraid that some persons affected by your publication, might inform the public that you were not a man of science, that you were not a man of letters, and that you were not qualified for scientific research. The length of the observations already made prevent me from giving even a *limited detail* of my information upon this point.

I, however, assure you that I shall wait with some impatience for your voluminous work; and shall willingly subscribe for it, when a reasonable price is fixed; but hope you will be cautious in magnifying trifles; and in giving too long and learned dissertations with respect to the "*Origin of Prairies,*" and "the cause of the muddiness of the Missouri." With respect to the latter, which you make one of your great points of investigation, Mr. Gass, who does not speak scientifically, only says, "At two, we proceeded again on our voyage, and passed a long chain of Bluffs on the north side, of a dark colour. From these and others of the same kind the Missouri gets its muddy colour. The earth of which they are composed dissolves like sugar; every rain washes down great quantities of it, and the rapidity of the stream keeps it mixing and afloat in the water until it reaches the mouth of the Mississippi." Now who can relish this homespun account without a spice of "scientific research!"

I must pass over the unhappy affair with the Indians

on the plains of Maria's river, also that very affecting one of your own posteriors,[10] and conclude with congratulating you that Mr. Gass's Journal did not fall into the hands of some wag, who might have insinuated that your wound was not accidental, but that it was the consequence of design,—that the *young hero* might not return without more scars (if not *honorable*, near the *place of honour*) to excite the curiosity and compassion of some favorite widow Wadman, who might have been languishing during his absence. In what a ludicrous situation he might have placed the *young hero* with his *point of honour* just past the *point of a rock*, with Crusatte taking aim!—perhaps there will be a representation in the plates embellishing your second volume!
Pittsburgh, 7th April, 1807.   The Editor of Gass's Journal

At the end, McKeehan added a request that newspaper editors insert the letter in their own papers. Apparently few, if any, complied, for McKeehan complained in the Pittsburgh *Gazette* of June 16 about "the conduct of those Editors of newspapers, who declined to publish his observations on captain Lewis's Notice,—especially of such as had given place to that Notice." So he offered an inducement: every editor who now ran the piece would receive two copies of the Gass journal.

"It is not yet clearly ascertained," McKeehan wrote, "how far the illiberal and indelicate notice of Captain Lewis has been injurious. In a few instances it has had a good effect; while in some parts of the country, there is no doubt, it has occasioned a temporary deception, which will vanish on correct information, and when the *price* of his work is made known." When McKeehan later learned that Lewis intended to ask thirty-one dollars for two volumes and a map, he ran another half-column advertisement in the *Gazette* to compare his own publication with Lewis's and to repeat that his price was only one dollar.

By July 7 McKeehan could announce that his book was ready for distribution. In many ways it was a miserable piece of work, for upon Patrick Gass's sketchy notes the editor had placed the burden of an elegant prose style. But it *was* a journal, the first to reach the public, and it sold well. The first edition, printed in

Pittsburgh by Zadok Cramer, was reportedly followed in 1808 by another Pittsburgh printing. A London edition appeared in 1808, and in 1810 the copyright apparently was purchased by Philadelphia publisher Mathew Carey, who published identical editions in 1810, 1811, and 1812, having added six plates to the original material. The French came forward with a Paris edition in 1810, containing the first map known to mention Lewis and Clark and to locate portions of their route.

Alexander Henry was carrying a copy of the work with him on a fur-trading expedition in 1810. "Put tongues to thaw, and perused Gass' Journal Across the Rocky Mountains," he wrote in his own journal.[11]

When the first edition appeared in Philadelphia bookstalls in the summer of 1807, Meriwether Lewis was still in that city making plans for his own publication. He was so much in demand socially, and had, through Jefferson, so many associations with the leading scholars and professional men of the city, that he accomplished little. By May 5, painter and museum curator Charles Willson Peale already had done his portrait and was writing to John Hawkins in London, "The drawings for Governor Lewis's Journal I mean to draw myself to be engraved for the work. It is a work that seems to excite much attention, & will I hope have a great sale & give considerable profit to this bold adventurer."[12]

The publishing house operated by John Conrad had contracted to produce the work, but, of course, they needed a manuscript. Later in the summer, when Lewis left to assume his governorship in St. Louis, there still was no manuscript and no prospect of one. There were thousands of pages of journal entries, kept by both Lewis and Clark, and the two explorers seem to have believed that these could somehow be transmuted into a printed book without further effort on their part. No one can say with certainty that the manuscript journals, as they exist today in the vaults of the American Philosophical Society, were produced during the expedition or, in a revised version, during the 1808–9 period when the men were together in St. Louis. Jefferson later declared that the journals were produced in the field, and indirectly attributed their fine state of preservation to the fact that they were sealed in metal containers.[13] In any event, we have John Conrad's testimony that at the time of Lewis's death in 1809, not a line of manuscript had been received from St. Louis.[14]

In the meantime, another "unauthorized" journal had appeared, and it was completely spurious. Published in Philadelphia by Hubbard Lester in 1809, it was entitled *The travels of Capts. Lewis & Clarke, by order of the Government of the Untied States, performed in the years 1804, 1805, & 1806.* Although it was designed to appear as an official report of the expedition, it was actually a compilation of odds and ends from Lewis and Clark letters and from the reports of Alexander Mackenzie, Jonathan Carver, and other travelers. It had the effect, however, of further satiating the public appetite for Lewis and Clark material and making more urgent the early issuance of Lewis's own account.

Lewis had other problems now, for he was not cut out to be a governor. As a public expression of gratitude, his appointment had been flattering, but he chafed under fiscal restrictions and showed little ability to cope with the wrangling that typified frontier politics. He soon made an enemy of Frederick Bates, the territorial secretary, who had a quick temper and a sharp tongue and who taunted Lewis publicly and privately.[15] He made some unwise decisions in Indian matters that irked Henry Dearborn, the secretary of war, although the calmer head of William Clark generally served him well here (Clark was territorial superintendent of Indian affairs). During the bothersome business of getting the Mandan chief back to his village against the opposition of the Arikaras, Lewis executed some drafts that were not honored by the secretary of war, and his personal finances suffered.

Finally, there was the matter of the unfinished manuscript. Conrad wrote him repeatedly about it and got no reply. European savants such as Humboldt and Volney were eagerly awaiting the edition. Jefferson, in his anxiety about the matter, seemed to feel that his choice of Lewis to lead the expedition would not be justified, in the eyes of his Federalist opponents, until the journals were published. He pressed Lewis for information and received none; Lewis wrote almost nothing to his old friend after leaving Washington, and the few extant letters are strictly about territorial affairs.

At last Lewis began an excessive use of alcohol—or so it was reported to Jefferson, and so Jefferson believed.[16] The mystery of

Grouse
are
about
Short
and eye.
Cock
Cock
which
on the
and
-hood
Mountains
to the Mountain
the Columbea
the Great falls
they go in large
or singularly
hide hide remarkably close when pursued.
Short flights &c.

the feathers about its head
pointed and stiff Some hairs
the base of the beak. feathers
fine and stiff about the ears,
This is a faint likeness of the
of the Plains or Heath
the first of those fowls
we met with was
Missouri below
in the Neighbour-
of the Rocky
and from
which pass
between
and Rapids
ganges
Gongues
and
make

The large Black & White Pheasant is peculiar
to that portion of the Rocky Mountains watered by
the Columbia River. at least we did not see them untill
we reached the waters of that river, nor since we have
left those mountains. they are about the size of a
well grown hen. the cantour of the bird is much
that of the redish brown Pheasant common to
our country. the tail is proportionably as long and is
composed of 18 feathers of equal length, of a uniform
dark brown tiped with black. the feather of the
body are of a dark brown black and white. the black

Gary E. Moulton, ed., *Journals of the Lewis and Clark Expedition*, vol. 6 (1990)

Portion of William Clark's journal entry, March 2, 1806

his violent death in October 1809 at a wayside tavern in Tennessee can never be solved now; it might have been murder, but the testimony leads most observers to conclude that Lewis took his own life.[17]

It would be 1814 before Clark, Jefferson, and Philadelphia litterateur Nicholas Biddle could bring about the publication of the work. By this time, John Conrad would be bankrupt, the country would be at war with England, and public interest in the expedition would understandably have ebbed somewhat. The so-called Biddle narrative was considered by Jefferson to be only a stopgap publication. He wanted the scientific observations of Lewis and Clark on natural history to be edited and published by Benjamin Smith Barton, a botanist and zoologist at the University of Pennsylvania, and he continued to hope that the journals themselves could still be put into print. Barton died before he could accomplish his assignment. Eventually, the journals were published, but not until 1904, exactly a century after the exploring party pushed westward from St. Louis toward the Pacific.[18]

If Lewis was a suicide, his death can be attributed to no single cause. Perhaps the early and singular achievement of this melancholy man led him to expect more of himself, and of his post-expedition career, than he was able to accomplish. Undoubtedly, the realization that he had disappointed Jefferson and the world by his failure to prepare his journals for publication added one more problem to the list of those he could not solve.

Notes

1. The draft in Lewis's hand, dated September 24, 1806, is at the Missouri Historical Society, St. Louis. The fair copy sent by Clark, dated September 23, 1806, is at the Filson Club, Louisville, Kentucky. Despite the earlier date of the fair copy, the internal evidence that it was copied by Clark from the Lewis draft is conclusive. The letter begins "Dear Brother" and bears no address. In printing it, the *Palladium* reported that it had been sent to "gen. Clark, near Louisville."

2. A holograph copy of the prospectus is at the State Historical Society of Wisconsin, in Madison. Printed versions also appeared in some newspapers, including Philadelphia's *Aurora* on December 13, 1806.

3. The manuscript map is in the Library of Congress and appears in facsimile in Carl Wheat, *Mapping the Transmississippi West* (San Francisco, 1957–63), 2:following p. 50.

4. A settling of their account with one another on August 21, [1809], shows the cost of Ordway's journal as $150; it further shows that the two explorers were dividing all such preliminary publication costs. See account in the Missouri Historical Society. Although Jefferson and his associates considered the project mainly Lewis's, Lewis himself thought of it as a joint undertaking which he called "Lewis & Clark's Travels."

5. When Lewis arrived in Washington on December 28, 1806, his party included Sheheke or Big White, a chief of the Mandans, with his family and an interpreter. It would be nearly three years before Sheheke could return home. A detachment of soldiers under Ens. Nathaniel Pryor, who had been a sergeant on the expedition, failed in its mission to return the Indians in the summer of 1807 when the Arikaras attacked the party. The expedition that finally pushed through in 1809 contained more than one hundred men. See Lewis's contract with the St. Louis Missouri Fur Company for the return of the Mandan, February 24, 1809, Missouri Historical Society.

6. Barlow's poem and an account of a dinner in Lewis's honor are in the Washington, D.C. *National Intelligencer*, January 14, 1807.

7. Alexander Mackenzie, *Voyages from Montreal, on the River St. Lawrence, through the Continent of North America, to the Frozen and Pacific Ocean; in the Years 1789 and 1793* . . . (London, 1801). Lewis and Clark were acquainted with this work and probably had a copy with them in the West.

8. Lewis was secretary to Jefferson from the spring of 1801 until he left Washington in July 1803. He was replaced by another Virginian, Lewis Harvie, and did not draw a salary from Jefferson after his departure.

9. Here McKeehan merely quotes from Gass's discharge. The same words are found in Private William Bratton's discharge, in Lewis's hand, in the Iowa State Department of History and Archives.

10. The very few unfortunate incidents on the expedition included the two singled out by McKeehan: an encounter with a small band of larcenous Piegan Indians, two of whom were killed, and the accidental shooting of Lewis by Private Pierre Cruzatte. Cruzatte was blind in one eye, and claimed to have mistaken Lewis, in his elkskin suit, for an animal in the dense underbrush.

11. Elliott Coues, ed., *New Light on the Early History of the Greater Northwest*, vol. 2, *The Manuscript Journals of Alexander Henry* . . . (New York, 1897), 591.

12. Charles Willson Peale, *Peale Letter Books, 1767–1827*, 18 vols., American Philosophical Society Archives, Philadelphia.

13. Jefferson to José Corrèa da Serra, April 26, 1816, microfilm, series 1, reel 49, Jefferson Papers, Manuscripts Division, Library of Congress, Washington, D.C. (hereafter Jefferson Papers).

14. C. & A. Conrad & Co. to Jefferson, November 13, 1809, microfilm, series 1, reel 44, Jefferson Papers.

15. Considering Bates's relationship with Lewis, his solicitude could not have been sincere when he wrote to Louisville publisher Joseph Charless, March 12, 1808: "I should esteem a particular favor your procuring for me, one, two or three of those western Papers, from different Presses, which contain the Prospectus of Frazier's Journal. The interest which I take in the compromise of those misunderstandings which have arisen from that Prospectus, urge me to trouble you with this request. If the Publication of Gov. Lewis on the subject of Gass' & Frazier's Journal can be procured, you would confer an additional favor by transmitting it." Bates Letter Books, Missouri Historical Society.

16. Captain Gilbert C. Russell to Jefferson, January 31, 1810, microfilm, series 1, reel 45, Jefferson Papers, discusses the possible contribution of Lewis's intemperance to his death. Jefferson acknowledged this in a letter on April 18, saying of Lewis, "He was much afflicted & habitually so with hypocondria. This was probably increased by the habit into which he had fallen."

17. The entire occurrence is well covered by Dawson A. Phelps, "The Tragic Death of Meriwether Lewis," *William and Mary Quarterly*, 13 (no. 3, 1956), 308-18. Phelps concludes that Lewis committed suicide.

18. Reuben Gold Thwaites, ed., *Original Journals of the Lewis and Clark Expedition, 1804–1806*, 8 vols. (New York, 1904–5). The 1814 edition, published in Philadelphia by Bradford and Inskeep in two volumes, was entitled *History of the Expedition under the Command of Captains Lewis and Clark, to the . . . Pacific Ocean*. It was written by Nicholas Biddle, with some final touches by Paul Allen, and was based partly upon the journals, partly upon personal interviews with Clark, Ordway, and Private George Shannon.

Captain Lewis in a Crossfire of Wit
John Quincy Adams v. Joel Barlow

Albert Furtwangler

IN EARLY 1807 THE POET JOEL BARLOW HAD WHAT HE THOUGHT
was an inspired idea in poetry and politics. Meriwether Lewis and
William Clark had just returned from their great expedition across
America to the Pacific Coast; a formal banquet was arranged to
honor them in Washington, D.C.; and Barlow wrote a poem to
celebrate the occasion. When he had it in finished form, he sent a
copy to President Thomas Jefferson with a letter repeating the
main idea he had put into verse. Since Lewis had led a new
exploration over the principal American river of the west, why not
rename that river after him? Why not name the Columbia the
Lewis River and make one of its main tributaries the Clark?

Unfortunately for Barlow, Jefferson refused to heed this
suggestion about renaming the Columbia. To make matters worse,
Barlow's poem soon came in for a drubbing. It served its purpose
at the banquet for Lewis (Clark did not come to Washington after
all); it was published in a newspaper account of the celebration
and reprinted elsewhere. Barlow thought it a fair specimen of his
talents as a poet and meant to include it in a collected edition of
his works.[1] But another writer soon began to tinker with his lines
and pull them apart with clever malice. After a few weeks a parody
appeared in a literary magazine in Massachusetts. The author of
this piece was not identified, but Barlow's poem was explicitly

mentioned and sorely ridiculed. Decades later it emerged that the satirical poet and critic was John Quincy Adams, already a prominent figure in American politics and eventually a successor of Jefferson's as president of the United States.

This incident thus reveals three major American figures in a curious conjunction of poetry and politics. Barlow, a poet with strong political connections, long had been ambitious to write the most distinctive, lofty verses to celebrate the new nation. Lewis, the brilliantly perceptive young captain, had just led a daring and arduous exploration of the West; there was good reason to celebrate him as a hero who had changed American knowledge and geography. But Adams, a politician with his own keen flair with a pen, saw Barlow's effort as mere puffery and pretense and swiftly cut it down to size: silly as verse, wrongheaded as praise, pernicious as a statement about American names and ideals.

For modern readers this clash of poems requires some patient explication of allusions and ideas current in 1807. But this incident brings to light some of the rough play of political life in Jefferson's time. It also reveals some strange and significant conceptions of poetry in early America.

Joel Barlow is read today chiefly because of an anthology piece, "The Hasty Pudding," his three-canto celebration of wholesome cornmeal mush. But for many decades he was renowned as the author of a grand epic about American history from the time of Columbus through the Revolutionary War. In 1807 he was near the peak of his celebrity. He had recently returned from seventeen years abroad, where he had made a fortune in various trading ventures and achieved notable successes as an American consul in Algiers and a defender of democratic principles during the French Revolution. Back in the United States he made arrangements to buy a splendid house in Washington, offer his counsel to the government, and take up a request from Jefferson and Madison to write a proper history of the early American republic. But he was putting off the latter project in order to bring out a revised and lavish edition of his great poem.

Barlow's fame made his poem about Lewis a high and almost official American honor. Barlow was doubtless the most celebrated literary figure of Jefferson's circle. He had been singled out by

Jefferson as the proper man to write the history of the founding. And he had long had an international reputation as a writer of many talents. In Europe he had been a conspicuous friend and ally of Thomas Paine and other radicals. He was the author of his own sharp answer to Edmund Burke, his *Advice to the Priveleged Orders* (1792). He had also been a notorious opponent of Federalist foreign policies under John Adams; one of his letters from France had been published in New England and attacked as a conspicuous outrage under the Alien and Sedition Acts. Barlow had traveled far from his roots in Connecticut, and, as he found when he returned to New England in 1805, he was no longer welcome there. His deism was as bad as atheism to many of his Yale classmates. His political ideas were associated (mistakenly) with the Terror and the guillotine. (In Boston, the *Repertory* reprinted a song praising the guillotine, attributed it to Barlow, and vilified him as a bloodthirsty agitator.)[2] But Barlow still saw an important place for himself elsewhere in America. From his college years to the time of his death, he felt a calling to write lofty American poetry. One major poem or poetic design emerged again and again to concentrate all his energies and hopes. And in 1807, that project was about to be fulfilled in its most elaborate form.

Already it was in the hands of printers in Philadelphia: a poem in ten books totaling over 8,300 lines in iambic pentament couplets—*The Columbiad*, an epic vision of the rise of freedom in the New World. The germ of its main design is plainly evident in Barlow's Yale graduation poem, *The Prospect of Peace* (1778). In a year when victory seemed within reach in the American revolution, Barlow wrote 234 lines celebrating the reemergence of the goddess Peace to reign over a realm of prosperity, science, and political freedom in America. That same idea reappeared in revised form—as an account of the discovery of America—at another Yale commencement in 1781; by then Barlow was enlarging this material into an epic. He supported himself by teaching school, serving as an army chaplain, starting a weekly newspaper, translating *Watts's Psalms* into American terms, practicing law, and traveling around Connecticut selling shares in the Ohio Land Company. In these years Barlow also collaborated on a satiric poem, *The Anarchiad* (1786–87), with a circle later known as the Connecticut Wits: John

Trumbull, David Humphreys, and Lemuel Hopkins.[3] But his main project was something unattained by any previous American author: a subscription edition that would give him national fame and a handsome profit for his poetry.

"All things considered," his biographer writes, "the poem was in a modest way the first American best seller after the Revolution, and Barlow was probably the first American writer to receive fair pay for a book."[4] In 1782 he had circulated subscription lists and traveled himself to Philadelphia to promote his poem in the national capital. In the end, he negotiated permission to dedicate his work to Louis XVI, and that king bought twenty-five copies. Subscribers also included George Washington, Benjamin Franklin, Alexander Hamilton, Robert Livingston, Aaron Burr, Thomas Paine, and fifteen generals of the Revolutionary army. Editions were brought out in London and Paris, and by this one work Barlow did become an American known abroad for his poetry.

In the view of most critics, then and later, his talents for poetry could not sustain a serious epic. But Barlow took himself very seriously, and many of his countrymen signed their names and put down their money to endorse his work. In 1807, when he came to write his poem on Lewis, Barlow was still taking pains with this epic—overseeing the new version, with costly plates, handsome bindings, and a further book of libertarian prophecy, a full twenty years after his first reaching international fame.

Thus in Barlow's terms his poem on Captain Lewis pays the explorer a supreme compliment. In both *The Vision of Columbus* and *The Columbiad* the main figure is, of course, Christopher Columbus. Released from a prison in Spain and carried to a Mount of Vision, the old explorer is inspired by an angel (or in the later version, by Hesper, a spirit of the West) to see into the future. He sees new settlements arise in the Americas, until a great revolution overthrows old tyrannies and opens the way to a final era of world peace and prosperity. In the poem on Lewis, Columbus again appears. But now he is called from heaven to bless Meriwether Lewis as his rightful successor. It is Lewis in this poem who sees into the West and brings fresh hopes of a millennium.

To some readers it has seemed odd, if not obtuse of Barlow, to want to change the name of the Columbia River when he himself was promoting his *Columbiad* at just this time. But Barlow had two good reasons for his suggestion; he states them very specifically in his letter to Jefferson. The first is that the name Columbia is already attached to so many geographical features that it is in no danger of being lost or forgotten: "We have so many towns, districts & counties, & I believe some smaller streams, called Columbia, besides its being the general name of the Continent, that it will tend to run our geography into some confusion, which may as well be avoided." The second is that another western river had just been named for its explorer: "The world has justly given the name of MacKensie to the great river of the north for the same obvious reason, the merit of discovery."[5] In other words, Barlow asserts a strong impulse of American patriotism in his proposal: the British are naming "the great river of the north" for Alexander Mackenzie, who traveled downstream to its mouth and recorded his exploration; America should name its own great river of the West for Lewis—who traveled downstream to its mouth—not for the ship *Columbia* which first crossed its bar (and certainly not for anyone connected with George Vancouver, who sailed deeper into the river a few weeks later).[6]

This idea, that Lewis properly discovered or explored the Columbia by tracing its course from the mountains to the sea, informs the opening stanzas of Barlow's poem. Rivers on other continents have defied complete exploration, but Columbus can now look down and see a chain of well-explored rivers, the Potomac, the Ohio, the Missouri, and the Columbia, linked in a path from sea to sea.

> Let the Nile cloak his head in the clouds, and defy
>   The researches of science and time;
> Let the Niger escape the keen traveller's eye,
>   By plunging, or changing his clime.
>
> Columbus! not so shall thy boundless domain
>   Defraud thy brave sons of their right:
> Streams, midlands and shorelands illude us in vain,
>   We shall drag their dark regions to light.
>
> Look down, sainted sage, from thy synod of Gods;
>   See, inspired by thy venturous soul,

Mackensie roll northward his earth-draining floods,
   And surge the broad waves to the pole.

With the same roaring genius thy Lewis ascends,
   And, seizing the car of the sun,
O'er the sky-propping hills and high waters he bends,
   And gives the proud earth a new zone.

Potowmak, Ohio, Missouri had felt
   Half her globe in their cincture comprest;
His long curving course has completed the belt,
   And tamed the last tide of the west.

Then hear the loud voice of the nation proclaim,
   And all ages resound the decree:
Let our Occident stream bear the young hero's name,
   Who taught him his path to the sea.[7]

A captious reader may here object that Barlow is misinformed.
Lewis and Clark did trace the Missouri to its headwaters. They did
descend some important tributaries of the Columbia, and they did
explore its course through the Cascade Mountains to the sea. But
they did not in fact completely explore the Columbia. In Barlow's
design such an objection is a mere cavil. The important point is that
Lewis completed the water route from the Atlantic to the Pacific,
that he explored the long-sought Northwest Passage. The Potomac
could be used as a pathway to the Ohio (as Barlow, the former Ohio
Land Company agent, knew very well). The Ohio, Mississippi,
Missouri system offered a splendid pathway for commerce and
settlement in the American interior (as Barlow well knew from long
friendship and collaboration with Robert Fulton). Now an explored
link with the Columbia River system united the recent Louisiana
Purchase with recent American claims to the Pacific Northwest.

To the mind of an idealistic poet, the way now lay open for a
new era in all of North America, from the Atlantic on the east to
the Pacific on the west, from Darien in Central America to the
Davis Strait in the Arctic (between Greenland and Baffin Island).
A new "zone" or belt of rivers would bind America as a continental
nation, growing in wealth and wisdom to confer peace round the
world. And the source of this new era was not an Old World

explorer but a homespun American hero, who deserved his nation's thanks in a permanent memorial.

> These four brother floods, like a garland of flowers,
>   Shall entwine all our states in a band,
> Conform and confederate their wide-spreading powers,
>   And their wealth and their wisdom expand.
>
> From Darien to Davis one garden shall bloom,
>   Where war's weary banners are furl'd;
> And the far-scented breezes that waft its perfumes,
>   Shall settle the storms of the world.
>
> Then hear the loud voice of the nation proclaim,
>   And all ages resound the decree:
> *Let our Occident stream bear the young hero's name,*
>   *Who taught him his path to the sea.*

If only Jefferson, Congress, and the mapmakers of the world had listened to Barlow: we would now have the Lewis River running between Oregon and Washington, and his poem would make much better sense. Instead, we still have the mighty Columbia (now flowing between several later monuments to Lewis and Clark). We also have a poem that seemed a glowing tribute for about one month.

No doubt the poem sufficed for its occasion, the celebration dinner in Washington. No doubt, too, the achievement of Lewis was worthy of poetry and praise. Even the deepest-dyed Federalists had to acknowledge that. Timothy Dwight, for example, came to hate Barlow and Republicans in general, but in attacking Jefferson and Madison as presidents he had to pause to grant that they did one thing right when they sent explorers into the Far West: "Except for the Missions of *Pike, Lewis, and Clark,* to explore the *Mississippi,* there is not a single measure originated by either, during the fourteen years of their reign, which has reflected the least credit upon their character, or produced the least benefit to the United States."[8] In his attack on Barlow's poem, John Quincy Adams also tried to spare Lewis, by adding an explanatory note: "There are *some* understandings, graduated on such a scale, that it may be necessary to inform them, that our intention is not to depreciate the merits of Captain Lewis's publick services. We think highly of the spirit and judgment, with which he has executed the duty undertaken by him, and we rejoice at the rewards bestowed by congress upon him and his companions."[9]

Nevertheless, Barlow's poem first appeared in print in a newspaper account that begged for a sharp reply. It appeared as the last touch in a long column about the Lewis dinner, beginning with the distinguished guest list and reporting every one of the twenty-odd formal toasts. The poem thus appeared as an elaborate, versified tribute, just a step above the florid speechifying that goes with raising a glass.

The celebrations had been put off until William Clark could get to Washington, but were held at last in his absence on Wednesday, January 14, 1807. The citizens of Washington drew together celebrities from east and west, including the St. Louis dignitaries Pierre Chouteau and Pierre Provenchère, and Sheheke, the Mandan chief who had come east with Lewis from his village on the upper Missouri. After dinner there were a reading of the poem, songs and instrumental music, and over two dozen toasts. Thirteen formal toasts honored the people; the Constitution; the president; Congress; Washington; Franklin; Columbus; the United States; the red people of America; the council fire; science; union; peace; the army and navy; agriculture, commerce, and manufactures; and the District of Columbia (the mayor of Washington presided over this whole affair). Later, glasses were raised to Captain Lewis ("Patriotic, enlightened, and brave; who had the spirit to undertake, and the valour to execute an expedition, which reflects honor on his country") and Captain Clark "and the other brave companions of Capt. Lewis" ("Their patriotic and manly perserverance entitles them to the approbation of their countrymen"). As if this were not enough of high sentence and high spirits, there were seven further "volunteers" or impromptu toasts. The first was by Lewis himself: "May works be a test of patriotism, as they ought of right to be that of religion." The second was by Barlow: "Victory over the wilderness, which is more interesting than that over men."[10]

Barlow and Lewis were old hands at this kind of palaver. The poet had been at many a diplomatic dinner, and the army captain had seen his share years earlier, when he was President Jefferson's private secretary and fellow bachelor in the White House. (Just two years later, alcoholism would be a factor in Lewis's mental breakdown and suicide.) But the *National Intelligencer* reported this evening in full detail as a grand social event. All the toasts were cataloged, a litany in praise of just about everyone present. And to wind up the account, Barlow's poem was described as "elegant and glowing stanzas" which were "recited at an early period of the entertainment." Here, in short, was an irresistible bundle of pomposity, praising everything Republican and Jeffersonian—a perfect target for any Federalist with malice, wit, and a pen.

The next March an anonymous contribution appeared in the *Monthly Anthology* in Boston. "Gentlemen," an explanatory note began: "The following 'elegant and glowing stanzas' are not from the pen of Mr. Barlow; nor were they recited by Mr. Beckley at the 'elegant dinner' given by the Citizens of Washington to Captain Lewis. *See National Intelligencer*, 16 January, 1807."[11] Two different sources have identified these *Anthology* verses as the work of John Quincy Adams: an anthology of American literature published in 1855 and an annotated run of the *Monthly Anthology* in which this piece is marked with the name J. Q. Adams.[12]

This identification is not absolute. Adams never stepped forward and explicitly claimed these verses in his own name; he kept to the usual eighteenth-century practice of publishing odd bits and controversial pieces either anonymously or under a pseudonym. But Adams surely matches this ascription on other circumstantial grounds. He had motives both public and private for attacking Barlow. He had the talents and propensities to write such verses. And, like Barlow, he was offered a wonderfully suitable occasion.

Perhaps Adams attacked Barlow for the same reasons other Federalists invoked—that he was an apostate New Englander, so tainted by his years in Europe that he abandoned the faith of his fathers, got mixed up with dangerous political radicals like Tom Paine, and came home to lend his pen to the service of Thomas Jefferson. Perhaps Adams had a score of honor to settle. His father the president had been particularly libeled by Barlow's notorious letters in 1798; they called John Adams an implacable enemy of France, who deserved to be sent to the madhouse. At about the same time, John Quincy's successor as minister to Holland was writing to him with particular complaints about Barlow's meddling in American-French diplomacy.[13]

But Adams's little poem has simpler, more obvious motives, too. It was good fun, and it fitted right into Adams's long-standing habit of contributing satiric verses to the press.

Adams is now remembered as the only son of a president to become president himself; as a brilliant ambassador and secretary of state; as a member of Congress for many terms after his years as president, one who annoyed southern adversaries by tirelessly presenting petitions against slavery. But he was also a playful and persistent man of letters. At the time of this incident, he was both a United States senator from Massachusetts and the first Boylston Professor of Rhetoric and Oratory at Harvard. And for many years before 1807 he had secretly contributed many essays, poems, translations, and critical reviews to American journals.

Years later, in 1831, Adams noted in his diary that he tried to throw off a nagging itch to scribble bad poetry. "At certain seasons, however, the propensity becomes too strong for me. I walk and muse and pour forth premeditated verse, which it takes me six or nine months to lay by and resume to find it good for nothing."[14] Adams goes on in this passage to reflect that he has allowed a few of his poems to be published. "Very short fugitive pieces and translations are the only rhymes I have ever committed to the press." Among these he lists an elegy, a translation of the thirteenth satire of Juvenal, and "one satirical song, overlooked when first published, [but] dragged to light twenty years afterwards, for political effect against me, because it laughed at the party Lama—Jefferson." These were the only poems that had any life beyond the moment. "All the rest of my published poetry has passed from the press into the waters of Lethe."

Adams's own volumes of a Philadelphia magazine, the *Port Folio*, is now preserved in the Boston Athenaeum, with initials to identify contributions made by members of the Adams family. This evidence reveals four important points about his writing in this period: that Adams was himself that journal's "most prolific and prominent correspondent" in its beginning stages; that he contributed poems, some of which match the description just quoted from his diary; that his interest in the *Port Folio* ended around 1805; and that he may have given his set of the *Port Folio* to the Athenaeum.[15] This latter point bespeaks an interest in the Athenaeum Society and in its own journal, the *Monthly Anthology*, where the satire on Barlow appeared.[16]

The *Port Folio* was the most widely circulated American magazine of its time (1801–12), a weekly that ran to fifteen hundred copies an issue at its height. It printed articles and selections on a variety of subjects including politics, literature, and science. Joseph Dennie, the editor, was an angry, witty Federalist, with an outlook much like that of his Harvard classmate and collaborator, Thomas Boylston Adams. The latter was John Quincy's brother and for a time (and secretly) the *Port Folio's* business manager. The magazine was founded in 1801, just after the bitter defeat of John Adams by Jefferson and the Republicans. It served sometimes as an organ of anti-Republican politics and satire, but it also aimed to raise the tone of American letters. Linda K. Kerber and Walter John Morris note that John Quincy Adams tried to moderate the passions of Dennie and his brother and give the *Port Folio* a more distinctive tone as a literary journal. In his own words, it would help remove "that foul stain of literary barbarism, which has so long exposed our country to the reproach of strangers, and to the derision of her enemies."[17]

Among his contributions, however, were poems that included some sharp satire. He published translations of Juvenal's seventh and thirteenth satires, and he translated one of Horace's odes in words that directly point to the current rumor that Thomas Jefferson had fathered slave children with his black slave, Sally Hemings. "Dear Thomas," Adams's translation begins, "deem it no disgrace/With slaves to mend thy breed."[18] This was the "political song" Adams says was dragged to light years later because it showed him ridiculing Jefferson.[19] As we shall see in a moment, this same barbed accusation appears in the parody of Barlow. This imitation of Horace also bears several other resemblances to the Barlow parody: it comes with a full apparatus of footnotes; its lines allude directly to quotations from Jefferson, the main object of attack; a full text of Horace's poem is appended for comparison; and the poem pokes fun at Thomas Paine as well as Jefferson (Paine is presented as the drunk and impotent speaker of the poem).

Despite their deep involvement with the *Port Folio*, both John

Quincy Adams and his brother had broken with this journal by 1805. Dennie had published materials so inflammatory that he was charged with seditious libel in 1803. At that point John Quincy advised his brother to abandon Philadelphia and "come where there is yet some sense of right, and some government to protect a citizen in his person, character, and property, against highwaymen and Jacobins."[20] His brother soon afterwards settled in Massachusetts.

At just about this time, another journal began publication in Boston, explicitly designed to rival the *Port Folio*. The *Monthly Anthology* first appeared in November 1803, and soon came under the editorship of an "Anthology Society," the same group that would found the Boston Athenaeum a few years later. Here, in embryo, was a New England circle of intellectuals—lawyers and churchmen who were sociable, Federalist, and generally more interested in literature than in science or politics. The full title of the journal was *Monthly Anthology and Boston Review, Containing Sketches and Reports of Philosophy, Religion, History, Arts, and Manners*, and the first editor to gather a successful group of contributors was William Emerson, pastor of the First Church and father of Ralph Waldo Emerson. Louis P. Simpson suggests that the founding of the *Anthology* corresponded with the decline of Philadelphia as the intellectual center of American life and the emergence of new stirrings of literary activity in Boston. He points out that John Adams had founded the American Academy of Arts and Sciences in Boston in 1780, as a more humanistic alternative to the American Philosophical Society of Franklin, Rittenhouse, and Jefferson.[21] The *Monthly Anthology* was another organ of vital literary life in New England.

A prejudice against Philadelphia, tailor-made for the *Anthology*, may explain the opening lines of Adams's satire on Barlow and Lewis. The poem seems to have three main objects to attack: scientific nonsense foisted on Lewis and Clark by Jefferson and his colleagues at the American Philosophical Society; Barlow's pretentiousness as a poet; and Barlow, Paine, and Jefferson as outrageous proponents of radical change. The first section pokes fun at many absurd things Lewis and Clark were sent west to find, and it now makes sense only to a reader familiar with scientific interests in the late eighteenth century. Charles Willson Peale had recently excavated a mammoth skeleton, and Lewis and Clark were encouraged to be alert for such animals in the West. Jefferson's *Notes on the State of Virginia* had repeated current theories that no new species were known to be created and none had ever become extinct; Jefferson had, in fact, given specific instruction to an earlier western expedition to look for living mammoths.[22] Jefferson had also heard and repeated a popular legend that there was an entire mountain of salt somewhere up the Missouri. According to some accounts, this mountain was 180 miles long and 45 miles wide. Jefferson had urged Lewis to read an official account of Louisiana which contained this information.[23] Philadelphia scientists also knew of legends that some Indian tribes might be descended from Madoc, a legendary Welsh leader. Lewis and Clark seem to have been alert for tribes with strange languages on this account.[24] These points explain most of the references in Adams's opening stanzas:

> GOOD people, listen to my tale,
>   'Tis nothing but what true is;
> I'll tell you of the mighty deeds
>   Atchiev'd by Captain Lewis—
> How starting from the Atlantick shore
>   By fair and easy motion,
> He journied, *all the way by land,*
>   Until he met the ocean.

> HEROICK, sure, the toil must be
>   To travel through the woods, sir;
> And never meet a foe, yet save
>   His person and his goods, sir!
> What marvels on the way he found
>   *He'll* tell you, if inclin'd, sir;
> But *I* shall only now disclose
>   The things he *did not* find, sir.

> He never with a Mammoth met,
>   However you may wonder;
> Nor even with a Mammoth's bone,
>   Above the ground or under—
> And, spite of all the pains he took
>   The animal to track, sir,
> He never could o'ertake the hog

With navel on his back, sir.

And from the day his course began,
   Till even it was ended,
He never found an Indian tribe
   From Welchmen straight descended:
Nor, much as of Philosophers
   The fancies it might tickle;
To season his adventures, met
   A Mountain, sous'd in pickle.[25]

Readers of Lewis and Clark's journals may take some exception here. The explorers did not travel by "fair and easy motion" or "all the way by land" or merely "through the woods." They endured hardships through years—a long pull up the Missouri River, through the treeless Great Plains; a dangerous crossing of the Rockies on a rugged path; and a descent of the Columbia to a cold, damp winter encampment with scanty provisions. As for "never met a foe": there was an angry confrontation with the Sioux on the way up the Missouri, a gunfight with Piegan Blackfeet on the return trip, and losses to Indian raiders and horse thieves along the Yellowstone, not to mention bears, buffalo, snakes, and swarms of mosquitoes. In fact, Lewis and Clark reported two licks containing mammoth bones, in present-day Kentucky and Missouri;[26] and in one encounter with Indians with a very strange and hard to interpret language, one sergeant speculated that there might be a touch of Welsh in the far Rockies.[27]

Adams is on surer ground when he attacks Barlow for his bad verses in the next two stanzas. Barlow strains his metaphors in saying that Lewis "seizes the car of the sun" to "give the proud earth a new zone," and that he "tamed the last tide of the west" and "taught" the Columbia its path to the sea. Adams catches these lapses and a poetic gaffe, to boot. As Adams explains in a footnote, Barlow has "obtained an interesting victory over verse. He has brought *zone* and *sun* to rhyme together; which is more than ever was attempted by his great predecessor in psalmody, Sternhold."[28]

He never left this nether world—
   For still he had his reason—
Nor once the waggon of the sun

Attempted he to seize on.
To bind a *Zone* about the earth
    He knew he was not able—
THEY SAY he did—but ask himself,
    He'll tell you 'tis a fable.

He never dreamt of taming *tides*,
    Like monkeys or like bears, sir—
A *school*, for teaching floods to flow,
    Was not among his cares, sir—
Had rivers ask'd of him their path,
    They had but mov'd his laughter—
They knew their courses, all, as well
    Before he came as after.

These lines seem crafted to separate Lewis from Barlow. Lewis "knew he was not able" to do all these silly things Barlow says he did. But in the final section of the poem, Lewis appears at best as Barlow's dupe, the willing or stupid accomplice who lends himself and his name to an absurd scheme for radical change.

And must we then resign the hope
    These Elements of changing?
And must we still, alas! be told
    That after all his ranging,
The Captain could discover nought
    But Water in the Fountains?
Must Forests still be form'd of Trees?
    Of rugged Rocks the Mountains?

We never will be so fubb'd off,
    As sure as I'm a sinner!
Come—let us all subscribe, and ask
    The HERO to a Dinner—
And Barlow stanzas shall indite—
    A Bard, the tide who tames, sir—
And if we cannot alter *things*,
    By G—, we'll change their *names*, sir!

Let old Columbus be once more
    Degraded from his glory;
And not a river by his name

> Remember him in story—
>   For what is *old* Discovery
>   Compar'd to that which new is?
>   Strike—strike *Columbia* river out,
>   And put in—*river Lewis!*

From here on, the poem rages to its conclusion with a series of angry swipes. How to take these lines depends on a reader's taste for satiric invective. To modern readers they may seem purely malicious. But they are quite in keeping with the rough play of eighteenth-century politics and poetry—not at all out of line with what Dryden, Pope, and for that matter Timothy Dwight, John Trumbull, and Barlow himself had been flinging at enemies for decades. And looked at patiently, these lines show a certain flair for turning Barlow's ideas back upon themselves.

Barlow says that good old names should be changed for new ones, and Adams takes that as a fine invitation for naming names and scoring Barlow, Paine, and Jefferson for what they are. If Lewis is the new Columbus, then Jefferson must be the new King Ferdinand—and his consort "the dusky Sally" Hemings, the black mistress currently named in poems and attacks on the president, including Adams's earlier poem in the *Port Folio*.

> Let dusky Sally henceforth bear
>   The name of Isabella;
> And let the mountain, all of salt,
>   Be christen'd Monticella—
> The hog with navel on his back
>   Tom Pain may be when drunk, sir—
> And *Joël* call the Prairie-dog,
>   Which once was call'd a Skunk, sir.

The next stanza picks up Barlow's toast at the Lewis dinner: "Victory over the wilderness, which is more interesting than that over men." It makes it into a sloppy utterance from someone drunk enough to throw a bottle against a wall. But the stanza goes on to make a richer point.

> And when the wilderness shall yield
>   To bumpers, bravely brimming,

A nobler victory than men;—
    While all our heads are swimming,
We'll dash the bottle on the wall
    And name (the thing's agreed on)
Our first-rate-ship United States,
    The flying frigate *Fredon.*

Clearly the figure here is the ship of state: a first-rate ship is now called the United States; should we change its name, too, if we call the Columbia River the Lewis? One of the proud accomplishments of the John Adams administration had been the authorization and financing of three new war ships to build up an American navy. Two of those ships, the *Constitution* and the *Constellation* are still preserved as monuments of the navy in the age of sail. The third was the U.S.S. *United States,* the sister ship of the *Constitution,* a forty-four gun frigate, 175 feet long, with a crew of 400.[29] It was with the *United States* that Stephen Decatur became an early hero in the War of 1812 by capturing H.M.S. *Macedonian.* Many years later, its most famous crewman was Herman Melville, who used experiences aboard the *United States* in his novels *White-Jacket* and *Billy Budd.*[30] Probably there was no frigate or ship of any kind named *Fredon* or *Fredonia* at this time. But Adams certainly knew that this name had been promoted by Samuel Latham Mitchill, his fellow senator (and fellow intellectual) from New York. Mitchill thought the name a proper term for "freedom's land," an idea that does seem in keeping with Barlow's views of America, and he had agitated to have America's name officially changed.[31] This proposal had also been debated and satirized in earlier letters in the *Monthly Anthology.*[32] But "Fredonia" now survives in the names of a few American towns and as an absurd country in the plot and anthem of the Marx Brothers movie *Duck Soup*: "All hail Fredonia, land of the brave and free!"[33]

True—Tom and Joël now, no more
    Can overturn a nation;
And work by butchery and blood,
    A great regeneration;—
Yet, still we can turn inside out
    Old Nature's Constitution,
And bring a Babel back of *names*—
    Huzza! for revolution!

This last stanza unfairly yokes Barlow with Paine as an advocate of violence and the French Reign of Terror. Like many Federalists, Adams makes a mistaken inference. Barlow did live in Paris during the Terror; he did call for an end to monarchy in his pamphlets; he was awarded French citizenship by the National Convention; and he did support Paine in his years in Europe. But he did not advocate the guillotine or all things French. Besides, Adams himself could hardly deny that American freedom derived from warfare, blood, and revolution. But here as throughout the poem he is attacking Tom Jefferson as well as Tom Paine, venting anger at many threats to conservative Federalist values. Changing names, the poem argues, is just a step away from silly alteration of things— from claiming that tides have been "tamed" or that an honest westward exploration has climbed to the sun. And that way madness lies, unholy madness. "As sure as I'm a sinner," says this poet, I will not be fooled by such deist irreverence. It leads to a confusion of tongues, a tower of Babel, the demolition of Columbus or anything worth preserving from the past.

Looking back on this entire incident, we can see that these poems sharply illuminate each other. Taken by itself Barlow's poem offers a deep compliment to a new American hero. It offers Barlow's own life work as a poet, his celebration of Columbus and his millennial hopes for America, in one brief tribute to Lewis's achievement. Yet to see the poem as Adams first saw it, as a misrhymed collection of anapests in a mismatched collection of toasts, is to see a mere ode for a fleeting occasion, one doomed to die aborning, along with its proposal to change a river's name. And Barlow, anatomized as he is in Adams's verses and notes, does appear to be a poet far past his prime.

Yet Adams, too, suffers by comparison. He attacks Barlow but tars Lewis with the same brush. And his allusions are hit and miss— here a direct hit on Barlow's absurdities of imagery, there a wide miss on what Lewis and Clark were all about, here and there a ricochet peppering Jefferson, France, Paine, Philadelphia science, deism, or anything newfangled.

Taken together, both poems also reveal a striking turn of mind in the literature of early America. In Meriwether Lewis both Barlow and Adams could find a hero to admire, safely returned from a genuinely courageous, intelligent, and productive American adventure. Both writers also yearned to make or promote an authentic American poem, something for all the world to admire. But both were brought up and habituated to think of poetry as rhyming argument; both were best qualified for engaging in political controversies; both were enmeshed in that limited way of thinking and writing.

In fact, this crux in their common outlook had been anticipated many years earlier in a letter about poetry by John Adams. In 1785 he wrote from Europe to thank John Trumbull (his former law student) for a copy of Trumbull's famous verse satire *M'Fingal*. Adams used the occasion to make two sharp points. One was that a talented American poet should try to rise above satire. "I wish you to think of a poem which may employ you for many years, and afford full scope for the pathetic and the sublime, of which several specimens have shown you master in the highest degree. Upon this plan I should hope to see our young America in possession of an Heroick Poem, equal to those most esteemed in any Country." In other words, the great Adams ancestor was just as eager as Trumbull or Barlow or John Quincy to see devoted labor bring forth a lofty epic on an American theme. But Adams's second point was a firm parental squelch. This letter, he wrote, would be carried back to America by his son—John Quincy was about to enter Harvard. "The passion for Poetry," the elder Adams wrote, "is not always proportioned to the Talent. In the former he would bear some comparison with you at his age, but he has not yet given such proofs of the latter, and probably never will. If he had it, which is not likely, he will not be so independent of Business as you, and therefore must not indulge it, but devote himself wholly to the Law."[34] That's the Great American Father speaking: poetry is fine in its place, young man, but not if it distracts from Business, Getting Ahead, or Public Duty! One can only wonder: could pure envy have been part of the younger Adams's animus against Barlow, an alter ego who also practiced law, diplomacy, and poetry, and attained international fame first and foremost by his verse?

In any case, decades would pass before poets who would achieve serious but appealing narratives on American subjects—the Longfellow of "Paul Revere's Ride," the Emerson of "The Concord

Hymn," the Whitman who preserved vivid scenes of the Civil War. No notable poet would touch Lewis and Clark again until Stephen Vincent Benét wrote a simple piece for his children in the 1930s, and Robert Penn Warren engaged Lewis and Jefferson in a tragic dialogue, *Brother to Dragons* (1953).[35] Between Barlow and Adams, Federalists and Republicans, Bostonians and Philadelphians, anglophiles and francophiles, a high moment in America was simply lost in a crossfire of topical wit. No poet anywhere in America could summon the muse to lift Lewis and Clark into song upon their return, even though two keen and ambitious writers were right there ready and willing to reach for their pens. After three centuries Columbus had become embodied in myth, legend, and epic in Europe and the Americas. Born to a different age, Captain Lewis would have to remain his own best chronicler—in unfinished prose.

Notes

1. *The Works of Joel Barlow*, ed. William K. Bottorff and Arthur L. Ford (Gainesville, Fla., 1970), 1:vii.

2. Boston *Repertory*, October 15, 1805, cited in James Woodress, *A Yankee's Odyssey: The Life of Joel Barlow* (Philadelphia, 1958), 238-39.

3. Woodress, *Yankee's Odyssey*, 84.

4. Ibid., 85-86.

5. Joel Barlow to Thomas Jefferson, January 13, 1807, in *Letters of the Lewis and Clark Expedition, 1783–1854*, ed. Donald Jackson, 2d ed. (Urbana, Ill., 1978), 1:362.

6. The depth of Barlow's belief in Lewis's achievement is open to question. If Lewis was the true successor to Columbus, it would be only fitting for him to make some appearance in *The Columbiad* itself. Other explorers do appear there, including "Vancouvre," Drake, Cook, and "Mackensie" (book 10, lines 18, 20, 59, and 219), but Lewis is mentioned nowhere. Probably the text of the entire epic was in the printer's hands if not in cold type or printed sheets by the time Barlow wrote his poem on Lewis. All the same, if this ambitious epic poet had a new vision of the West after Lewis, he had the means to alter his poem accordingly, then or later.

7. Joel Barlow, "Of the Discoveries of Captain Lewis," *National Intelligencer and Washington Advertiser*, January 16, 1807, p. 3, col. 1; the poem is reprinted in Mark Anthony De Wolfe Howe, "The Capture of Some Fugitive Verses," *Proceedings of the Massachusetts Historical Society*, 43 (1910), 238-39.

8. Timothy Dwight, *Remarks on the Review of Inchiquin's Letters* (1815), quoted in Leon Howard, *The Connecticut Wits* (Chicago, 1943), 395.

9. *Monthly Anthology and Boston Review*, 4 (March 1807), 143-44; Adams's notes to his poem seem to have been reprinted only in Howe, "Fugitive Verses," 240-41.

10. *National Intelligencer and Washington Advertiser*, January 16, 1807, p. 2, col. 5.

11. *Monthly Anthology and Boston Review*, 4 (March 1807), 143.

12. Evert A. Duyckinck and George L. Duyckinck, eds., *Cyclopaedia of American Literature* (New York, 1855), 1:395; Howe, "Fugitive Verses," 239.

13. Woodress, *A Yankee's Odyssey*, 194-95, 199, 202.

14. *Memoirs of John Quincy Adams*, ed. Charles Francis Adams (1874–77; reprint, New York, 1970), 8:399.

15. Linda K. Kerber and Walter John Morris, "Politics and Literature: The Adams Family and the *Port Folio*," *William and Mary Quarterly*, 3d ser., 23 (1966), 450-76.

16. Lewis P. Simpson notes that Adams was proposed for membership in the Athenaeum Society in 1809, but by that time his political allegiances had changed. President James Madison appointed him ambassador to Russia that year, and when he left the country he relieved the society from the necessity of confirming or rejecting his membership. See Lewis P. Simpson, ed., *The Federalist Literary Mind: Selections from the Monthly Anthology and Boston Review* (Baton Rouge, La., 1962), 229.

17. John Quincy Adams to T. B. Adams, March 21, 1801, quoted in Kerber and Morris, "Politics and Literature," 452.

18. "Horace, Book II, Ode 4, to Xanthia Phoceus," *Port Folio*, 2 (October 30, 1802), 344.

19. Another poem on the same theme, "Song Supposed To Have Been Written by the Sage of Monticello," had appeared in the *Port Folio* a few weeks earlier, in vol. 2 (October 2, 1802), 312. A headnote says it was copied from the Boston *Gazette* and notes that it is set to the tune of "Yankee Doodle." Merrill D. Peterson identifies this as another poem that was used against Adams but says that he probably did not write it: Peterson, *The Jefferson Image in the American Mind* (New York, 1960), 462. For this reason it is listed as a doubtful attribution in Lynn H. Parsons, *John Quincy Adams: A Bibliography* (Westport, Conn., 1993), 36; Kerber and Morris do not discuss it, though they note that another scurrilous translation of Horace's ode, also aimed at Jefferson, appeared in the same issue as Adams's; in fact, it appears on the same page of the *Port Folio* (Kerber and Morris, "Politics and Literature," 457). The charge of Jefferson's sexual liaison with Sally Hemings is a much-vexed question in current discussions of Jefferson; its origins, ramifications, and implications

take up much space, for example, in the recent compilation, Peter S. Onuf, ed., *The Jeffersonian Legacies* (Charlottesville, Va., 1993). Literary echoes include reprints of Adams's poems in the presidential campaign of 1828 (Peterson, *The Jefferson Image*, 22, 182).

20. J. Q. Adams to T. B. Adams, August 19, 1803, quoted in Kerber and Morris, "Politics and Literature," 464.

21. Simpson, *The Federalist Literary Mind*, 3-4.

22. Thomas Jefferson, *Notes on the State of Virginia*, ed. William Peden (Chapel Hill, N.C., 1954), 43, 54; Thomas Jefferson to André Michaux, April 30, 1793, in Jackson, *Letters*, 2:670.

23. John Logan Allen, *Passage through the Garden: Lewis and Clark and the Image of the American Northwest* (Urbana, Ill., 1975), 51-52; Thomas Jefferson to Meriwether Lewis, November 16, 1803, in Jackson, *Letters*, 1:136.

24. The legendary Welsh Indians were sought by Lewis and Clark's predecessors on the Missouri, James Mackay and John Evans (Allen, *Passage through the Garden*, 207 n). Jefferson pointed this out when he enclosed a map made by Evans in his letter to Lewis of January 22, 1804 (Jackson, *Letters*, 1:165, 2:515-16).

25. "On the Discoveries of Captain Lewis," *Monthly Anthology and Boston Review*, 4 (March 1807), 143-44. The hog with its navel on its back may be a strained allusion to Aristophanes's account of humans split apart and twisted around in Plato's *Symposium* 190e, but such an animal was also reported at Rio de Janeiro by Magellan and his crew in 1519; see *The First Voyage round the World by Magellan*, ed. Henry E. Stanley (1874; reprint, New York, 1963), 101. Of course, strange new animals were being reported in the far West. Adams refers to the prairie dog later in the poem. Lewis and Clark were the first to make a scientific description of this animal, and they succeeded in sending a live specimen back to Jefferson, who sent it on to Charles Willson Peale's museum in Philadelphia in 1805. See Paul Russell Cutright, *Lewis and Clark: Pioneering Naturalists* (Urbana, Ill., 1969), 79-80, 375-83; *Journals of the Lewis and Clark Expedition*, ed. Gary E. Moulton (Lincoln, Nebr., 1983–96), 3:52-54 (hereafter JLCE).

26. Lewis to Jefferson, October 3, 1803, in Jackson, *Letters*, 1:126-32; JLCE, 3:340.

27. JLCE, 5:189 n.

28. Howe, "Fugitive Verses," 240. This satiric point has two barbs. Barlow is reduced from epic poet to psalm-maker, a reflection on his translation of *Watts's Psalms* years earlier. Then he is reduced to the level of a bad psalm-maker; the verses of Thomas Sternhold had been scorned by Dryden and Pope and many other wits.

29. Ralph Adams Brown, *The Presidency of John Adams* (Lawrence, Kans., 1975), 72.

30. Howard P. Vincent, *The Tailoring of Melville's White-Jacket* (Evanston, Ill., 1970), 71-78.

31. Mitchill was not a mere crank but a convivial, wealthy, public-spirited polymath with notable talents as a politician, editor, poet, scientist, and physician (his name is sometimes maddeningly misspelled Mitchell, even by careful correspondents like Jefferson). Henry Adams describes him as a professor at Columbia who could have held every chair there in succession (see *History of the United States under the Administrations of Thomas Jefferson and James Madison* (New York, 1891–96), 1:111). In 1807 he was a Jeffersonian senator and also editor of the *Medical Repository*, a journal that took special interest in such projects as the Lewis and Clark Expedition. Just a week before the dinner for Lewis he had invited the explorer to dinner to discuss such phenomena as coal burning under the plains near the Missouri River. See "Dr. Mitchill's Letters from Washington, 1801–1813," *Harper's Magazine*, 58 (April 1879), 750. Mitchill proposed his ideas about Fredonia in an 1804 pamphlet, "An Address to the Fredes or People of the United States," with a parenthesis on the title page: "The modern and appropriate name of the people of the United States is Fredes or Fredonians, as the geographical name is Fredon or Fredonia, and their relations are expressed by the terms Fredonian or Fredish" (see Duyckinck, *Cyclopaedia*, 1:518). This pamphlet was written in verse, and Mitchill was also known for his verse translations of the third and fifth piscatory eclogues of Sannazarius (Duyckinck, *Cyclopaedia*, 1:520). As a sociable, learned, energetic, playful, and ingenious political figure, Mitchill probably amused John Quincy Adams more than he irritated him.

32. *Monthly Anthology and Boston Review*, 1 (1804), 217-18, 293-94, 342-45. These letters were reprinted in 1950 as *A Proposal of a General Name for the United States*, a project of the Industrial Arts Laboratory Press at San Jose State College in California.

33. An obscure poet named Richard Emmons also published an enormous epic poem on the War of 1812 entitled *The Fredoniad; or, Independence Preserved*, 4 vols. (Boston, 1827).

34. John Adams to John Trumbull, April 28, 1785, in *Historical Magazine*, 4 (July 1860), 195. Robert A. Ferguson reads this letter somewhat differently, as an early statement of a long-running tension between law and literature in American intellectual life; see his *Law and Letters in American Culture* (Cambridge, Mass., 1984), 3-4.

35. Members of the Lewis and Clark Trail Heritage Foundation have helped me trace about thirty titles of works in verse about Lewis and Clark and their party. Most are song-pageants or children's programs or verses to fit a statue or an occasion. See Albert Furtwangler, "Lewis and Clark in Verse," *We Proceeded On*, 22 (February 1996), 12-15, 30.

Pompey's Pillar, 1902, photographed by L. A. Huffman

Part Six

Looking Back

THROUGHOUT THE PAST TWO CENTURIES the Lewis and Clark Expedition has suffered a strange fate at the hands of both professional historians and the wider American public. Jefferson's explorers have been either ignored or overpraised, neglected or lionized. Textbook writers, novelists, and film-makers have bounced from one extreme to the other, making the Lewis and Clark company either invisible nobodies or invincible heroes.

In recent years popular culture has adopted the explorers as convenient shorthand for western adventure and national triumph. For all sorts of reasons—some laudable and others less praiseworthy—Americans have become deeply invested in the Lewis and Clark story. And that investment has ensured the continued appeal of the subject. It has also meant that each generation of historians and fellow travelers will tell their own version of the journey. While some might look askance at such constant revision, we might also see the constant retelling as a sign of intellectual vigor and the inherent vitality of the expedition story.

The essays that conclude this volume trace the course of Lewis and Clark scholarship and comment on recent work in the field. More than anything else, these essays suggest that the story has become more than just a tale of high adventure and personal courage. Told with sensitivity and an awareness of larger stories, the Lewis and Clark story is an emblematic one. The "writing" that the captains began in September 1806 continues into our own time. And the power of this story, as well as its broad appeal, shows no sign of diminishing into the next century.

'Of This Enterprize'
The American Images
of the Lewis and Clark Expedition

John L. Allen

Of this enterprize, planned by our own government, and achieved
through great dangers by our own countrymen, little need be said to
attract the attention of the American people.
—from *The Prospectus*, C. A. Conrad, May 1810

LEWIS RIVER, CLARK'S FORK, FLOYD'S RIVER, the Musselshell and
Judith and Marias, Great Falls, White Bear Islands, Walla Walla
and Hungry Creek: the names and experiences are spread across
the maps of our western landscape just as they are spread across
the maps of our collective consciousness. That these names continue
to exist—on our maps and in our minds—is testimony to the
strength and durability of the images of Lewis and Clark and their
expedition in the American mind. They are images which have
been, like all images, created out of real world experiences and
which have been continually modified and refined from their
beginnings nearly two centuries ago down to the present. The
images of the Lewis and Clark Expedition and its major protagonists
are models representing a people's referral to their past; they are
patterns of belief and perception, and they are not rational—or at
least they are not, nor have they been, controlled and shaped by
what we take to be logic. Rather, they have been based on faith
and belief and opinion instead of reason, on ideas and ideals instead
of realities. They have been passed on from one generation to the

next via an unconscious and nonrational process and, in that process, have been changed and adapted to meet new interpretations of what we believe to have been reality. A part of the truth about what we Americans are as a people resides in both the images and the realities which have created and shaped them. If we would understand our world better, we must therefore understand these images, among others, for they are a part of our world, just as they were part of the world of our grandfathers and grandmothers.[1] I would hope that what will follow in this essay will enhance that understanding.

At the very outset of this attempt at understanding the images of the Lewis and Clark Expedition it must be noted that the use of the plural term "images" rather than the singular "image" to refer to the pattern of beliefs about the Lewis and Clark Expedition is an advised and necessary usage, since what we are dealing with is not a single image at all but a set of images representing different patterns of belief about the same historical events and realities. The mind is a mirror which reflects an image of what it perceives; the nature and appearance of the reflected image is determined by the conditions of the mirror—whether it is cracked, warped, spotted, or otherwise modified by both collective and personal experience. Thus are all images distorted and discolored by the quality of the minds in which they have been lodged.[2] It is for this reason that we cannot speak accurately of an "image" of the Lewis and Clark Expedition. Rather, we must speak of images; for there has never been a single, universally accepted and comprehensive image of Lewis and Clark and their great exploratory epic. What there has been is a set of images, varying in character depending upon the minds housing them. When taken together, this set of images provides us with a group of elements—the captains, their party, the journey itself, and its purposes and results—which constitutes the bulk of what we know or think we know about the expedition of Lewis and Clark.

It may be helpful to think of the disparate images of the Lewis and Clark epic as divisible into three categories: the "personal images," containing elements or representing beliefs held only by the individual or, at the most, by small groups of individuals; the "consensual images," containing elements and patterns of belief held collectively by any large segment of American society at any particular time; and the "universal images," containing elements which may be truly universal or shared by all.[3] For example, those gathered at an institution which bears the name "Lewis and Clark College" would probably agree with the prominent Lewis and Clark scholar Paul Cutright that the expedition "stands, incomparably, as the transcendent achievement of its kind in this hemisphere, if not in the entire world."[4] Our agreement constitutes a consensual image, held by this group at this particular time. But each of us, at some time in the past or in the future, may hold a personal image which is at some variance with the collectively shared viewpoint. And while Cutright's statement may be fair a summation of our consensual image of the Lewis and Clark Expedition, it is far from a universally accepted element in the overall universal image as it may exist now or as it may have existed in the past. Not all Americans since 1806 have held such high opinion of Lewis and Clark and their epic trek; indeed, not all Americans since 1806 have held opinions on the matter of Lewis and Clark at all—high or otherwise.

Before this line of reasoning threatens to plunge us all into intellectual darkness, let me try to shed some enlightenment on the matter by suggesting that, while it is true that there are and have been nearly as many American images of the Lewis and Clark Expedition as there are and have been Americans, we need concern ourselves only with a few of them. The images that are important for our discussions are neither the personal ones—which are difficult to define and, with some few exceptions, are not terribly important—nor the universal ones—which contain so few elements as to be comparatively meaningless. Rather, the images upon which we might most profitably dwell are the consensual or collective images, those which contain elements that are shared by large groups of people and which, therefore, are the images most likely to influence thought and behavior and thus the world of which they are a part. Additionally, the collective images are the most readily defined and bear the most obvious relationships to the beliefs, hopes, aspirations, and goals inherent in the mind-set of the groups holding them.

To simplify matters even further, let me suggest that of all the collective images of the Lewis and Clark Expedition held by

Americans during the nineteenth and twentieth centuries, two were the most operative and had the greatest influence on thought and action by Americans. These two collective images I will define as "the literate elite image," held by the American scientific and scholarly community and based primarily on the literary tradition of the expedition, and the "folk image," held by the common populace and containing elements of both literate and nonliterate traditions. Let us examine these two images—their inception, their changing character, and the degree of convergence or divergence between them from 1806 to the present.

The first of the images of the Lewis and Clark Expedition to be fully operative was the literate elite image. This image, due in large measure to the role played by the American scientific community in the planning and preparation stages of the expedition, placed it from the very beginning in the position of a real-world application of Enlightenment scientific tradition. Thomas Jefferson, perhaps the foremost representative of the Enlightenment in the United States and president, concurrently, of both the nation and the American Philosophical Society, the country's premier Enlightenment scientific association, had tried for years prior to Lewis and Clark to bring to fruition his ambitions for the discovery of a water passageway between the Upper Missouri and the source region of some Pacific stream.[5] The last of these attempts was carried out through the auspices of the American Philosophical Society and, as a consequence, the leading scientists in the country were quite familiar with Jefferson's scientific objectives even before he became president and had, finally, the capacity to carry them forward.[6] When Jefferson's message to Congress of January 18, 1803, laid the foundations of the expedition, the familiarity of American science with the president's objectives soon became involvement.[7] Jefferson dispatched Meriwether Lewis to Philadelphia for training in scientific observation, measurement, and reporting under the tutelage of such men as Andrew Ellicott, Robert Patterson, Dr. Benjamin Rush, Dr. Benjamin Smith Barton, and Dr. Caspar Wistar, all members of the American Philosophical Society.[8]

After Lewis had left Philadelphia and Washington for the West to join Clark and establish the expedition's base camp at Wood

River in the winter of 1803–4, the involvement of the scientific community with the expedition continued in the form of correspondence between Jefferson, Lewis, and the scientists.[9] It is noteworthy that, although one of the later criticisms leveled at the Lewis and Clark Expedition was "the lack of some trained scientist," the members of the society had enough confidence in Lewis's scientific abilities—and faith in the scientific nature of his forthcoming exploration—to elect him to membership in that prestigious organization in November of 1803.[10] In this act is seen the clearest evidence of the pre-expeditionary image as held by the literate elite. Although American science could not have been unaware of at least some of Jefferson's geopolitical ambitions with regard to the West, for most of the scientists the expedition's central objective was, as Jefferson had stated it: "to enlarge our knowledge of the geography of our continent, by adding information to that interesting line of communication across it, and to give us a general view of its population, natural history, production, soil and climate."[11] Jefferson's statement aptly expressed patterns of belief that constituted the literate elite image of the expedition at this stage; these patterns of belief would not suffer much erosion until after the expedition's return and the nearly intolerable delays in presenting to the intellectual community its scientific results.

Of the nature of the folk image of the expedition, little direct evidence exists prior to the return of Lewis and Clark in September of 1806. Lewis had left Washington for the West at the same time as the official announcement was made regarding the Louisiana Purchase; news of the impending expedition was overshadowed in the public press by the magnificent acquisition. For weeks following the news of the purchase, American newspapers (a primary source of the folk image) carried descriptive accounts of Louisiana, many of them being extracted directly from Jefferson's own "Official Account" which constituted the government's "press release" on the lands so fortuitously acquired by the young Republic. Frequently, in papers carrying an account of the new territory, there appeared a brief addendum to the effect that "Captain Meriwether Lewis, the President's secretary, and his party are even now preparing to explore the territory."[12] It is natural that the expedition should have been overshadowed, at this juncture, by the purchase itself. For Louisiana had burst upon the public consciousness—and it was a consciousness ill prepared to understand just what the United States had acquired. The public press attempted to mitigate general ignorance of the lands west of the Mississippi by dredging up and reprinting every available piece of information about them.[13] Small wonder that an exploratory expedition, dispatched without great fanfare, would be lost in the overwhelming public debate that followed the purchase. Nor is it any wonder that the expedition—conceived, planned, and actually in its early stages well before release of the news of the purchase—should have been, from this time on, inextricably linked in the public image with the purchase of Louisiana. To this very day, an important component of the public or folk image of the expedition holds that Lewis and Clark were sent forth for the explicit purpose of exploring and evaluating the newly acquired lands.[14]

Another component of the public image began to take shape during the public debate over the Louisiana Purchase, a component that colored, for a good part of the nineteenth century at any rate, the folk image of the expedition. This was the notion of the expedition as ill conceived and ill managed and undertaken purely as the consequence of Jefferson's greedy attempt to acquire territory which many Americans felt nearly worthless. Not all Americans had viewed the purchase of Louisiana with enthusiasm; particularly among the Federalist papers of Philadelphia, New York, and Boston was found a great deal of criticism leveled at the administration for spending public funds on what the non-expansionist Federalists viewed as a "Pig-in-a-poke."[15] This negative view of the purchase led to a negative view of the expedition itself, a view expressed even more clearly in the years following Lewis and Clark's return to St. Louis in September 1806.

During the years 1804–6, as Lewis and Clark traversed two-thirds of a continent to the Pacific and back again, little modification occurred in either the image held by the literate elite or that held by the folk. Unlike our modern explorers who, from as far away as the moon, are in constant communication with "mission control," Lewis and Clark were completely cut off from Monticello, Washington, or Philadelphia during their journey. Immediately upon their return, however, the process of image modification began; and two new images, elite and folk, began to take shape on the basis of the completed fact of the successful journey.

The image of the literate elite, as it took shape during the years from 1806 to 1814 when the accounts of the expedition were finally published, reflected the essential features of the pre-expeditionary image. It contained as its central elements patterns of belief regarding the successful completion of the expedition's cardinal objective—the discovery of a water route to the Pacific—and its corollary objective of expanding scientific knowledge of the interior. On both counts, the general tone of the developing elite image was one of disillusionment. Both Lewis and Jefferson had commented favorably on the expedition's results vis-à-vis the discovery of the water passageway. In a letter to Jefferson from St. Louis immediately upon his return, Lewis wrote: "We view this passage across the Continent (the route followed on the return journey) as affording immense advantages to the fur trade . . . We believe that many articles not bulky, brittle nor of a very perishable nature may be conveyed to the United States by this rout with more facility and at less expense than by that at present practiced."[16] Jefferson repeated this claim in his message to Congress of December 2, 1806: "The expedition of Messrs. Lewis and Clarke for exploring the river Missouri, and the best communication from that to the Pacific ocean, has had all the success which could have been expected . . . The desideratum therefore of the interior of our continent along this important channel of communication with the Pacific is now obtained."[17] Such commentary should have excited enthusiasm and produced a highly positive image. But Lewis's letter to Jefferson contained a qualifier as to the successful completion of the search for the Passage to India: "[We] fear that the advantages which it offers as a communication for the productions of the East Indies to the United States and thence to Europe will never be found equal on an extensive scale to that by way of the Cape of Good Hope."[18]

It was the qualifier which became operative, and although later generations would tend to speak of Lewis and Clark as having "opened the way west," for the scientists and scholars of the immediate post-expeditionary period no such illusions prevailed.

One authority, for example, commented that the fur trade which followed Lewis and Clark into the mountains had already (by 1814) located a number of passes which, far from being the water route that had been hoped for, were still better than the torturous route followed by the captains.[19] There is almost a note of petulance in the response of the intellectual community to the perceived (and, it must be noted, actual) failure of the expedition to locate the Passage to India. American science had for decades based its view of the western interior on such a connecting link between Atlantic and Pacific streams. That it did not exist in the form in which it had been envisaged was not good news; and, as bearers of bad news, Lewis and Clark suffered from detractions among the scientific elite.

A similar, although less emotional, situation prevailed with regard to the scientific results of the expedition. Having been led to expect great things from the outset, American science continued to be tantalized for the years intervening between the captains' return and the final publication of the accounts of their travels in 1814. Jefferson wrote to colleagues in the American Philosophical Society referring to "the additions he [Lewis] brings to our knowledge of the geography and natural history of our country, from the Mississippi to the Pacific."[20] To a European scientist resident in the United States, he wrote, "I can assure you that the addition to our knowledge . . . has entirely fulfilled my expectations . . . and that the world will find that those travellers have well earned its favor."[21] But the president's protestations to the contrary, the scientific community had received little of a scientific nature in the few halting reports that were emerging from the expedition. As a consequence, they developed a largely negative and critical view of the effectiveness of the expedition in scientific terms. Indeed, toward the end of the period 1806–14 even Jefferson himself grew surly over the combination of events which had delayed the release of the party's scientific contribution. In a letter of 1813 to Alexander von Humboldt, the world's premier scientist, Jefferson lamented: "You will find it inconceivable that Lewis's journey to the Pacific should not yet have appeared; nor is it in my power to tell you the reason . . . The botanical and zoological discoveries of Lewis will probably experience greater delay, and become known to the world through other channels before that volume will be ready."[22] This, in fact, is exactly what happened. The delay in publication of the accounts of the Lewis and Clark Expedition, coupled with the fact that, when their accounts did appear they contained little scientific information, had allowed Lewis and Clark to be scooped scientifically by the reports of other early American scientists working in the West. The result was that the elite image of the expedition was not a terribly positive one in regard to the intellectual contributions made by the captains. This basically negative view of the role of Lewis and Clark as contributing scientists prevailed in the elite image throughout the nineteenth century.

The folk image of the expedition during the same period of 1806–14 suffered from the same malaise affecting the literate elite image: disillusionment arose from the failure to locate the passage and, early in the period, the public may have felt cheated at not being able to acquire cheap and readable accounts of the explorers' exploits. In spite of this, the expedition did have its public proponents; and newspaper commentary appeared about evenly divided as to the overall success and benefits to the nation contributed by Lewis and Clark. And within the folk image another element crept in to distort the nature of the shaping image—this was the controversy over western expansionism which was still an item in American thought several years after the Louisiana Purchase.

In general, there was a tendency for those who favored western expansion to see the Lewis and Clark Expedition in a favorable light and to agree with the citizens of Fincastle, Kentucky, who presented to the captains a memorial which read in part: "You have navigated bold and unknown rivers, traversed mountains; which had never before been impressed with the footsteps of civilized man, and surmounted every obstacle, which climate, Nature, or ferocious savages could throw in your way. You have the further satisfaction to reflect that, you have extended the knowledge of the Geography of your country; in other respects enriched Science; and opened to the United States a source of inexhaustible wealth."[23]

The initial public fame of the expedition rested upon the newspaper publication of a letter which Clark had written to his brother upon the return to St. Louis, a letter in which he claimed that the exploration had uncovered the passage: "We were completely successful and have therefore no hesitation in declaring that such as nature has permitted it we have discovered the best route which does exist across the continent of North America in that direction."[24]

The citizens of Fincastle apparently agreed with that conclusion—as did poet Joel Barlow:

> Let the Nile cloak his head in the clouds, and defy
> The research of science and time;
> Let the Niger escape the keen traveller's eye,
> By plunging or changing his clime.
> Columbus, not so shall thy boundless domain
> Defraud thy brave sons of their right;
> Streams, midlands and shorelands illude us in vain.
> We shall drag their dark regions to light.[25]

Those Americans who had viewed the purchase with disfavor and who were against western expansion in general had, on the other hand, a disparaging tone in their voices and in their writings about the expedition. Barlow's laudatory poetry was followed in the papers by this effort, reputedly authored by none other than John Quincy Adams:

> Good people listen to my tale, 'tis nothing but what true is;
> I'll tell you of the mighty deeds achieved by Captain Lewis—
> How starting from the Atlantic shore by fair and easy motion,
> He journeyed, all the way by land, until he met the ocean.[26]

And while the first prospectus for the publication of the Lewis and Clark travel accounts, issued in 1807, had stressed "the immense advantages which would accrue to the Mercantile interests of the United States, by combining the same with a direct trade to the East Indies through the continent of North America,"[27] and had spoken in high terms of the expedition's success, a detraction referring to the prospectus had been widely published: "With respect to the hazardous nature of the enterprize and the courage necessary for undertaking it, candour compels me to say that public opinion has placed them on too high ground."[28] Jefferson had referred to the initial public reaction to the Lewis and Clark Expedition by claiming that "never did a similar event excite more joy thro' the United States."[29] While surely true for part of the public, it just as surely was not true for another part which was critical of the expedition, its results, and the compensation received by the returned explorers. An editorial comment in an independent newspaper (neither Republican nor Federalist) noted that the expedition had "excited more curiosity in Europe than it has in this country."[30]

Images based on faulty or limited information are often disparate, and therefore it might be expected that the publication of the first official account of the Lewis and Clark Expedition in 1814 would have resolved the disparities in both the literate elite and the folk images, producing a collective American image at once more favorable and more accurate. Such, unfortunately, was not the case. Jefferson had claimed that the humblest of American citizens "had taken a lively interest in the issue of this journey, and looked forward with impatience for the information it would furnish."[31] And the prospectus for the official account, the *History of the Expedition Under the Command of Captains Lewis and Clark*, compiled by Nicholas Biddle of Philadelphia and finally published in 1814, claimed that "Of this enterprize, planned by our own government, and achieved through great danger by our own countrymen, little need be said to attract the attention of the American people."[32] Yet, it is indicative of both the literate elite and the folk images of the expedition that when the *History* finally was published, the volumes languished on the booksellers' shelves. For all the high language in the prospectus and for all of Jefferson's concern that the journals appear as quickly as possible, when they became available in 1814, they simply did not sell well. Nicholas Biddle wrote to Clark in May 1816: "I cannot express to you how much I am disappointed at the unfortunate result of this business."[33] An accounting late in 1816 revealed that sales had continued small; and, indeed, the final accounting showed that Clark would have received the munificent sum of $170.18 1/2 for his efforts.[34]

The failure of even the publication, at long last, of the Biddle narrative to unify the American images of the expedition may be

the consequence of the combined effects of three factors. First—
and this is particularly true for the elite image—the narrative and,
therefore, the expedition itself, simply did not deliver on its promise
to locate a commercial passage. The prospectus for the Biddle
volumes had enthused that: "The sources of the Columbia and
Missouri rivers, which had eluded all former research, had been
fully explored, and a line of intercourse—the future path of
civilization—connects the Atlantic and Pacific oceans. Vast regions
are now opened, to reward the spirit of commercial adventure,
and to receive, hereafter, the overflowing tide of our own
population."[35]

A careful reading of the *History*, however, coupled with a
knowledge of what had passed in the West since 1806, would bring
even the enthusiast to the conclusion that Lewis and Clark had
not really discovered a passage at all. The holders of both elite and
folk images could not but have been affected by the final recognition
of the failure of the expedition's ultimate goal, the discovery of a
water passageway across the continent for the purposes of
commerce.

The second factor in the failure of the publication of the *History*
to produce a uniform and positive image of the expedition in the
American mind was the overall lack of scientific data in the Biddle
narrative. The prospectus had reported that "Entire nations, varying
at once from ourselves and from each other, have been revealed to
the curiosity of the civilized world, while science is enriched by
new and valuable acquisitions."[36] But once again there was a failure
to deliver on promises, and the narrative contained precious little
information on the expedition's remarkable achievements in
geography, biology, and ethnology. Jefferson admitted as much in
a letter to a member of the American Philosophical Society:

> A part of the information of which the expedition of Lewis
> and Clark was the object has been communicated to the
> world by the publication of their journal; but much and
> valuable matter remains yet uncommunicated. The
> correction of the longitudes of their map is essential to its
> value; to which purpose their observations of the lunar
> distances are to be calculated and applied. The new subjects

they discovered in the vegetable, animal and mineral departments are to be digested and made known.[37]

Unfortunately, they would not be made known for quite a number of years; and this failure did little to unify the elite and folk images, and it did little to produce in either image a favorable interpretation of the expedition.

The third factor in the Biddle narrative's failure relative to a positive American image simply stemmed from the delay in its publication. Produced initially by Lewis's preoccupation with government matters, compounded immeasurably by his suicide in 1809, and compounded even further by Clark's difficulties in obtaining proper editorial help in compiling an account from the manuscript field notes, the delay in publication simply let too much water go under the bridge. A lot had happened in the West between 1806 and 1814. Several important travel accounts, such as those of Zebulon Pike, had already appeared and the efforts of the Astorians were becoming public knowledge in the period 1810–14. These events diverted attention, both elite and folk, away from Lewis and Clark and toward other concerns. To make matters worse in terms of representing fairly and accurately the expedition's unique contributions, the publication of the *History* was preceded by a series of spurious and/or highly limited accounts of the expedition in the form of the published journals of Patrick Gass (Gass was one of the sergeants of the Corps of Discovery),[38] and the so-called "Apocrypha," a work calling itself *The Travels of Capts. Lewis and Clarke.*[39] While the Gass journal presented a reasonably accurate account of the essential facts of the expedition, the work was limited in its content; and the information from it was ambiguous enough to be inconsequential for the shaping of a coherent image of the expedition. And the "Apocrypha" constituted such an aberration that it did irreparable damage to the public view of the expedition for much of the remainder of the nineteenth century.

The "Apocrypha" was quite popular in both the United States and Europe and went through many reprintings between 1809 when it was first issued and the middle of the century.[40] The bulk of this spurious work consisted of an account of the expedition's ascent of the Missouri as far as the Mandan villages (this extracted from

Lewis's letter to Jefferson from the Mandans in the spring of 1805), a summary of the expedition (extracted from Clark's 1806 letter to his brother), and a plagiarized version of the description of western Indians from Jonathan Carver's *Travels in the Interior*, first published in the 1780s. Unfortunately, much of what the public knew or thought they knew about Lewis and Clark they learned from the "Apocrypha." It is therefore little wonder that the images of the great expedition appeared so ambiguous throughout a good portion of the nineteenth century. In their ambiguity, the literate elite and the folk images had begun to converge into a single and unified image which, if not fully negative was certainly not completely positive either—an image in which neither the captains, their journey, or its results emerged in anything like an accurate light. It was an unfortunate convergence.

A final note needs to be added about the character of American images—both literate and folk—of the expedition during the middle years of the 1800s. Quite simply, the expedition of Lewis and Clark was an Enlightenment venture which failed to enlighten. As such, it was quickly lost sight of among a population for whom enlightenment was much less important than utilitarianism. Americans demanded results from their heroes. When those results were slow in forthcoming or did not appear at all, the representatives of the Enlightenment—the scientific community—moved to other things. They shifted their attention to the growing literature of western exploration, to Pike and Long and Bradbury and Nuttal and Brackenridge and, later, to the reports of the U.S. Army Corps of Topographical Engineers. The representatives of the utilitarian viewpoint—the folk—reacted to the lack of applied results of the expedition by either ignoring the contributions of Lewis and Clark, by actively disparaging them, or—in perhaps the most fascinating extension of the Lewis and Clark image to public behavior—by inventing for the expedition results simply not there.

When the name "Oregon" began to appear on American lips and in American minds in the 1830s, the accounts of Lewis and Clark were dragged, dusty, off bookshelves where they had rested for two decades. Proponents of Oregon settlement used them to prove that Oregon was the end of the settler's rainbow, the savanna land for which Americans had been searching since Jamestown and Plymouth. To use the Lewis and Clark narratives in this way distorted fact; the captains had been generally unenthusiastic in their reports on the Pacific Northwest, seeing it as a dark and gloomy region, poor in many resources when compared with the plains and prairie country of the Missouri valley. Yet Oregon boosters like Hall Jackson Kelley, founder and general agent of the American Society for Encouraging the Settlement of Oregon, read in the Biddle narrative what they wanted to see. In 1830 Kelley published "A Geographical Sketch of that Part of North America Called Oregon" in which, according to his own commentary, he utilized the Biddle *History* to paint a glowing, rosy picture of the Oregon country. That country, he learned (or said he had) from the Biddle account, was: "generally uneven . . . [and] an undulating surface of territory, or a surface chiefly broken into hills and mountains is, in almost every consideration, preferable to one that is level; because the former abounds with springs and rivers of pure water. Consequently the air is more salubrious and the country better furnished with natural facilities for the application of labour . . . [The climate] is remarkably mild . . . Providence has made Oregon the most favoured spot of his beneficence."[41]

In their journals Lewis and Clark had entered precious few comments favorable to the Oregon country. But Kelley seems to have found them all. With objectives similar to those of Kelley, other Oregon boosters did the same thing. Archibald McVickar, editor of a "new" edition of the *History* in the fall of 1842, justified it on the grounds that Lewis and Clark had said good things about "that portion of the North American Continent known by the name of the Oregon Territory" and that their accounts deserved to be placed once more before the public eye.[42]

While men like Kelley and McVickar used Lewis and Clark to "prove" the value of Oregon settlement, opponents of that settlement used the Biddle narrative of the expedition to "prove" just the opposite—that Oregon, in the words of William Joseph Snelling: "is to the last degree rugged and mountainous . . . Lewis and Clark say that they often found the natives in extreme want, if not actually starving, and their own party, though provided with fishing tackle and guns, which they well knew how to use, were glad to buy a few small dogs wherewith to quiet the cravings of nature. Mr. Kelley says the climate is excellent; Lewis and Clark say it is wet and uncomfortable."[43]

Obviously, in shaping American opinion and policy, the Kelleys and McVickars had their way and the Snellings did not. Oregon was settled—and it was settled at least partially on the strength of the supposedly favorable nature of the great captains' reports on the territory between the Rockies and the Pacific. This process is not only an interesting commentary on the character of the American image of the expedition in the middle of the nineteenth century—it is also a commentary on the very real role played by that image in conditioning the behavior of a westering people.

After the debates on the value of Oregon Territory were settled by the occupation of that region by an American population and its ultimate cession to the United States, Lewis and Clark receded into the American memory, for both the literate elite and folk segments of society. Little held the captains in the forefront of memory for the scientists, whose view of the scientific accomplishments of Lewis and Clark continued to pale beside the brilliance of nineteenth-century western exploration after 1806. And the folk memory required heroes larger than life. Lewis and Clark were not, during the nineteenth century, the kind of folk-heroes that Americans favored; they were not like Davy Crockett or Paul Bunyan or Mike Fink or Kit Carson. They were, perhaps, too workaday in their competence, in their matter-of-factness, in their simple approach to doing their job. Significantly, during the long portion of the nineteenth century between the publication of the Biddle account in 1814 and the appearance of the next "official" narrative in 1893, virtually no important works appeared in the American literature dealing with either the captains or their travels. During those years publishers had periodically reprinted the Biddle *History*, the *Journals of Patrick Gass*, or the apocryphal *Travels of Capts. Lewis and Clarke*. But nothing new appeared until the arrival on the literary scene of a former army physician and natural historian named Elliott Coues.

During his service as a field surgeon and a naturalist with the U.S. Army, Coues had considerable field experience in the American West. In addition, he had served as a naturalist and secretary to the United States Geological and Geographical Survey of the Territories and had written a number of books and articles in the field of natural history.[44] In 1891 Francis P. Harper, a New York publisher, approached him with the idea of reediting the Biddle *History*; nothing much came of this suggestion and, a year later, Harper again wrote Coues: "we are anxious to have this matter under way, as I am informed that another publisher has under consideration the republishing of this work."[45] Coues has often been credited with reawakening American interest in Lewis and Clark—and this may be. But it also may be that the interest was quickening anyway, if Harper's allusion to another publisher's potential interest in the Biddle narratives is any indication. At any rate, the lack of attention paid to the Lewis and Clark Expedition by the American scientific community had spanned three-quarters of a century, a fact brought home in the strongest terms by what may have been Coues's greatest contribution to the images—both elite and folk—of the expedition. This was his discovery, in 1892, of the manuscript field journals of the explorers in the collections of the American Philosophical Society where they had lain "unknown, unheralded, and untouched" since Nicholas Biddle had given them to the society in 1818.[46]

Whether or not the publication, in 1893, of the Coues edition of the *History* had an impact on the folk image of Lewis and Clark cannot be properly assessed. There certainly did not appear in the public literature a great outpouring of interest in the captains or their travels immediately after the appearance of the Coues edition in booksellers' shops. But Coues's impact on the character of the elite image was significant: as its major outcome, the Coues edition fostered the opinion that the Lewis and Clark Expedition had suffered immeasurably from "the lack of some trained scientist."[47] The quarrel that Coues had was, of course, not really with Lewis and Clark but with Jefferson who, in the editor's opinion, had expressed unrealistic confidence in Lewis's scientific abilities. Since Coues, other writers, taking their cue from him, have spoken out similarly. No less a historian than Walter Prescott Webb, for example, had this to say: "Why a man of Jefferson's philosophical and scientific turn of mind should have been unable to select more capable men for the enterprise, keen observers with trained minds, is hard to understand . . . Throughout the journal there is a lack of specific detail, a vagueness, an absence of names of persons and places in connection with episodes related. The records fail to reveal in their authors much knowledge of geology, physical geography, botany, zoology, or anthropology."[48]

This opinion, an outgrowth of Coues's criticism, was petty and mean—not to mention just plain wrong. It also demonstrates a very considerable lack of understanding of the nature of Enlightenment science under which the expedition was conceived, planned, and executed. But wrongheaded or not, this critical evaluation of the expedition was a major outgrowth—for the elite image—of the Coues edition.

On a more positive note the Coues edition also awakened scholarly and scientific interest in the expedition for about the first time since the captains' return in September of 1806. This awakening of interest can be partly attributed to the inclusion, in the Coues edition, of a significant mass of scientific data omitted from the Biddle edition. But it can also be said to have been a function of Coues's rather cavalier editing of Lewis and Clark material—an editing which began to produce the feeling that a full-blown, scholarly treatment of the expedition, using the captains' original field notes, was necessary. Such a treatment followed shortly after the appearance of the Coues edition. That event changed, probably forever, the nature of American images of the expedition and brought, finally, the images of the elite and folk into closer conjunction.

If the shaping of the contemporary image of the Lewis and Clark Expedition gained its initial impetus by the Coues edition of the *History*, the really critical piece of scholarship upon which our present image depends was the first edition of *The Original Journals of the Lewis and Clark Expedition*, magnificently edited and annotated by Reuben Gold Thwaites and released for public consumption in 1904. The Thwaites edition of the *Original Journals* could not have come at a better time. It was the centennial of the Louisiana Purchase and of the expedition's beginning and, being great ones for celebrating "centennials" (perhaps a short history demands such attention), Americans had already been gearing up for a celebration. In fact, it was partly the centennial that prompted the American Philosophical Society—in whose possession rested the captains' manuscript field journals and the bulk of their scientific notes resulting from their data collection—to approve plans to publish the journals and scientific materials. The society selected distinguished historical editor, Reuben Gold Thwaites, to carry out the project. At this point an entirely new phase in the shaping of the scholarly, scientific, elite image of the expedition began.

The Thwaites edition of the *Original Journals* suffered in some slight regard from the fact that its compiler was a historian rather than a scientist; nevertheless, the overall scientific content of the Thwaites journals, particularly in geography, biology, and ethnology, was immeasurably greater than anything that had ever appeared in print related to the expedition. And, in addition to the daily field entries containing the above-mentioned data, Thwaites included several appendices with invaluable geologic and meteorological information.[49] From Thwaites on, the Lewis and Clark Expedition has been viewed by the scientific community— with some few curmudgeonly exceptions—as one of the most productive exploratory journeys ever taken. The contributions to all branches of natural science made by the captains have been, since Thwaites, looked upon with something akin to awe by most American scholars. Moreover, Thwaites set a pattern of scholarship which has been followed by Lewis and Clark scholars down to this very day. It is noteworthy that, where no significant scholarly works on the expedition preceded Thwaites, the years since his editing have seen a proliferation of thematic works on various aspects of the scientific accomplishments of Lewis and Clark. In this sense, Thwaites has been the direct intellectual forebear of the great Lewis and Clark scholars of this century—Milo M. Quaife, Ernest Staples Osgood, Donald Jackson, and Paul Cutright. And through their work, he also figures prominently in the ancestry of those present Lewis and Clark scholars contributing to this volume and continuing the attempt, really begun by Thwaites, to enlarge upon our intellectual appreciation of the Lewis and Clark Expedition.

But if Thwaites achieved a unification of the elite image and fostered the view of the Lewis and Clark Expedition as one of the most remarkable examples of Enlightenment scientific ventures, what did the publication of the *Original Journals* mean for public image, still fuzzy and incoherent at the beginning of the twentieth century? Unhappily, the answer is "relatively little." The publication of the Thwaites volumes may have been a signal event for scholarship, but the work—eight volumes in size—was too expensive to be available to the general reader or even the smaller public library. Much more available, again unhappily, during the first half of the twentieth century were those popular works dealing with the expedition and its members which, in a few instances, may have been stimulated by the publication of the *Original Journals* but were far more likely the result of the centennial interest in the expedition. As with the scholarly literature, the bulk of the popular material about the expedition has been written since the turn of the century. But unlike the scholarly literature, which attempted to clarify the characteristics of the expedition, the popular literature tended to cast a haze of romanticism and half-truth and outright fiction over the real story of Lewis and Clark. While the listing of Lewis and Clark popular works is too lengthy to deal with in detail,[50] several salient elements in the folk image that still exist have derived directly from those volumes produced since 1900. Chief among those elements, and perhaps the one most representative of the influence of the literature on the folk image, is that of Sacagawea, still viewed in the folk image as "Lewis and Clark's guide to the Pacific Ocean and back."

Beginning with Eva Emery Dye's *The Conquest: The True Story of Lewis and Clark*, published in 1902, and continuing down to the present, a sizeable body of literature has focused on the role of Sacagawea in the expedition.[51] The popularity of this "Sacagawea literature" in the general body of material on the expedition has produced within the public image a significant distortion: for many contemporary Americans, the name Sacagawea is at least as familiar, if not more so, than those of the captains themselves; and the Shoshone Indian woman has been variously presented as the central figure in the expedition's success. Even in much of the popular literature which does not deal exclusively with Sacagawea, her role in the expedition is magnified beyond the bounds of reality. For example, Donald Culross Peattie's *Forward the Nation* makes the crossing of the Rockies at Lemhi Pass the key to the expedition's success—and makes the presence of Sacagawea the key to that crossing:

What key, then, will open for Meriwether Lewis the door in the mountains? It must be of nothing less than gold, of the truest metal. And it must be curiously shaped, for the lock is an intricate one. To fit it, find then an Indian without a lot of Indian deceit, venality, cowardice . . . It must be one—if such an Indian can be imagined—who cannot be bought nor bribed, who will not suddenly quit the party altogether to chase buffalo or a girl . . . So the gold must be beaten into a woman's shape.[52]

It is on this point that the greatest divergence has existed in the twentieth century between the elite and the folk images of the expedition, with the scientists and scholars generally refuting the popular and romanticized version of the public's view of the Lewis and Clark Expedition as the Sacagawea Expedition, sometimes ably assisted by the two captains.

Even in those popular works which do not fictionalize and enlarge upon the Sacagawea saga, the expedition is treated romantically and viewed more as a great adventure than as a magnificent accomplishment of Enlightenment science. These works are filled with tales of narrow escapes from storms, grizzlies, savages, and the like, making of the captains and their men heroes cast more in the mold of Romanticism than the mold of Enlightenment: "All alike possessed the same hero-qualities— courage and endurance that were indomitable, the strength that is generated in life-and-death grapple with naked primordial reality, and that reckless daring which defies life and death. Those were hero-days; and they produced hero-types which flung themselves against the impossible—and conquered it."[53]

Lewis and Clark would have been most embarrassed at such statements. And even when the popular literature has not made romantic heroes out of the captains, the West they explored has been overromanticized:

Meriwether Lewis and William Clark/Wrote in their journals after dark, Of all they had seen in the livelong day/Up the Missouri all the way. Of the surly Sioux in their feathers and pride/Stalking down to the riverside, Out

of the Plains and the High Black Hills/In their wampum
and beads and porcupine quills./Of beavers and bears and
buffalo herds/of pelicans, swans, and sweet-singing birds/
Of black bears robbing the honey bees/And chasing the
hunters up the trees./Of white bears charging with foaming
jaws/And fiery eyes and terrible claws./Of plunging ponies
with flying manes/And Buffalo thundering over the plains./
They drank of the wilderness mystery/And the wild sweet
wine of liberty./Its splendor and beauty filled their eyes/
With sunset pageants in western skies. [54]

Dreadful poetry perhaps—but typical of major elements of the
folk image of the Lewis and Clark Expedition throughout much
of the twentieth century.

Until very recently, then, the American images of the Lewis
and Clark Expedition have been divided into the elite image—
which has become increasingly focused on the expedition as
Enlightenment science—and the folk image—which has fallen prey
to the effects of the romantic filters through which Americans have
tended, perhaps since the seventeenth century, to view the West.
But of late, there has been a rediscovery of Lewis and Clark in
both the scholarly and public segments of our society that has
begun a merging and melding of the elite and folk images. Since
1960, the resurgence of interest in Lewis and Clark has resulted in
a number of scholarly publications which have had as large an
impact on the public mind as they have on the scholarly
community; and an unprecedented number of popular works
which, by and large, have presented the expedition in a light more
similar to that of the elite image than did earlier popular histories.
We have also witnessed "the birth of Lewis and Clark societies,
the creation of national and state Lewis and Clark Trail
commissions, the designation of Lewis and Clark National
Historical Landmarks, the erecting of numerous trail markers, and
the institution by an internationally known travel agency of Lewis
and Clark tours."[55]

It has taken time for the American image of the Lewis and
Clark Expedition to become just that: an image instead of images,
a collective and more consensual pattern of belief rather than the

widely divergent elite and folk viewpoints which have characterized most of American thought about the expedition since 1806. Divergences still exist, most notably on the role and relevance of "the Indian woman Sacagawea" for the expedition. But the divergence is narrowing and by the time we celebrate the Lewis and Clark bicentennial, we may see a unified and near-universal image of the Lewis and Clark Expedition, one that has its elements of romanticism, derived from the folk images of the past, but also one that contains, as a derivative of the scholarly image, a coherent view of the expedition as the "transcendent achievement" of exploration in the Age of Enlightenment. After two centuries, it may finally come to pass that "of this enterprize, planned by our own government, and achieved through great dangers by our own countrymen, little need be said to attract the attention of the American people."

Notes

1. An excellent statement on the role of image and myth in American history is James Oliver Robertson, *American Myth, American Reality* (New York, 1980).

2. One of the earliest, and still one of the best statements on the nature of images is John Kirtland Wright, "Where History and Geography Meet," in *Human Nature in Geography: Fourteen Papers, 1925–1965* (Cambridge, Mass., 1966), 24-32.

3. See David Lowenthal, "Geography, Experience, and Imagination: Toward a Geographical Epistemology," *Annals of the Association of American Geographers*, 51 (no. 3, 1961), 241-60.

4. Paul Russell Cutright, *Lewis and Clark: Pioneering Naturalists* (Urbana, Ill., 1969), 393.

5. See Donald Jackson, *Thomas Jefferson and the Stony Mountains: Exploring the West from Monticello* (Urbana, Ill., 1981), 42-85.

6. This was the aborted mission of the French botanist, André Michaux. See Jackson, *Thomas Jefferson*, 74-78.

7. See *Jefferson's Message to Congress*, January 18, 1803, in *Letters of the Lewis and Clark Expedition with Related Documents, 1783–1854*, ed. Donald Jackson (Urbana, Ill., 1962), 10-14.

8. Thomas Jefferson to Benjamin Smith Barton, February 27, 1803, in Jackson, *Letters*, 16-17; Jefferson to Caspar Wistar, February 28, 1803, in ibid., 17-18; Jefferson to Benjamin Rush, February 28, 1803, in ibid., 18-19; Jefferson to Robert Patterson, March 2, 1803, in ibid., 21; Andrew Ellicott to Jefferson, March 6, 1803, in ibid., 23-25.

9. See Jefferson to Meriwether Lewis, July 4, 1803, in Jackson, *Letters*, 105-6; Lewis to Jefferson, July 8, 1803, in ibid., 106-7; Jefferson to Lewis, July 11, 1803, in ibid., 107-8; Caspar Wistar to Jefferson, July 13, 1803, in ibid., 108-9; Jefferson to Lewis, July 15, 1803, in ibid., 109-10; Lewis to Jefferson, July 22, 1803, in ibid., 111-12; Lewis to Jefferson, July 26, 1803, in ibid., 113-15; Lewis to Jefferson, September 8, 1803, in ibid., 121-23; Wistar to Jefferson, October 6, 1803, in ibid., 133-34.

10. Elliott Coues, ed., *History of the Expedition under the Command of Lewis and Clark . . . by Order of the Government of the United States* (New York, 1893), 1:xx.

11. Jefferson to Bernard Lacépède, February 24, 1803, in Jackson, *Letters*, 15-16.

12. Boston *Gazette*, July 13, 1803, p. 2.

13. See John L. Allen, "Geographical Knowledge and American Images of the Louisiana Territory," *Western Historical Quarterly*, 2 (April 1971), 151-70, reprinted in this volume, 39-58.

14. Donald Jackson, "The Public Image of Lewis and Clark," *Pacific Northwest Quarterly*, 57 (January 1966), 1-7.

15. See, for example, selected issues of the Boston *Gazette* during the period from July to November 1803.

16. Lewis to Jefferson, September 23, 1806, in Jackson, *Letters*, 319-25.

17. *Jefferson's Annual Message to Congress*, December 2, 1806, in Jackson, *Letters*, 352-53.

18. Lewis to Jefferson, September 23, 1806, in Jackson, *Letters*, 321.

19. See the Pittsburgh *Western Gleaner*, May 1, 1814, p. 1.

20. Jefferson to Jonathan Williams and Charles Willson Peale, January 12, 1807, in Jackson, *Letters*, 361.

21. Jefferson to Lacépède, July 14, 1808, in Jackson, *Letters*, 443.

22. Jefferson to F. H. Alexander von Humboldt, December 6, 1813, in Jackson, *Letters*, 596.

23. Reprinted in Reuben Gold Thwaites, ed., *Original Journals of the Lewis and Clark Expedition, 1804–1806* (New York, 1904–5), 7:351-52 (hereafter Thw).

24. Thw, 7:338-42.

25. Washington, D.C. *National Intelligencer*, January 16, 1807, p. 1.

26. Philadelphia *Monthly Anthology*, March 1807, p. 3.

27. From a broadside printed and issued by C. A. Conrad, Booksellers, Philadelphia, April 1, 1807.

28. Pittsburgh *Gazette*, April 14, 1807, p. 2.

29. Jefferson to Paul Allen, August 18, 1813, in Jackson, *Letters*, 591.

30. *Monthly Anthology and Boston Review*, April 1810, 3.

31. Jefferson to Allen, August 18, 1813, in Jackson, *Letters*, 591.

32. C. A. Conrad booksellers broadside reprinted as "The Nicholas Biddle Prospectus," in Jackson, *Letters*, 547.

33. Nicholas Biddle to William Clark, May 29, 1816, in Jackson, *Letters*, 614.

34. Thomas Astley to Charles Chauncey, September 18, 1816, in Jackson, *Letters*, 622.

35. "The Nicholas Biddle Prospectus," in Jackson, *Letters*, 547.

36. Ibid.

37. Jefferson to Peter S. Du Ponceau, November 7, 1817, in Jackson, *Letters*, 632.

38. Patrick Gass, *A Journal of the Voyages and Travels of a Corps of Discovery, under the Command of Capt. Lewis and Capt. Clarke of the Army of the United States*, ed. David McKeehan (1807; reprint, Minneapolis, 1958).

39. An excellent discussion of the "Apocrypha" may be found in Paul Russell Cutright, *A History of the Lewis and Clark Journals* (Norman, Okla., 1976), 33-39.

40. The authorship of these spurious accounts is not known. Most of them carried no compiler or editor or author credit. The exception is a series, printed in Philadelphia and Baltimore in 1812 and 1813, which were supposedly authored by a "William Fisher, Esq." A search of city registries for Philadelphia and Baltimore in those two years revealed no William Fisher.

41. See Jackson Kelley, *Geographical Sketch*, 20th Cong., 1st sess., 1828, H. Doc. 139.

42. From the advertisement for McVickar's edition of the *History of the Expedition under the Command of Captains Lewis and Clark: To the Sources of the Missouri, . . .*, ed. Nicholas Biddle (Philadelphia, 1814), published by Harpers and Brothers, New York, 1842.

43. Reprinted in Archer Butler Hulbert, *The Call of the Columbia: Iron Men and Saints Take the Oregon Trail, 1830–1835* (Colorado Springs, 1934), 67, et seq.

44. For an excellent account of Coues and the editing of the 1893 edition see Cutright, *History of the Journals*, 73-103.

45. Ibid., 82.

46. Elliott Coues, "Description of the Original Journals and Field Notes of Lewis and Clark," *Proceedings of the American Philosophical Society*, 42 (no. 140, 1893).

47. Coues, *History of the Expedition*, 1:xx.

48. Walter Prescott Webb, *The Great Plains* (New York, 1931), 143-44.

49. The appendix was volume seven while the eighth volume was an atlas which contained cartographic materials reportedly associated with the expedition.

50. For a good rendering of the major publications dealing with Lewis and Clark and the expedition, see Cutright, *History of the Journals*, 202-23.

51. See, for example, the 1969 edition of the *Encyclopedia Americana* which states that "Sacagawea displayed remarkable ability as a guide, threading the way accurately to her country." And in the *World Book* (also a 1969 edition) we find that "Sacagawea was the principal guide of the expedition to the Pacific Ocean and back." Fortunately, in a recent edition of *The World Book* the article on Lewis and Clark, contributed by the author of this essay, contains no such misinformation.

52. Donald Culross Peattie, *Forward the Nation* (New York, 1942), 56-57.

53. Agnes C. Laut, *Pathfinders of the West* (Freeport, N.Y., 1904), 332.

54. James Daugherty, *Of Courage Undaunted* (New York, 1951), 33.

55. Cutright, *History of the Journals*, 177.

On Reading
Lewis and Clark
The Last Twenty Years

Gary E. Moulton

THE LEWIS AND CLARK EXPEDITION is one of the great adventure stories in American history. Everyone knows about the two captains' trek across the continent with their band of intrepid explorers. And who has not heard about Sacagawea, the young Shoshone girl who accompanied the party with her newborn baby strapped to her back? The journey is filled with tales of high excitement: of dangerous encounters with the natives; of hair-raising river crossings and precipitous mountain traverses; of hunger, thirst, and bodily fatigue. It remains for all time a story of endurance, discovery, and achievement.

Yet, what sets this romantic and stirring event apart from other western epics is the true and undisputed evidence upon which it is based. Had the captains and several enlisted men not kept daily journals of their activities—recording events, observations, and impressions—their important discoveries might just be more wide-eyed tales spread by would-be adventurers. There is, then, a literary adventure awaiting the reader of Lewis and Clark. Not only can we vicariously relive the experiences of the Corps of Discovery in the men's own words, but we can also read exciting literature by writers who have thrilled to the story.

LEWIS AND CLARK RENASCENCE

In 1968, Don Jackson reviewed Lewis and Clark literature in an essay published in *Montana The Magazine of Western History*. Because of the significant flowering of literature on the expedition since, and to acknowledge the debt owed Jackson for the current state of Lewis and Clark scholarship, it is appropriate now to view again the literary landscape of the expedition.[1] The quantity and quality of writing on the subject during the last two decades is largely due to Jackson's efforts, for he not only provided new primary sources with his magisterial *Letters of the Lewis and Clark Expedition* in 1962, but he also contributed significantly to the literary renascence of Lewis and Clark studies. In his own work and as editor of the University of Illinois Press, where he guided important books about Lewis and Clark into print, Jackson set a high standard. And in *Among the Sleeping Giants*, his last published book before his death, Jackson brought together his final reflections on the expedition.[2]

The Lewis and Clark renascence also owes a heavy debt to three periodical publications. Since 1974, the Lewis and Clark Trail Heritage Foundation has published *We Proceeded On*, a quarterly periodical devoted entirely to the study of the expedition, containing feature articles by scholars and enthusiasts.[3] The *Bulletin* of the Missouri Historical Society, St. Louis, now titled *Gateway Heritage*, has also been an important vehicle for writing on Lewis and Clark. Since the 1960s, it has carried numerous articles and essays by Lewis and Clark scholars on the expedition. And *Montana* has been an outlet for at least twenty-five Lewis and Clark articles that have been published since its first issue in 1951.[4]

THE ORIGINAL DOCUMENTS

One of the most important recent events for Lewis and Clark scholarship was the decision to publish a new edition of the journals. Playing a key role, Don Jackson expressed what others had believed for some time when he told Missouri Historical Society members in 1967 that it was time to produce a new and standard edition of the journals. A decade later, an editor at the University of Nebraska

Press took up Jackson's challenge and enlisted the support of the university's Center for Great Plains Studies, which hired Jackson as a consultant. After a year's work, Jackson had obtained the cooperation of the manuscript-holding repositories and written the first proposal for federal funding. By July 1979, I began directing *The Journals of the Lewis and Clark Expedition*, and to date an *Atlas* and three volumes of journal material have been published.[5]

Ironically, the new edition comes not at the beginning of the renaissance of expedition scholarship but during its growth. As one reviewer of the edition queried, "Are we on the verge of a new burst of Lewis and Clark material? Or has the wave already crested, with these *Journals* the culmination rather than the incubator of inquiry?" Lewis and Clark enthusiasts hope it is the former.[6]

This new edition differs from earlier ones because it is not the result of a discovery of original documents, even though we have recently seen a most important discovery of new material. In 1953, in St. Paul, Minnesota, descendants of a Civil War general discovered sixty-seven loose sheets of expedition field notes in an antique attic desk. The first pages cover the period from December 1803 to May 1804 while the party was camped in Illinois across from St. Louis; the remaining documents take up the writing in May 1804 and continue sporadically until April 1805, when the party left Fort Mandan in present-day North Dakota. A court case to determine ownership, which Calvin Tomkins thoroughly discussed in *New Yorker* magazine, delayed publication of these important documents. Eventually, Ernest S. Osgood edited the documents—some of the most difficult from the exploration—as *The Field Notes of Captain William Clark*. Osgood also presented his findings about the provenance of the documents, their place among the expedition's records, and why Clark kept such notes.

Discussions of the journals themselves must include Paul Russell Cutright's *A History of the Lewis and Clark Journals*. Cutright traced the provenance and distribution of the diaries by the two captains and four enlisted men, followed the publication history of the journals, and evaluated the editors of the various editions, from Nicholas Biddle in 1814 to Osgood and Jackson in the 1960s. Cutright also collaborated with Michael J. Brodhead in a biography of Biddle's editorial heir, Elliott Coues, and he worked with original material when he compared a fair copy of Private Joseph Whitehouse's journal found in 1966 with its original version. Because the copy extended the soldier's journal writing nearly five months, it was an important discovery and is discussed by Cutright in his *History* and in an article, "The Journal of Private Joseph Whitehouse: A Soldier with Lewis and Clark." This new Whitehouse material will appear in print in its entirety for the first time in the new edition of the journals.

How to interpret the journals has also been a subject for writers on Lewis and Clark. Don Jackson's "Some Advice for the Next Editor of Lewis and Clark," for example, asks two intriguing questions: do we have all the journals and other documents, and how and when were the journals produced? I have tried to answer these questions in the introduction to volume two of the *Journals*, while declaring that a final answer may not be possible. The first question I addressed in an article in *Montana*, "The Missing Journals of Meriwether Lewis," where I concluded that there are probably no lost journals. We seem to have the full corpus of Lewis's journal writing, with the exception of some lost notes possibly kept during the trip over the Rocky Mountains and during the fall of 1805. In "The Specialized Journals of Lewis and Clark," I investigated the six notebooks that included the men's observations on astronomy, botany, zoology, and weather.

New cartographic materials have also come to light in recent years. W. Raymond Wood and I described a long-lost series of maps that had been made for Prince Maximilian in 1833 from originals owned by Clark at St. Louis. In the care of the Joslyn Art Museum, Omaha, since 1962, these maps show Clark's detailed charting of the Missouri River below Fort Mandan—an area for which no large-scale maps from the expedition are known to exist. The Clark-Maximilian maps also fill important gaps in Clark's mapping of the Yellowstone River on the return trip in 1806. In another essay, Wood follows Clark's mapping across the state of Missouri and reveals a previously hidden map from Clark's field notes. Scholars have also reinterpreted some existing maps, such as Stephen A. Chomko's determination that a map printed by Reuben Gold Thwaites is in fact a post-expeditionary work, probably made about 1807 or 1810.

THE PARTY

During the resurgence in Lewis and Clark studies, the expedition leaders have not received the biographical attention they deserve. Existing biographies are inadequate and concentrate mostly on the day-to-day activities during the expedition, and they are not well documented. Clark has yet to receive a full-scale biography. We need modern studies of the men, of their lives before the exploration, and of their careers afterward. Although the expedition was the high point of the men's lives, authors must understand that the captains' lives, characters, and careers were not entirely formed or devoted to those few years.

The short and tragic life of Lewis has inspired more writing than that of Clark. Rochonne Abrams wrote three articles on Lewis's youth and his life after the expedition, but she added no new facts, advanced no new interpretations, and was unable to take advantage of Don Jackson's important discovery that Lewis may not have been enlisted as Jefferson's secretary specifically to prepare him for western exploration. It appears that Jefferson wanted to use Lewis's knowledge of military personnel to strengthen the officer ranks. Jackson's essay, "Jefferson, Meriwether Lewis, and the Reduction of the United States Army," is exactly the sort of special study that needs to be done on the men.[7]

The circumstances of Lewis's death continue to be a fascinating question for study, despite general acceptance that it was suicide. For most, evidence included in Jackson's *Letters* settled the matter; and in "A Footnote to the Lewis and Clark Expedition," Jackson discussed Lewis's death at length, convincingly reiterating his conviction that Lewis died by his own hand. Howard I. Kushner approached the question of "The Suicide of Meriwether Lewis" as a psychoanalytic investigation, using psychological studies of suicide, and found an explanation in the effects of "incomplete mourning." Kushner surmised that because of his youth Lewis had not completed the process of mourning his father's and stepfather's deaths. Kushner also scrutinized Lewis's relationship with his mother. Lacking documentary evidence to support his conclusion, Kushner built his case almost entirely on supposition, a weak device for historical inquiry, and he is wrong on an important point—that few historians accept the suicide theory.

Jerome O. Steffen's *William Clark: Jeffersonian Man on the Frontier* is a thematic study rather than a traditional biography. Steffen was less interested in Clark's actual career than he was in how that career mirrored changes in American society as it moved from Jeffersonianism to Jacksonianism. John L. Loos provided better information on Clark's years after the expedition in "William Clark: Indian Agent." It is easy to forget that Clark spent the greater part of his career in St. Louis as a federal agent of Indian affairs. An effective and conscientious officer, Clark promoted the best interests of his Indian wards and gained the respect of his white contemporaries. "Although Clark's treatment of the Indians may now be considered to have been paternalistic and patronizing," Loos concluded, "by the standards of his own time and place it was fair and often compassionate."

Although abundant information exists about the captains, most of the corpsmen lived obscure lives before and after their season of glory and hardly qualify for biographies. One member of the party, however, has recently received book-length treatment: Clark's black slave, York. Robert Betts went *In Search of York* and discovered the specter of racism. Tales of York's sexual prowess, for instance, rest largely on racial bias; his relations with Indian women were similar to other men in the party. York seems to have performed his full share of duties and even carried a gun, a privilege not allowed Virginia slaves.

Charles G. Clarke gave brief sketches of all *The Men of the Lewis and Clark Expedition* and also provided a count of the men that is probably as accurate as can be achieved considering the difficulty of identifying the French *engagés*. His short biographical sketches yield about as much information as may ever be known about many of the men. Biographies of ten expedition members or persons closely connected with the expedition are included in LeRoy R. Hafen's *The Mountain Men and the Fur Trade of the Far West*, due largely to their later fur-trading careers.

Some expedition members appear only infrequently and insignificantly in the journals, but Joseph and Reubin Field are mentioned repeatedly. One or both brothers seemed always to draw special assignments and difficult tasks, as Lewis later noted: "It was their peculiar fate to have been engaged in all the most dangerous and difficult scenes of the voyage, in which they uniformly accquitted themselves with much honor."[8] Roy E. Appleman discovered and presented what scant evidence is available about them in "Joseph and Reubin Field, Kentucky Frontiersmen of the Lewis and Clark Expedition and Their Father, Abraham." Wisely, he concentrated on their early and later years, especially Joseph's, writing that their lives belong "to the short and simple annals of the poor—and forgotten."

Sacagawea has probably received more attention than any other member of the expedition, save the captains. The devotion lavished on her led Bernard DeVoto to observe that some may believe that "Lewis, Clark, and their command were privileged to assist in the Sacajawea Expedition."[9] During the last two decades her acclaim has not diminished and no amount of historical scholarship has been able to correct the distortions. Despite incontrovertible evidence to the contrary, for instance, the belief still persists that she lived into the 1880s at the Wind River Reservation in Wyoming. She actually died at Fort Manuel in South Dakota in 1812, a fact that has been known since 1920 and confirmed beyond doubt from a document by Clark in Jackson's edition of *Letters*.

Obvious and seemingly trivial items, such as the spelling of her name and its meaning and pronunciation, generate heated debate. The captains' journals give it as Sacagawea—or some close approximate—and translate it as a Hidatsa name meaning Bird Woman. Their rendering of the word shows that they pronounced it Sa-ca-ga-we-a, stressed each syllable equally, and sounded the *a*'s and the *g* hard. Alternate spellings, pronunciations, and translations of the word have had to rely on complicated interpretations that argue against the original records.

Most of what we know about Sacagawea is in the expedition journals and is very meager material on which to build a legend. She and her husband, Toussaint Charbonneau, were not hired as guides, but as interpreters and were indispensable in that capacity among her people and other Shoshonean-speaking Indians in the Rockies. She recognized some geographic features when the party reached her homeland in southwestern Montana, and her presence with a baby calmed Indian fears that the party was a war expedition. Beyond this, she may have been a pleasant companion, and her child, Jean Baptiste, probably delighted the men, but romantic links between Clark and her have no foundation in the record and are latter-day fantasies.

James P. Ronda in his work on *Lewis and Clark among the Indians* superbly took up these matters and also listed the major sources on the Shoshone woman. The paragraphs above borrow from his short essay and from the several works of Irving W. Anderson, the ablest student of the Charbonneaus. A good place to start is Anderson's essay, "A Charbonneau Family Portrait," which follows the life of Sacagawea, as well as the interesting careers of father and son. His other articles on Sacagawea form the basis for much of the current, undramatized view of the woman, as do E. G. Chuinard's "The Actual Role of Bird Woman" and Blanche Schroer's "Boat-Pusher or Bird-Woman? Sacagawea or Sacajawea?" The best single book-length account is Harold P. Howard's *Sacajawea*, although the spelling of her name and some of his interpretations are dated. Ella E. Clark and Margot Edmonds's *Sacagawea of the Lewis and Clark Expedition* is a regrettable book. Although the correct information was available, they perpetuate the notion that Sacagawea lived into the 1880s, basing it on more faulty evidence. Readers still await the full, unfictionalized account of the only woman to make the continental crossing.

THE TRAIL

Studies of the explorers' route have concentrated mainly on retracing the trail. Most are travel accounts that describe to armchair travelers the changes wrought upon the land since the expedition. These works can quickly devolve into stories of "how I spent my summer vacation." Serious readers may not be interested in such books—a shelf-full of such books already exists—but creative accounts of this sort do provide enjoyable reading. Most recently Dayton Duncan followed the trail *Out West* and tied his own experiences to those of Lewis and Clark. This New Englander's encounters with western folk and with history are both entertaining and thoughtful.

Two other works stand out as the best in this genre: Roy E. Appleman, *Lewis and Clark*, and Gerald S. Snyder, *In the Footsteps of Lewis and Clark*. Commissioned by the National Park Service, Appleman's book contains appendices that include discussions of major historic sites along the route. The first part of his book is probably the best brief, single account of the expedition in print. Snyder's book comes from the National Geographic Society and is typical of its publications—well illustrated and personalized. Archie Satterfield also followed *The Lewis and Clark Trail* the full distance, while Ann Rogers pursued *Lewis and Clark in Missouri*. Gerald W. Olmsted's *Fielding's Lewis and Clark Trail* is the most recent work of this type. Less well done is David Freeman Hawke's survey of *Those Tremendous Mountains*.

Among specialized books about the trail, John L. Allen's *Passage through the Garden* will remain a classic. More important to Allen than the general route or the location of campsites or events are several larger questions. Allen investigated the captains' image of the broad continent they were exploring. At strategic points, Allen explained, they took time from their march to look ahead to a geography of expectation and to look beyond to a geography of imagination. Images before, during, and after their exploration colored the men's vision of the West. Allen's study opened new doors of understanding of the leaders' geographic preconceptions, of their reordering of ideas in the face of topographic realities, and of their attachment to certain incorrect theories.

Writers have also been interested in particular locales along the party's traverse. Bob Saindon cleared up some confusion about the identification of rivers in his essay, "The River Which Scolds at All Others." He revealed that Lewis and Clark were correct all along in declaring the present Milk River to be the one that the Hidatsa Indians called *Am-mah-tah ru-shush-sher*, "the scolding river." Editor Nicholas Biddle mistakenly presumed it to be the Marias River, causing some confusion over the years. In "Lewis and Clark on the Upper Missouri: Decision at the Marias," John Allen described how the captains' keen geographic intuition led them to distinguish correctly between the Marias and Missouri rivers.[10] More than a week's worth of investigation at the rivers' confluence proved the leaders correct.

John J. Peebles in three articles in *Idaho Yesterdays* examined the route and campsites of the party in his state on both their outbound and return trips; the essays were later published as a single pamphlet, *Lewis and Clark in Idaho*. His impressive work is augmented by excellent maps, especially the large folded map of the Lolo Trail. Harry M. Majors, in "Lewis and Clark Enter the Rocky Mountains," disputed Peebles's reconstruction of the party's route near Lost Trail Pass, arguing that Clark's compass readings were off. In other areas, Majors concurred with Peebles. Improving on Peeble's work, Ralph Space gave his own account of the party's difficult passage over the Lolo Trail. Writing from more than a half-century of personal experience on the Lolo Trail, Space brought insights to this portion of the expedition's route that probably cannot be matched by anyone for any other area.

In other essays on the trail, Roy E. Appleman rediscovered "The Lost Site of Camp Wood," Ernest S. Osgood followed "Clark on the Yellowstone," and John Francis McDermott discussed "William Clark's Struggle with Place Names in Upper Louisiana." Knowing the captain's carefree style with English, his difficulties with a foreign language seem guaranteed. One confusing French term for Clark was Dubois, the name of the river where the party camped during the winter of 1803–4, across from St. Louis, and in present-day Illinois. McDermott showed that the term comes from *Rivière à Dubois*, apparently named for a forgotten Frenchman (Wood) rather than after the trees; Wood's River would be a more accurate English version. McDermott also corrected a previously misidentified map from the expedition and called attention to the use of *dit* names (or nicknames) among the engagés of the party.

THE INDIANS

One of the most critical aspects of the expedition's mission, the party's relations with native peoples, has been almost entirely overlooked until recently. This is particularly surprising considering Jefferson's careful and lengthy instructions to Lewis on Indians, which read like an ethnologist's brief to a star pupil. The captain was to learn their names and number, extent and limits, intertribal relations, trading patterns, languages, occupations, food, clothing, health, types of shelter, traditions, laws, customs, morality, and religion. And Lewis was to record it all, as Jefferson put it, "at leisure times."[11]

James P. Ronda's *Lewis and Clark among the Indians* eliminates this deficiency in the literature. Not content to guide readers over well-worn paths, Ronda ventured into new territory and delved deeply into ethnographic literature, borrowing from the fields of anthropology, archaeology, and linguistics. The familiar themes and events are here also, but many are viewed in new and refreshing ways. Ronda recounted the party's confrontation with the Teton Sioux, the men's sexual relations with native women, the long days among Mandans, Hidatsas, Clatsops, and Nez Perces, the fortuitous meeting with the Lemhi Shoshones, and the deadly encounter with the Blackfeet; but he added an ethnological perspective by trying to see events from both sides. Ronda displayed admirable objectivity and was not afraid to offer controversial interpretations that go against accepted notions. These tribes had their own views on trade relations, intertribal associations and conflicts, and internal tribal politics; and many of the subtleties of these attitudes were not noticed or were misunderstood by the American leaders.

Ronda also recognized the important contributions of Indians to Clark's mapping in his essay, "'A Chart in His Way': Indian Cartography and the Lewis and Clark Expedition." In another essay, "Lewis and Clark and Enlightenment Ethnography," he discussed the Enlightenment philosophy that permeated Jefferson's instructions to Lewis regarding Indians. Here also Ronda showed that Lewis and Clark were transitional figures between the hit-and-miss ethnographers of the early nineteenth century and the trained ethnologists of later decades. Not totally unbiased observers, the captains did rise above cultural relativism and were not nearly as ethnocentric as some of their contemporaries. The expedition, Ronda found, "pioneered not only a new road across the continent but a fresh approach to the study of Indian America."

Other authors have dealt with the expedition's Indian relations from the Indian viewpoint. John C. Ewers, in "Plains Indian Reactions to the Lewis and Clark Expedition," emphasized that Plains Indians were quite accustomed to white traders and may have associated the gift-bearing captains with these merchants, thereby missing the Americans' special mission.[12] Because of such confusion, Ewers concluded, Lewis and Clark were handicapped in Indian diplomacy and were not as successful as in other endeavors. Ewers might be faulted on one point because he seemed to accept that Lewis's confrontation with the Blackfeet was the cause of the tribe's later animosity toward Americans. That assumption has since been rejected, no doubt by Ewers also.

William Nichols in "Lewis and Clark Probe the Heart of Darkness" discovered a "darker, more elusive story of failure" in the expedition's relations with native people. He contended that there was a definite change during the return journey in the explorers' treatment of and attitudes toward Indians. "They went out as explorers," he declared, "they came back as imperialists, or worse." According to Nichols, the change was nearly pathological, and he accounted for the shift by surmising that it related to the disappointment of the men not finding a water route to the coast. Gone, for Nichols, are Lewis and Clark's detached, descriptive, and scientific view of Native Americans on the return trip. Critics have commented that readers may get more of Joseph Conrad than of Lewis and Clark in his essay.

Archaeologists who study Indian sites along the Lewis and Clark route have used the captains' journals and maps as important resources. In some instances, Lewis and Clark were the first and last to describe native villages, material culture, and tribal practices just before contact with whites altered these things. Later investigators had to sift through layers of acculturation and post contact clutter to get a true picture of early native life. Two archaeological studies have focused on the captains' findings: W. Raymond Wood for the middle region of the Missouri River valley, and Robert C. Dunnell for the Bonneville area of the Columbia River.

Haruo Aoki in "What Does 'Chopunnish' Mean?" and Roderick Sprague in "The Meaning of 'Palouse'" considered some linguistic items in the journals. We have come to know the Nez Perce Indians by the French name that translates "pierced nose" rather than by their present self-designation, *Neemeepoo* (variously spelled), meaning "the people." Although a debate still continues as to whether the people actually did pierce their noses, Lewis and Clark observed them with nasal ornaments, and the best authorities today acknowledge the practice. Aoki discovered that Lewis and Clark's word "chopunnish" may derive from an obsolete self-designation, *tsoopnitpeloo*, meaning "piercing people," thus confirming the practice and Lewis and Clark's rendition of the tribe's early name. Sprague's aim was to correct the notion that the "Pelloat Pallah" (variously written) Indians of Lewis and Clark were the Palouse Indians of present-day southeastern Washington. By studying the captains' versions of the name and the tribe's location on expedition maps, he determined that the Pelloat Pallah were actually Nez Perces from villages on the Snake River.

THE EQUIPMENT

Interest in the equipment of the expedition has largely been directed toward the party's weapons. Lewis's airgun has generated as much curiosity among modern writers as it did among Indians during the trip. Mentioned about twenty times in the journals, it was used principally for impressing natives with its repeating capabilities. It may also have been used for hunting purposes, as airguns were certainly lethal weapons. Pumped up to nine hundred p.s.i., the thirty caliber rifled weapon could get off up to forty shots. Henry M. Stewart, Jr., a gun collector of Philadelphia, discovered that a Philadelphia gunsmith made Lewis's piece. He also tracked the actual airgun to a collector in Milwaukee, Wisconsin, and was able to purchase it for his personal collection.

Stewart wrote of his find and of airguns generally in a short article, "The American Air Gun School of 1800," while Ashley Halsey wrote a more detailed account of the gun's story for a larger audience in *American Rifleman*. That publication later featured an article by Kirk Olson, "A Lewis and Clark Rifle," in which he described the party's standard weapon, the Harpers Ferry Model 1803, and suggested the possibility that he may have found one that had made the historic trip. The essay is also a nice introduction to the production of the Model 1803 and to the variations in the weapon that became a standard military piece and that was in use until the 1840s. Olson's main point was that the fifteen rifles made for Lewis "were not prototypes or patterns of the Model 1803, but were instead predecessors in the evolution of the 1803 rifle."

Scientific and astronomical equipment used on the expedition is an interest of Silvio Bedini of the Smithsonian Institution, one of the premier scholars of Jeffersonian science. In "The Scientific Instruments of the Lewis and Clark Expedition," Bedini explained that by Lewis and Clark's time the science of astronomy was fairly advanced and instruments were quite sophisticated. Latitude could be determined with some precision, but discovering exact longitude suffered for want of a reliable timepiece. Lewis and Clark were plagued not only with a malfunctioning chronometer but also with neglect in winding it. In their scientific baggage, the captains also carried artificial horizons, octants, quadrants, sextants, and compasses. Bedini discussed these instruments, Lewis's training in their use, his method of "shooting the stars," and the results of the work, which suffered because of time constraints, unreliable equipment, inexperience and insufficient skills, and difficult field conditions.[13] In spite of this imprecision, Clark's maps are masterfully executed and are models of field cartography.

THE MEDICAL ASPECTS

Lewis and Clark were their own physicians. For twenty-eight months and across eight thousand miles of wilderness they doctored themselves and their party. Starting out in the company of "robust, healthy young men," the captains nonetheless had to face the ills that human flesh is heir to—abscesses and boils, dysentery, malaria, pleurisy, and rheumatism. Injuries and accidents were also recurring daily events—bruises and dislocations from spills and falls, frostbite, and snakebites. Contagious diseases troubled the party as well; colds and venereal disease were not uncommon ailments. Yet at the end of the trip Lewis could happily report that they had returned in good health; during the entire expedition only one man died.

In spite of such success, there has been criticism of President Jefferson for not adding a medical doctor to the party. E. G. Chuinard answered the critics in "Thomas Jefferson and the Corps of Discovery: Could He Have Done More?" and in *Only One Man Died*. Chuinard emphasized that Lewis received tutoring from the nation's best medical authorities prior to setting out and, perhaps more importantly, he accorded the men great care and concern. As Jefferson would observe, Lewis was "careful as a father of those committed to his charge," which is confirmed in the captains' care for ill men during the sickly days at Fort Clatsop.[14] Chuinard concluded that it is "doubtful that any medical practitioner of the time could have done any better or even as well, as did the two captains."

Chuinard's impressive book treats the medical practices of Lewis and Clark's day, enabling us to understand the captains' choice of bleeding and purging as routine expedition remedies: It was the accepted practice of the period. Chuinard also examined Lewis's background for medicinal knowledge, gained partly from his mother who grew and dispensed vegetable drugs. During the continental crossing, Lewis occasionally concocted a strong brew of local plants for his own relief. Finally, Chuinard carefully and critically followed the captains' transcontinental medical practices and explained their procedures in the light of modern medical knowledge.

Other authors have examined the doctoring captains. Paul Russell Cutright in "I gave him barks and saltpeter . . . ," concentrated on the captains' medicines, while noting the more significant illnesses, as does Drake W. Will in "Lewis and Clark: Westering Physicians." Best known from the captains' medical chest are the six hundred bilious pills—an effective and fast-acting laxative made from calomel and jalap—that they got from Dr. Benjamin Rush of Philadelphia. Their pharmacopoeia also included quinine, diuretics, laudanum, poultices, astringents, and emetics. Herb therapy was also an available remedy, found on the nearest bush or shrub. Donald Snoddy compiled all references from the journals relating to medical problems and practices, and Cindy Fent wrote a brief overview of the party's health procedures. Fent faulted the leaders for not keeping better records of medical matters, but considering the range, depth, and constancy of their journal-keeping labors the criticism seems trifling at best.

THE NATURAL HISTORY

Realizing that Lewis and Clark could become discoverers of a host of new plants and animals, Jefferson instructed Lewis carefully. He told Lewis to be particularly conscientious in recording "the soil & face of the country, it's growth & vegetable productions . . . [and] the animals of the country generally, & especially those not known in the U.S." He also sent his young protégé to Philadelphia for rudimentary training in botany, zoology, and other sciences. Occasionally in the journals Lewis categorized species under the Linnaean system, which had gained acceptance by his time.

Jefferson has been criticized for not sending a naturalist as well as a physician with the expedition. As the noted ornithologist and editor of the journals, Elliott Coues, commented: "the most serious defect in the organization of the Expedition was the lack of some trained scientist." But the consummate student of the corps' naturalist work, Paul Russell Cutright, defended Jefferson's decision in his *Lewis and Clark: Pioneering Naturalists*. He pointed to the paucity of trained naturalists in America at the time, among whom Lewis was nearly equal, and that few of them could have stood up to the rigors of wilderness travel. Cutright declared that Lewis was blessed with "an outstanding, inherent observational competence, an all-inclusive interest, and an objective, systematic, philosophical approach to understanding the natural world." For example, when Lewis counted eighteen tail feathers on the western blue grouse he recalled that the familiar ruffed grouse had exactly the same number. Cutright stressed that few of Lewis's contemporaries would be so keen in observation or knowledgeable about species. Chuinard echoed these points in his essay, "Thomas Jefferson and the Corps of Discovery: Could He Have Done More?" Lewis's discourses on the animals of the West written during the winter at Fort Clatsop and his botanical writings, especially his acute ecological distinctions, confirm the wisdom of Jefferson's decision.

Cutright's *Lewis and Clark: Pioneering Naturalists*, surely his most significant scholarly achievement, is one of the most important books on the expedition in our time. Concerned primarily with new discoveries, Cutright did not attempt to catalog all journal references to plants and animals. He wrote the book principally to demonstrate the importance of Lewis and Clark's scientific work, particularly in the fields of botany and zoology. In this he succeeded marvelously. Since Cutright's book, which will not soon be superseded, no one can question the natural history contributions of the captains, especially Lewis.

During the last two decades, the range and quality of Lewis and Clark studies have been impressive and our knowledge has increased substantially. The expedition continues to fascinate us, and Don Jackson's advice of twenty years ago to anyone interested in Lewis and Clark is still the best: "to read everything you can lay your hands on." Because of Jackson and the burst of writing about the expedition, we now have much more to read, and much of it the best writing on the Corps of Discovery.

Notes

1. This essay was originally published in 1988 and thus does not review material published after that date.

2. Donald Jackson, "On Reading Lewis and Clark," *Montana The Magazine of Western History*, 18 (Summer 1968), 2-7. Some of the items that are mentioned in this essay were published before 1968. This was done in order to show the influence of Jackson's work in the *Letters* and to pick up some sources that he did not mention in the earlier article; his essay did not include periodical items, for instance.

3. For many years, *We Proceeded On* was superbly edited by Robert E. Lange of Portland, Oregon; it is now headquartered in Great Falls, Montana. I have decided not to discuss articles in *We Proceeded On* in this essay, because space will not allow an adequate discussion of its many excellent articles. No one doing serious study of the expedition can overlook it, and anyone interested in the Lewis and Clark story ought to be a subscriber. I also do not consider children's literature or fiction in this essay.

4. Other trail state periodicals have also carried important essays about the expedition, including *Idaho Yesterdays, Nebraska History, North Dakota History, Missouri Historical Review, Oregon Historical Quarterly, South Dakota History,* and *Pacific Northwest Quarterly.*

5. As of 1997, eleven volumes of the journal material have been published.

6. Harry Fritz reviewing volume three of *The Journals of the Lewis and Clark Expedition*, in *We Proceeded On*, 13 (November 1987), 31. Reviews of the new edition are being carried volume-by-volume in that and many other historical periodicals, including *Montana The Magazine of Western History.*

7. Donald Jackson, "Jefferson, Meriwether Lewis, and the Reduction of the United States Army," is reprinted in this volume, 59-71.

8. Lewis to Henry Dearborn, January 15, 1807, in *Letters of the Lewis and Clark Expedition with Related Documents, 1783–1854*, ed. Donald Jackson, 2d ed. (Urbana, Ill., 1978), 1:367.

9. Bernard DeVoto, *The Course of Empire* (Boston, 1952), 478.

10. John L. Allen, "Lewis and Clark on the Upper Missouri: Decision at the Marias," is reprinted in this volume, 119-42.

11. Jefferson's instructions to Lewis, June 20, 1803, in Jackson, *Letters*, 1:63, reprinted in this volume, 31-38.

12. John C. Ewers, "Plains Indian Reactions to the Lewis and Clark Expedition," is reprinted in this volume, 171-82.

13. Silvio A. Bedini, "The Scientific Instruments of the Lewis and Clark Expedition," is reprinted in this volume, 143-65.

14. Jefferson's "Memoir of Meriwether Lewis," in *The History of the Expedition under the Command of Lewis and Clark, to the Sources of the Missouri River, Thence across the Rocky Mountains and Down the Columbia River to the Pacific Ocean, Performed during the Years 1804–5–6, by Order of the Government of the United States*, ed. Elliott Coues (1893; reprint, New York, 1965), 1:xxi.

'The Writingest Explorers'
The Lewis and Clark Expedition in American Historical Literature

James P. Ronda

ON SEPTEMBER 26, 1806, JUST FOUR DAYS AFTER RETURNING from the Pacific Coast, Meriwether Lewis and William Clark settled into a rented room at Pierre Chouteau's and "commenced wrighting."[1] Journal entries, scientific observations, ethnographic notes, and detailed maps—a virtual encyclopedia of the West—needed to be examined, catalogued, and arranged for further study. Surveying the literary remains of their expedition, Lewis and Clark surely would have agreed with historian Donald Jackson that they were the "writingest explorers" the West had yet seen.[2] The struggle to understand the meaning of what Clark once called a "vast, Hazidous and fatiguing enterprize" began in that St. Louis room and continues into our own time.[3]

Both the explorers and those who followed them sensed that the expedition occupied a special place in American history. But the exact character of that place has often proved elusive. Confusion and ambiguity about the meaning of the venture surfaced no more than two days after the party's return. St. Louis townspeople, bent on celebrating the homecoming, hosted a grand dinner and ball at William Christy's city tavern. Those festivities included a round of toasts. Such expressions were an indicator of the expedition's public image, a kind of initial evaluation of what the explorers had accomplished. And if the drinking at Christy's meant anything, merchants and traders were not quite sure what Lewis and Clark had done. The toasts that night praised the nation and the Louisiana Territory, memorialized Christopher Columbus and George Washington, and lauded "the fair daughters of Louisiana—May they ever bestow their smiles on hardihood and virtuous valor." Once Lewis and Clark withdrew, as custom required, they were cheered for "their perilous services" to the nation.[4]

The exuberant townspeople of St. Louis were not alone in their confusion about the expedition's significance. Was the great trek nothing more than a grand adventure at public expense? When a group of citizens at Fincastle, Virginia, sent their congratulations, the testimonial emphasized daring against terrible odds. "You have navigated bold and unknown rivers, traversed Mountains which had never before been impressed with the footsteps of civilized man, and surmounted every obstacle, which climate, Nature, or ferocious Savages could throw in your way." A passing mention of extending geographic knowledge was overwhelmed by a burst of patriotic rhetoric comparing Lewis and Clark to Columbus. Fincastle residents were ready to predict that the explorers would enjoy "pure and unsullied" fame. But the reasons for that reputation seemed hard to define.[5]

St. Louis merchants and Fincastle well-wishers could be excused for their uncertainty about the journey. They had seen nothing of the journals, maps, and specimens brought back from the West. Yet the public confusion about the expedition was shared by Lewis and Clark as well as Jefferson. Had the undertaking achieved its central purpose? From its inception the enterprise had one goal. As the president put it to Lewis in June 1803: "The object of your mission is to explore the Missouri river, & such principal stream[s] of it, as, by it's course and communication with the waters of the Pacific ocean, whether the Columbia, Oregan, Colorado, or any other river may offer the most direct and practicable water communication across this continent for the purposes of commerce."[6] When Lewis appeared to stray from that objective, Jefferson reined him in with a sharp reminder that "the object of your mission is single, the direct water communication from sea to sea formed by the bed of the Missouri and perhaps the Oregon."[7] Whatever else his Corps of Discovery might accomplish, whether in science or diplomacy, Jefferson was intent on tracing that Passage to India.

Sitting in their St. Louis rooms, the president's men had to face an unpleasant reality. They had failed to find that "direct water communication from sea to sea." Indeed, what they had come upon were mountain barriers that made such a passage virtually impossible. Torn between accurate reporting and the desire to satisfy their patron, the explorers sought to put the best face on failure. Writing to Jefferson just one day after the end of the journey, Lewis assured the president that the expedition "penitrated the Continent of North America to the Pacific Ocean, and sufficiently explored the interior of the country to affirm with confidence that we have discovered the most practicable rout[e] which dose exist across the continent by means of the navigable branches of the Missouri and Columbia Rivers." But what the explorer gave with one hand he snatched away with the other. Lewis admitted that the passage, while valuable for the fur trade, was hardly a plain path across the continent. There was no direct water communication and the northern overland route charted by the captains would never take the place of sea lanes around the Cape of Good Hope. As Lewis delicately put it, the overland path was useful only for goods "not bulky brittle nor of a very perishable nature."[8] Clark walked the same tightrope. Writing a letter he knew would be quickly printed in many western newspapers, the explorer pronounced the venture "completely successful." But there was the inevitable hedge. Clark had "no hesitation in declaring that such as nature has permitted it we have discovered the best rout[e] which does exist across the continent of North America in that direction." But what nature had permitted was not quite what Jefferson had in mind.[9]

The president's own understanding of the expedition proved equally selective. Jefferson's initial reaction—"unspeakable joy"— at the safe return of the party was reflected in his December 1806 annual message to Congress. Legislators were told that the expedition "had all the success which could have been expected." The measure of that success came as the explorers "traced the Missouri nearly to it's source, descended the Columbia to the Pacific ocean, ascertained with accuracy the geography of that interesting communication across our continent, learnt the character of the country, of it's commerce and inhabitants."[10] By the time Lewis got to Washington in January 1807, Jefferson must have begun to realize that his "interesting communication" was still more hope than reality.

When the expedition was in its earliest planning stages, Attorney General Levi Lincoln warned Jefferson about the high price of failure. Lincoln evidently had seen an early draft of expedition instructions, a draft containing little about ethnography and natural history. Lincoln suggested that "some new aspects be usefully given to the undertaking, and others made more prominent." As Lincoln saw it, the expedition ought to pursue scientific objectives so that if the passage to the Pacific proved illusory there would still be much to claim.[11] The attorney general's suggestions were both politically astute and strangely prophetic. By the summer of 1808 Jefferson was busy reshaping the meaning of the Lewis and Clark Expedition. Writing to French naturalist Bernard Lacépède, he asserted that "the addition to our kno[w]le[d]ge, in every department, resulting from that tour, of Messrs. Lewis and Clarke, has entirely fulfilled my expectations in setting it on foot."[12] As the hope of a water passage faded, the image of the expedition as a great scientific enterprise grew brighter. Jefferson's correspondence with Bernard McMahon and Charles Willson Peale pointed to that new understanding of the expedition's central mission. Levi Lincoln had been right. Science, the shape of strange animals, exotic Indians, and useful plants might rescue the whole venture from oblivion.

The emphasis on scientific accomplishment fit Lewis's personal conception of what he always called his "tour" of the West. Although he once told guests at a Washington dinner that the establishment of an American trading post on the Columbia would prove the expedition's greatest attainment, that bit of geopolitical fortune-telling was not at the heart of Lewis's writing.[13] In the spring of 1807 Philadelphia printer John Conrad issued a prospectus for Lewis's proposed three-volume expedition report. Lewis intended that the first volume be "a narrative of the voyage, with a description of some of the most remarkable places in those hitherto unknown wilds of America . . . together with an itinerary of the most direct and practicable rout[e] across the Continent of North America." Here was the tale of adventure sought by an enthusiastic public. But in keeping with the new emphasis on expedition science, Lewis promised two full volumes packed with ethnography, botany, zoology, and "other natural phenomena which were met with in the course of this interesting tour."[14] In many ways this prospectus was the formal announcement of the new wisdom about the expedition. Jefferson's desired passage and the failure to find it was lost in glowing promises of memorable scientific advances.

The success of this new interpretation depended on the timely publication of Lewis's history of the expedition. By mid-1807 he had made preliminary arrangements for printing the work. Plans were also underway for engraving maps and plates. The only thing lacking was a completed manuscript. Nearly a year later an impatient Jefferson prodded Lewis for news. "We have no tidings yet of the forwardness of your printer." The president could only hope that "the first part will not be delayed much longer." A full year after administering that polite scolding, Jefferson admitted that "every body is impatient" for the great work.[15]

Word of Lewis's suicide at Grinder's Stand on the Natchez Trace in 1809 was shocking enough. Almost as stunning was news that Lewis had made virtually no progress on his literary project. In late 1809 Lewis's publishers wrote Jefferson with the sorry news that "Govr. Lewis never furnished us with a line of the M.S. nor indeed could we ever hear any thing from him respecting it tho frequent applications to that effect were made to him."[16] Lewis's failure as an author and his untimely death now set off a complex series of events that finally led William Clark to obtain the services of Philadelphia lawyer and litterateur Nicholas Biddle. What Biddle finally brought to press in 1814 was essentially what Lewis had proposed as his first volume. Here, in an edition of only 1,417 copies, was the story of the expedition as a glorious western adventure. Readers would find a powerful story but no science. As Jefferson lamented to Alexander von Humboldt, "the botanical and zoological discoveries of Lewis will probably experience greater delay, and become known to the world thro other channels before that volume will be ready."[17]

Publication delays, omission of the vital scientific data, and poor sales all conspired to produce an expedition record with little public appeal. Stripped of its intellectual achievements, the Lewis and Clark Expedition was increasingly viewed by Americans as a great national adventure. Jefferson's bold western thrust had been transformed into a symbol for a westering nation. But the symbol lacked substance. No wagon trains followed the expedition's overland track. American diplomats caught up in the Oregon question used the voyages and travels of Captain Robert Gray and the Astorians to justify Yankee claims on the Columbia. An occasional eastern promoter might call up the captains' ghosts but even those appearances were few and far between. Americans had not lost a national fascination with exploring the West. Lewis and Clark simply could not compete with the much-publicized exploits of John Charles Frémont and other pathfinders. Jefferson's Corps of Discovery had been eclipsed by Frémont and explorer-scientists like John Wesley Powell, Clarence King, and F. V. Hayden. Eliminated from the scientific lists, Lewis and Clark fared poorly against popular heroes like Jesse James and Kit Carson. By the late nineteenth century the expedition had almost disappeared from the historical landscape.[18]

The struggle to recover the expedition and its meanings for American history began in June 1891 when New York publisher Francis P. Harper wrote naturalist and ex-army surgeon Elliott Coues asking if he would be interested in editing a new printing of the Biddle narrative. What pushed Harper to make such a suggestion has never been clearly explained. Harper and Brothers had obtained copyright to the Biddle edition in 1842 and had over the years issued printings of an abridged version of the narrative. In 1891 Harper evidently intended no more than a reprint of Biddle with some explanatory notes. Whatever Harper's motives and plans, the choice of Coues was an inspired one. During the 1860s Coues served as an army surgeon at a number of frontier posts. That western exposure and later work for the Northern Boundary Commission and the United States Geological and Geographical Survey of the Territories gave Coues's lifelong interest in ornithology a wider field. Here was a man who knew much of the Lewis and Clark West from personal experience and was ready to appreciate the expedition's scientific labors.

Coues's "discovery" of the original Lewis and Clark journals at the American Philosophical Society and his cavalier treatment of those documents is a familiar story. What is important is the refurbished image of the expedition that emerged when the Biddle-Coues edition appeared in 1893. Coues centered his extensive annotations on three subjects. The eighteenth century had defined natural history in the broadest terms, encompassing everything from botany to zoology. Coues found that definition congenial to his own scientific method and busied himself annotating expedition observations on western plants and animals. Lewis had once promised a full accounting of western Indian life and material culture. Little of that ethnography made it into the Biddle narrative. The late nineteenth-century frontier had seen valuable work done by soldier-ethnographers like John Bourke and John Wesley Powell. Influenced by those examples, Coues spent considerable annotation space commenting on native customs, behavior, and objects. Finally, Coues sought to identify as many Lewis and Clark campsites as possible. He did this neither from an antiquarian passion nor a boosterism that shouted "Lewis and Clark slept here." Rather, he wanted to place Lewis and Clark at the center of western exploration. More than Frémont and the post-Civil War surveys, Lewis and Clark had scientific primacy. As Paul Cutright observed some seventy years after Coues's work first appeared, that new edition "focused attention for the first time on the vast amount of unpublished and virtually unknown scientific data in the original journals and, thereby, on the salient roles played by Lewis and Clark as outstanding pioneer naturalists."[19]

Any significant reassessment of the Lewis and Clark Expedition required publication of the original journals. Coues's annotations might suggest new directions, but they were no substitute for the captains' own words, maps, observations, and specimens. In 1901, with the twin centennials of the Louisiana Purchase and the expedition at hand, the American Philosophical Society decided to seek publication of its treasured expedition records. Negotiations with Dodd, Mead and Company followed as did a search for an editor. Reuben Gold Thwaites, then superintendent of the State Historical Society of Wisconsin, was eventually chosen for the task. Thwaites had just completed a massive edition of the *Jesuit Relations* and enjoyed a growing reputation as a documentary editor. Equally important, he had at Madison a skilled staff of research associates, including Louise Phelps Kellogg and Emma Hunt Blair. Thwaites's work on the Lewis and Clark manuscripts is well known and has received careful commentary in Paul Cutright's comprehensive *History of the Lewis and Clark Journals*. Thwaites predicted that his edition would prompt "a new view of Lewis and Clark." He was especially sanguine about prospects for a thorough evaluation of expedition science. "The voluminous scientific data here given—in botany, zoology, meteorology, geology, astronomy, and ethnology—is almost entirely a fresh contribution."[20] But Thwaites had more than science on his mind. Like his friend Frederick Jackson Turner, he believed that explorers were the vanguard in the steady westward march of the young republic. Thwaites and Turner shared the notion of sequential development on the frontier. Lewis and Clark were at the head of an irrepressible American advance to the Pacific, an advance that promised political democracy, economic prosperity, and civilized values. For Thwaites, the expedition represented "that notable enterprise in the cause of civilization."[21]

The *Original Journals of the Lewis and Clark Expedition*, published by Dodd, Mead in 1904–5, quickly found its place on library shelves and in private collections. But the volumes did not spark a substantial reevaluation of the expedition. In fact, Thwaites's own writing about Lewis and Clark remained traditional in narrative style and emphasis on high adventure. In 1904, while still working on the journals, he wrote *A Brief History of Rocky Mountain Exploration, with Especial Reference to the Expedition of Lewis and Clark*. The book offered a chronological treatment of the journey, spiced with quotes from the then-unpublished journals. Perhaps Thwaites thought reading those lines would be reward enough since the Lewis and Clark chapters never rose above simple storytelling. Thwaites claimed that the expedition was "the most important and interesting of Rocky Mountains explorations" but let readers struggle to define that import and interest.[22] Several years later Thwaites had another opportunity to explain the expedition to a wider audience. In collaboration with Calvin Noyes Kendall, he wrote *A History of the United States for Grammar Schools*.

Here was a chance to give young students a glimpse of that "new view of Lewis and Clark" promised some seven years before. But it was a promise largely unfulfilled. Seventh- and eighth-graders got a meager outline of the expedition's progress across the continent. Thwaites's own Turnerian interpretation came to the surface when students were instructed about the venture's larger meaning. "The path having now been broken by Lewis and Clark, wandering fur traders soon thronged into the Far West. Many American settlers also opened farms in what became known as the Oregon Territory, and their presence furnished a basis for our later claim to the Northwest Coast."[23] Thwaites's new view ended up as nothing more than a vision of the expedition as an agent of a triumphant Manifest Destiny.

In the four decades that followed publication of the Lewis and Clark journals, American historians paid little attention to the West in general and Jefferson's explorers in particular. Edward Channing, the first professional historian to use the Thwaites edition, saw the expedition as a scientific venture. But the dimensions of that science eluded him, and he quickly fell back on the expedition-as-great-adventure approach, concluding that the journals "read like a romance."[24] The standard school text for the period, David S. Muzzey's *American History*, gave one scant paragraph to the expedition. Like Thwaites, Muzzey saw Lewis and Clark as part of an inevitable American conquest of the West.[25]

While textbook writers and some historians continued to believe that the expedition had some significance—however hard to define—others were beginning to doubt that Lewis and Clark were anything more than adventurers. Frederic L. Paxson's influential *History of the American Frontier, 1763–1893*, argued that the expedition produced neither lasting scientific results nor the basis for future settlement. Paxson insisted that "the results of the Lewis and Clark Expedition were not commensurate with the effort or the success that attended it."[26] Other frontier historians tended to agree. What really mattered in the history of the West was land, cattle, railroads, and the Indian wars. Dan Elbert Clark, a prominent western historian in the 1930s, found that the expedition failed to publish its findings, findings that had no lasting significance.[27] But no scholar in those years fashioned so negative an image of the expedition as did Walter Prescott Webb. In his *The Great Plains*, Webb insisted that the Lewis and Clark journals were "meager and unsatisfying." Pressing his indictment, Webb maintained that a reading of Lewis and Clark revealed a "lack of specific detail, a vagueness, an absence of names of persons and places in connection with episodes related." Webb was convinced that neither explorer knew anything about geology, botany, zoology, or ethnography. "Why a man of Jefferson's philosophical and scientific turn of mind," Webb wondered aloud, "should have been unable to select more capable men for the enterprise, keen observers with trained minds, is hard to understand."[28]

In the midst of cliché-ridden textbooks and professional historians either indifferent or openly hostile to the expedition, the 1930s saw two scholars offer serious studies of the journey. John Bartlett Brebner's carefully researched and well-written *Explorers of North America* was a thoughtful narrative history of the major expeditionary probes from coastal margins to interior plains and mountains. Brebner defined his geographical arena as North America, breaking from the parochial limits of the United States. He argued persuasively that French Canada, Russian Alaska, and the Spanish Southwest were essential parts of the wider story. Brebner saw the Lewis and Clark Expedition as the conclusion of imperial conflicts that had shaped the history of the continent since the Age of Columbus. More important, he portrayed the expedition as the beginning of professional, scientific studies of the West. "It is impossible," he asserted, "not to feel that the Lewis and Clark Expedition opened a new era in North American exploration." Brebner's Lewis and Clark were hard-eyed pragmatists supported by the best available technology and a national treasury. There was no romance here, no chasing after myths of Welsh Indians or elusive northwest passages. Lewis and Clark were wholly "unlike the daring dashes of the French and the Canadians or the grand cavalry marches of the Spanish." In the end, Brebner offered an expedition suited to a rational, technological society. "Its success," he wrote, "was a triumph of the elaborate co-ordination of geographical and technical knowledge and of the expenditure of public money without interest in material return."[29]

Brebner's evaluation of Lewis and Clark was based on reading the Thwaites edition as well as a broad knowledge of North American exploration. No scholar had yet undertaken the sorts of specialized studies Thwaites envisioned in 1905. Those studies might have begun with botany, zoology, or ethnography. That the first specialized expedition monograph was in linguistics proved a considerable surprise. In the 1930s Elijah H. Criswell came to the University of Missouri to pursue graduate studies in English. At Missouri Criswell fell under the influence of Professor Robert L. Ramsay. Ramsay, one of the foremost scholars of American regional language, suggested that Criswell study the Lewis and Clark journals as a means to probe "what is truly American in our language."[30] Challenged by Ramsay, Criswell began a thorough study of the language in expedition records. This was no narrow undertaking. Criswell and Ramsay defined language in the broadest terms. Scientific names, nautical phrases, military commands, medical jargon, frontier slang, and geographic descriptions all drew Criswell's attention. Employing the advice of several professional botanists and zoologist, he compiled the first comprehensive list of Lewis and Clark flora and fauna. Perhaps most valuable, the dissertation contained an extraordinary "Lewis and Clark Lexicon." From aborigines to Yellowstone, Criswell defined words as they were used in the period and gave the necessary Lewis and Clark references.

Published as part of the University of Missouri Studies in 1940, Criswell's *Lewis and Clark: Linguistic Pioneers* drew scant notice from historians. But its achievement should not be measured by that lack of attention. At a time when few scholars were studying the expedition, Criswell produced a book of genuine range and imagination. With little support from historians and no models on which to pattern his work, Criswell defined a crucial aspect of the expedition and wrote about it with grace and skill.[31]

Brebner's technocrats and Criswell's pupils of American English seemed remote from the West Bernard DeVoto sought to chronicle. Journalist, novelist, and magazine editor, DeVoto was also a passionate student of those lands beyond the Mississippi. His trilogy—*Year of Decision: 1846* (1942), *Across the Wide Missouri* (1947), and *The Course of Empire* (1952)—remains required reading on subjects as diverse as the Rocky Mountain fur trade, the conquest of California, and Jefferson's vision of an American empire. In the 1930s DeVoto was primarily interested in Mark Twain and western literature but Lewis and Clark were never far from mind. When the Christmas 1936 issue of the *Saturday Review* lacked a lead essay, editor DeVoto decided to write a Lewis and Clark piece. Titled "Passage to India: From Christmas to Christmas with Lewis and Clark," it tracked the expedition from Fort Mandan's bountiful holidays to the lean celebrations at Fort Clatsop. Here was DeVoto at his storytelling best, filling the reader's mind with images of firelight and shadow. But behind the dancing language was a real idea, what he would jokingly call years later an important "Historical Idea." The expedition touched "a crisis of world polity." Jefferson's dream of an American Passage to India meant something central about the imperial destiny of the young republic.[32] In 1936 DeVoto was not quite sure how the fabled Northwest Passage, Jefferson's imperial vision, and a band of tattered soldiers all fit together. Making the connections would take another decade and a half.

More than once in the years that followed, DeVoto gave thought to writing a full narrative history of the expedition. But other books kept getting in the way. Manifest Destiny, the Mexican War, and California all seemed more compelling. Those events and places came together in *Year of Decision: 1846*, a book that sought to "realize the pre-Civil War, Far Western frontier as personal experience."[33] That book forced DeVoto to confront the origins of empire in the West. The more he thought about it, the more he became convinced that Jefferson and his captains were at the heart of that powerful drive west. In the mid-1940s DeVoto seemed ready to write his book on Lewis and Clark. He confidently told Henry Steele Commager that he was "eyeing" the explorers.[34] And there was ample evidence of DeVoto's growing Lewis and Clark interest in a 1945 essay for *Harper's Magazine* on the meaning of the expedition. He was increasingly convinced that Lewis and Clark's wilderness errand said something fundamental about the history of North America, perhaps even the history of the world. The expedition was, he asserted, "conceived by the earliest, most farseeing of American geopoliticians, Thomas Jefferson, as a necessary step in the defense of the United States against expanding, rival empires in the Western Hemisphere."[35] But as chance had it, Lewis and Clark were shouldered aside by the Rocky Mountain fur trade. What began as a simple assignment providing captions for recently discovered paintings by Alfred Jacob Miller blossomed into a masterful book. *Across the Wide Missouri* was DeVoto's evocation of the western fur trade. Lewis and Clark had gotten lost in the presence of Jim Bridger, Black Harris, and Tom Fitzpatrick.

The mountain men and their wild Green River rendezvous only temporarily overshadowed Lewis and Clark. By late 1946 DeVoto was busy "filling his tank" for a book about the expedition.[36] That tank was getting far more than readings of the Lewis and Clark journals. DeVoto now believed that a simple narrative could not do justice to the larger history of the expedition. Garrett Mattingly, DeVoto's closest historian friend, once wrote that "American history was history in transition from an Atlantic to a Pacific phase."[37] DeVoto's problem was to trace that transition without becoming mired in the travels of every explorer from Columbus and Cabot to Pike and Frémont. Lewis and Clark were important, but DeVoto now knew that they were at the end of the transition, not at its beginnings.

What had started as a traditional history of the great expedition became DeVoto's most important and most complex book. *The Course of Empire* was dominated by two powerful, interconnected ideas. Struggling to find meaning in that Atlantic to Pacific shift, DeVoto settled upon the search for the Passage to India as his unifying theme. But he was not interested in following a northwest passage through Arctic waters. DeVoto's route was the Missouri River, Marquette's "Pekitonoui," the river of the big canoe. He had once told Catherine Drinker Bowen that American history was "the most romantic of all histories."[38] That romance meant leading the reader through all the myths, dreams, and mad schemes that drove everyone from the Sieur de la Vérendrye to Lewis and Clark into "the Northwestern Mystery."

But *The Course of Empire* was far more than a fascinating catalog of geographic delusions. DeVoto wanted the book to explain how the United States had become a continental nation, how it had come to occupy what Abraham Lincoln called a "national homestead." DeVoto had been thinking about continentalism since the 1930s. His Lewis and Clark research convinced him that geographic realities—river systems and mountain ranges—shaped American expansion. Here DeVoto danced with a dangerous idea. Geographic determinism, the likes of which had been proposed earlier in the century by Ellen Churchill Semple and Albert P. Brigham, reduced history to mathematical precision. DeVoto always affirmed the primacy of individuals in history. His continentalism, rooted in a sure sense of western geography, focused on Thomas Jefferson. DeVoto had been saying for years that Jefferson was the first American geopolitician, and in *The Course of Empire* he set out to prove it.

Thomas Jefferson, Meriwether Lewis, and William Clark occupied a mere 170 pages in a book of well more than 500 pages. But those concluding chapters were the crucial ones. Here was the culmination of a three-century quest for the Northwest Passage. Those pages made plain the first move by the United States to dominate the continent. Recounting Jefferson's 1803 message to Congress proposing a western expedition, DeVoto found a president bent on making the United States a Pacific power. Challenged by Anglo-Canadian moves carried out by Alexander Mackenzie and driven by his own understanding of western geography, Jefferson fashioned an enterprise that would wrest an empire from rival hands. The explorers were engaged in an "imperial necessity," a "heavy national responsibility."[39] In the midst of writing *Course of Empire* DeVoto told Mattingly that he wanted to "chock up American history on blocks, turn it around and give it a new orientation."[40] The Lewis and Clark Expedition was a grand adventure and DeVoto related it with zest and delight. But he knew that Jefferson and the captains meant to achieve more than a daring western tour. The expedition made the United States a continental power, a force in world history.

Course of Empire gave the Lewis and Clark Expedition context and meaning. DeVoto had succeeded in making the expedition into something more than a company of soldiers bound for the great western sea. The book brought its author critical acclaim but most academic reviewers missed its central message. Accustomed to a literary DeVoto, scholars found it easy to dismiss or ignore the book and its themes. Historians in the 1950s did not have the West on their research agendas. The Western History Association was years away. *Course of Empire*, the book that might have revitalized studies of Lewis and Clark, had the misfortune to fall into a vacuum. Praised and purchased, *Course of Empire* had no immediate heirs.

DeVoto's grand sweep of western history excited little interest in the 1950s. John Bakeless certainly found nothing compelling about such a synthesis. Drawn to the expedition as a way to write biography, Bakeless began his research in 1939. Wartime service interrupted his progress, and it was not until 1947 that *Lewis and Clark: Partners in Discovery* was finally published. This was the descriptive history of the expedition DeVoto had once assayed. Bakeless wrote traditional narrative largely untouched by larger questions of meaning and interpretation. His readers got a rattling good tale but remained innocent about questions of science, Indian relations, geography, and international politics. Bakeless's version of the expedition fit the optimism of postwar America, an America confident about its place in the world. DeVoto's disturbing questions about imperialism seemed as out of place as did his spirited defense of wilderness and conservation issues.[41]

Perhaps more than fresh ideas, the study of the expedition needed new evidence. There had been important documentary discoveries including the publication of Sergeant John Ordway's diary and Lewis's Ohio River journal in 1913.[42] More dramatic was the 1953 discovery of Clark's field notes covering the period from December 1803 to April 1805. After extended litigation the Clark materials were published by Ernest S. Osgood in 1964.[43] At the same time New York's Antiquarian Press reprinted the Thwaites edition, bringing the journals back into print for the first time in some forty years. Here was fuel enough to rekindle expedition fires.

One person was largely responsible for fanning that flame. In the mid-1950s Donald Jackson was editor at the University of Illinois Press. While busy shepherding other authors' manuscripts through publication, he had also done considerable research and writing on his own. Custer's 1874 Black Hills reconnaissance and the early history of Fort Madison in present-day Iowa captured his attention. When the press decided to reissue the autobiography of Black Hawk and could find no one eager to edit the book, Jackson took it on. Lewis and Clark drifted through this and other projects, more as federal officials than as explorers. Jackson knew that the expedition had produced a large body of documents beyond the party's official journals. While Thwaites had printed some of those letters, many more awaited discovery. By November 1958 Jackson's Lewis and Clark letters project had taken shape and direction. Jackson defined his task as compiling and annotating "an edition of all letters pertaining to the expedition and to the production of the original Biddle edition and transfer of the journals to the American Philosophical Society."[44]

When the University of Illinois Press published *Letters of the Lewis and Clark Expedition with Related Documents, 1783–1854* in 1962, the hefty volume contained 428 documents, well over half previously unpublished. A two-volume, revised edition, issued in 1978, added 29 more documents. Perhaps no documentary find both revealed more about Jackson's painstaking scholarship and proved more valuable to later scholars than his discovery of the Biddle Notes. In April 1810 Nicholas Biddle traveled to Virginia to interview William Clark. Those conversations amounted to a post-expedition debriefing. Biddle asked about everything from Indian linguistics to botany and geography. Those questions and Clark's answers were all duly recorded in Biddle's peculiar, hard-to-decipher handwriting. Working through Lewis and Clark manuscripts at the American Philosophical Society, Jackson came upon those notes. With an acute eye for handwriting, he quickly recognized the author. Equally important, Jackson grasped the significance of his discovery. Here was William Clark being queried by an intelligent scholar about major expedition matters just four year after the venture's end. Every student of the expedition, whether probing Indian relations or geography, soon came to recognize the Biddle Notes as a major source.[45]

Jackson's *Letters* proved far more than a skillfully presented collection of documents. The items themselves, their arrangement, and the editor's masterful annotations amounted to a scholarly transfusion for Lewis and Clark research. More important than any single monograph, the collection expanded the Lewis and Clark horizon. As Jackson put it, "it is no longer useful to think of the Lewis and Clark Expedition as the personal story of two men." Jackson's documents portrayed "an enterprise of many aims and a product of many minds."[46] Those many minds were reflected in letters from Jefferson, Albert Gallatin, Benjamin Rush, Benjamin Smith Barton, and a host of lesser-known scientists, politicians, army officers, and frontiersmen. Here were letters and reports on botany, zoology, ethnography, and physical geography. Knowing that Jefferson had planned other western exploring ventures before 1803, Jackson presented a full range of documents detailing those enterprises. Diplomacy and international relations were not ignored. Spanish reactions were traced in a number of important letters. Jackson's collection urged scholars to get beyond the great journey itself to see its consequences in the wider worlds of science, Indian relations, politics, and diplomacy.

Donald Jackson once wrote that "an editor's work is meant to be pillaged."[47] That pillaging began almost at once. In the 1950s DeVoto had complained that "it is still impossible to make a satisfactory statement about the scientific results of the expedition."[48] Challenged by both DeVoto and Jackson, a qualified scientist began such studies. Paul Cutright, a professor of biology at Beaver College, took up the task. Although Criswell and Jackson had compiled fairly complete lists of plants and animals encountered by the explorers, Cutright undertook a comprehensive examination of expedition science. His work, published as *Lewis and Clark: Pioneering Naturalists*, made plain the substantial achievements of the expedition. Cutright noted each plant and animal found by the explorers, recorded the names used by the expedition, and identified each by its modern binomial. Other writers had given expedition science an obligatory mention. Cutright did more. He clearly demonstrated both the depth and range of those accomplishments.[49]

Cutright's book fueled the blaze sparked by Jackson. The Lewis and Clark bonfire got fresh wood in 1975. Today Lewis and Clark each wear the title "explorer," a word neither man used to describe himself. No student of the expedition had carefully examined the nature of the exploratory process. Equally telling, there had been no systematic analysis of expedition cartography. Those gaps were filled when John Logan Allen completed his doctoral dissertation at Clark University in 1969 and subsequently published that work in revised and expanded form as *Passage through the Garden: Lewis and Clark and the Image of the American Northwest.*[50]

Allen's ambitious and provocative book probed the nature of the exploration by looking at field decisions made by the captains. At the same time he examined the geographical images that shaped the expedition. But the book was neither a simple catalog of choices made at this river or that mountain pass nor a study of disembodied "landscape images." As a historical geographer, Allen brought the two topics together by posing three vital questions. Following ideas set out by John K. Wright, Allen examined in great detail the ways knowledge—"lore" was Wright's word—from previous travelers fashioned an image of western geography. Here Allen provided an illuminating discussion of conceptual geography, the notions of river systems and mountain ranges that formed Jefferson's mental picture of the West. Allen then took that image and tracked it along the Lewis and Clark trail. As he envisioned it, the expedition was guided by geographic images constantly tested, modified, or discarded. Finally, Allen devoted considerable space to the role of Lewis and Clark as creators of new geographic imagery.

Passage through the Garden was an extraordinary book. Allen had not only discovered new cartographic evidence but he also had put Lewis and Clark in the mainstream of geographic thought. The emphasis on exploration as a "programmed enterprise" gave meaning to daily decisions about course and distance. Deeply influenced by DeVoto, Allen paid tribute to *Course of Empire* as "the major conceptual foundation" of his own work. Jackson's *Letters* had an importance, Allen wrote, "readily apparent" throughout his book.[51] *Passage through the Garden* was proof that the Lewis and Clark renewal sought by DeVoto and Jackson was now in full flame.

The course of historical research is often guided by lucky chance, and nothing was more serendipitous than the way Allen's work prompted the next major Lewis and Clark book. In 1976 *Ohio History* asked James P. Ronda to review *Passage through the Garden.* Ronda had previously written ethnohistorical accounts of Indian-missionary relations on eastern frontiers. Impressed by Allen's book,

Ronda set out to write what he called "exploration ethnohistory."[52] *Lewis and Clark among the Indians*, published in 1984, used a wide variety of historical and anthropological sources to reveal the full range of relations between the expedition and its Indian neighbors. As Ronda imagined it, the expedition was one human community moving through and living among other human communities. Lewis and Clark traversed a crowded West already explored and settled by many native peoples. The story of the expedition could not be told apart from the lives of scores of Mandans, Shoshones, Nez Perces, and Chinookans. *Lewis and Clark among the Indians* probed everything from diplomacy and ethnography to trade and sexual relations. The book argued that the expedition was a shared enterprise, one that united different peoples with the bonds of common experience. Ronda's book offered two new interpretive directions for the study of the expedition. The traditional telling of the voyage had a small cast of characters. Ronda increased that cast and expanded the stage. He urged readers to listen to Indian voices and watch native people as active participants in the venture. Equally important, the book suggested that the expedition was a microcosm for the larger world of cultural relations in North America.

Books by Cutright, Allen, and Ronda filled major gaps in Lewis and Clark literature. At the same time it was clear that a modern edition of the journals was needed. Discoveries of new manuscript materials and more exacting annotation standards made Thwaites increasingly out-of-date. At the 1967 centennial meeting of the Missouri Historical Society, Donald Jackson issued a public call for such a new edition.[53] Jackson's prompting and suggestions from others finally caught the attention of Stephen F. Cox, executive editor at the University of Nebraska Press. Jackson was engaged as a consultant to prepare plans for a multi-volume edition sponsored by the University of Nebraska Press, the Center for Great Plains Studies at the University of Nebraska, and the American Philosophical Society. Professor Gary E. Moulton was selected as the new editor for the journals. The first volume, a Lewis and Clark atlas, was published in 1983 and three journal volumes have appeared thus far.[54]

Now that a substantial portion of the new edition has been

published it is important to step back and evaluate what has been accomplished. Perhaps that evaluation might begin with a commonsense question. What does it mean that these are the journals of the Lewis and Clark Expedition? Questions about what to include determine later decisions about presentation and annotation. As Moulton explains in his introduction, the new edition will eventually print "the journals of Lewis, Clark, Charles Floyd, John Ordway, Patrick Gass, and Joseph Whitehouse (all the extant journals associated with the expedition); and a volume of the expedition's natural history materials."[55]

How that intention works out in practice can best be judged by looking at a sample day in the life of the expedition. On July 30, 1804, the explorers made camp at Council Bluff along the Missouri River some fifteen miles north of present-day Omaha, Nebraska. There Lewis and Clark prepared for their first Indian conference, a meeting with Oto and Missouri headmen. The new edition prints entries made by both captains. In addition there is the entry from Clark's field notes.[56] But the reader who assumes that this was the whole sum of writing done by the expedition that day will be wide of the mark. Sergeants Ordway and Floyd as well as Privates Whitehouse and Gass commented on the day's events. Their observations have been put off to be printed in a later volume. Although Moulton probably made a wise decision not to clutter each day with too many documents, the neglect of Ordway is a real loss. Ordway was the only member of the expedition to pen a journal entry every day. Ordway's importance lies not only in his comprehensive coverage but in his keen eye for detail. The young soldier could capture a scene or event with colorful, memorable language of the sort that often eluded his superiors.

The canons of documentary editing demand accurate transcription and clear printing of the original. Thwaites and his associates produced a reasonably clean reading of expedition journals. There were some errors, as when the phrase "cut my hand" was rendered as "cue my hare" in Clark's November 13, 1805, entry. The new edition locates and corrects those errors. At the same time the integrity of the originals, with all their delightful spellings and peculiar punctuations, has been honored. What readers are given is a reliable transcription. The chapter divisions, while not in the originals, are retained from Thwaites as they have become a useful research convention. Important scientific matter, relegated to volume six in Thwaites, is placed at the appropriate date and place.

No historical document can stand by itself. Obscure words need definition, little-known individuals require identification, and remote places demand location. Annotation provides that essential context. Documents without annotation are little more than disconnected fragments from a dark past. A generation ago documentary editors believed that their mission was to write long, learned footnotes. While some still cling to that tradition, the tide has turned toward a more restrained approach. Thanks in large part to the example of Donald Jackson in his Lewis and Clark, Pike, and Frémont editions, editors now annotate and avoid essay-length notes.

Moulton's annotation method can best be understood by returning to the events of July 30, 1804. An alert editor will surely find much to comment upon for that day. Thwaites wrote one note; Moulton has seven. A voyage of discovery is all about place and location. Any Lewis and Clark scholar must have a sure sense of place. Using both contemporary and modern maps, Moulton tells readers just where the expedition was on that July day. Locations throughout the edition are done by state, county, and closest present-day town. Unique terrain features that might further pinpoint a particular campsite are also included. One of the central reasons for this edition is the renewed emphasis on expedition science. Moulton has used a whole corps of specialists in botany, geology, and zoology to make his scientific annotations both informative and accurate. When Clark mentioned the "coffeenut" among a number of well-known trees, Moulton identifies it as the Kentucky coffee tree, *Gymnocladus dioica* (L.). Throughout the edition plants and animals, especially those discovered by Lewis and Clark, are carefully identified by both common and scientific name. When Joseph Field killed and brought to camp an animal the French *engagés* called a *Brárow*, the critter quickly drew Lewis's attention. Moulton identifies the badger and tells the reader something about the French and Pawnee derivations of its name.[57]

Mention of the Pawnee word *cuhkatus* for badger raises the

question of linguistic and ethnographic annotation. Expedition journalists filled their notebooks with important observations on native cultures as well as hundreds of Indian words and names. One of the lasting contributions of this edition is that it takes seriously those ethnographic and linguistic contributions. The entry for August 3, 1804—the day of the Oto-Missouri conference—is a good example of Moulton's Indian annotations. Here the editor briefly discusses Indian-Spanish relations, the protocol of Indian diplomacy, and the proper meaning of Oto and Missouri personal names listed by Clark. Moulton draws on the best recent anthropological and archaeological information to make these annotations of real value.[58]

In 1905 Reuben Gold Thwaites confidently predicted that "we shall henceforth know Lewis and Clark as we never knew them before."[59] With this new edition of the journals, that prophecy edges toward reality. What the Moulton volumes offer is not so much a new image of the expedition as a refurbished one. Donald Jackson once observed that the editor's task was like that of a specialist seeking to restore a fine painting. Generations of dirt, abuse, and misunderstanding had to be peeled away to reveal the splendid original. The new edition brings readers back to Jefferson's conception of the venture. Here is an expedition with many missions. Readers now see more clearly Lewis and Clark's diverse roles as advance agents of empire, geographic explorers and cartographers, federal Indian diplomats, ethnographers, and scientists. Almost two centuries after the fact, we are beginning to comprehend Jefferson's western vision.

What might justly be called the golden age of expedition scholarship began in 1962. Is the new journals' edition the conclusion to that burst of scholarly creativity or will these handsome volumes advance Lewis and Clark research into unpathed territories? Simply put, what remains yet unexplored? In recent years much emphasis has been placed on the expedition as a scientific reconnaissance. Cutright has gone so far as to insist that Lewis had scientific attitudes "more consistent with scientists of the twentieth century than those of his own."[60] While the expedition did make important botanical and zoological discoveries, its science was firmly rooted in eighteenth-century Enlightenment and natural history traditions. "Scientist" has become a convenient label to hang on the captains without much examination of the meaning and techniques of science in the Lewis and Clark years. As John C. Greene makes plain in his recent *American Science in the Age of Jefferson*, the expedition moved in an intellectual world quite unlike our own.[61] Now that scholars properly appreciate the natural history contributions made by the explorers, it is time to place those achievements in their historical context.

For all the public interest in the lives of expedition members, the shelf of biographies is indeed short. The captains themselves have suffered from a remarkable scholarly neglect. All to often students of the expedition have fallen into the habit of writing about that composite personality called "Lewisandclark." Richard Dillon's 1965 biography of Lewis is a fairly straightforward account but one that hardly fulfills the demands of modern biography.[62] Lewis was a person of extraordinary complexity, and too many writers have spilled ink on the circumstances of his death while ignoring larger and more important issues. William Clark, whose career went well beyond the expedition, has fared no better. Jerome Steffen's brief *William Clark: Jeffersonian Man on the Frontier* looks only at Clark's post-1806 career and tends to submerge him in Steffen's own theory about frontier politics and social change.[63] Clark's slave York has done better at the hands of the biographers than either of the captains. Robert Betts's *In Search of York* is a sensitive treatment of the man Indians called "Big Medicine."[64]

Meriwether Lewis once described the expedition as a family. Indeed, the Corps of Discovery was a community. We need to know much more about the life of that community. Eldon G. Chuinard's *Only One Man Died* suggests the medical dimension of that common life.[65] More remains to be said. How did a racially and culturally diverse group become a harmonious body ready to bend all energies to reach a common goal? Where did that remarkable social cohesion come from? Historians busy examining frontier communities might well study this expedition for clues about what Robert V. Hine has called the western tension of "separate but not alone."[66]

Lewis and Clark moved through lands claimed by others. Expedition relations with native peoples have been given a broadbrush treatment by James Ronda. But there is much room left for deeper study of the complex interactions between explorers and individual villages, bands, and tribes. Equally important, some scholar fluent in Spanish and knowledgeable about Iberian and Mexican archives must undertake a thorough study of Spain's reactions to the various American expeditions in the Jeffersonian period. A. P. Nasatir has gathered some important documents in his *Before Lewis and Clark*. Warren Cook's *Flood Tide of Empire: Spain and the Pacific Northwest, 1543–1819* makes some preliminary evaluation of Spanish attempts to halt the Lewis and Clark Expedition.[67] In his most recent book, *Among the Sleeping Giants*, Donald Jackson speculates about the consequences of a successful Spanish interdiction of the expedition. Because Jefferson had pinned so many personal and national hopes on the expedition, he might have reacted with considerable fury had Spanish forces arrested the man they called "Captain Merry." Jackson's thought-provoking "what if" points to the need for a major study of Spanish efforts to defend threatened borderlands.[68]

Jefferson's explorers have found their place in the history of North America. They have yet to be put in the wider context of eighteenth-century exploration. Lewis and Clark lived in the age of Cook, Vancouver, La Pérouse, and the incomparable Sir Joseph Banks. Enlightenment science and imperial power pushed voyagers to fill in the map of mankind. Recent books by David Mackay, Richard Van Orman, and P. J. Marshall and Glyndwr Williams all reveal important aspects of that worldwide exploration enterprise.[69] Lewis and Clark need to stand in company with Cook and Mackenzie if we are to gain a fuller understanding of both the American explorers and their European counterparts.

What remains to be written about the Lewis and Clark Expedition suggests that DeVoto was right. The expedition was a turning point in world history. Here are the beginnings of an American empire. That westering would transform the political and cultural boundaries of North America and eventually the wider world. Fresh readings of the Lewis and Clark journals, readings with new eyes, guarantee a continuing exploration of what Lewis once called his "darling project." What Lewis and Clark began in that rented room shows no sign of losing power and fascination.

Notes

I wish to thank James Axtell, Kay Graber, Gary Moulton, and the late Donald Jackson for their comments. This essay is dedicated to the memory of Dr. Donald Jackson.

1. Reuben G. Thwaites, ed., *Original Journals of the Lewis and Clark Expedition, 1804–1806* (New York, 1904–5), 5:395 (hereafter Thw).

2. Donald Jackson, ed., *Letters of the Lewis and Clark Expedition with Related Documents, 1783–1854*, 2d ed. (Urbana, Ill., 1978), 1:v.

3. William Clark to Meriwether Lewis, July 24, 1803, in Jackson, *Letters*, 1:112.

4. Frankfort, Kentucky, *Western World,* October 11, 1806, reprinted in this volume, 203-5.

5. Citizens of Fincastle to Lewis and Clark, January 8, 1807, in Jackson, *Letters,* 1:358-59.

6. Jefferson's Instructions to Lewis, June 20, 1803, in Jackson, *Letters*, 1:61, reprinted in this volume, 31-38.

7. Jefferson to Lewis, November 16, 1803, in Jackson, *Letters*, 1:137.

8. Lewis to Jefferson, September 23, 1806, in Jackson, *Letters*, 1:319-24.

9. Clark to [George Rogers Clark?], September 23, 1806, in Jackson, *Letters*, 1:326.

10. Jefferson to Lewis, October 26, 1806, in Jackson, *Letters*, 1:352.

11. Lincoln to Jefferson, April 17, 1803, in Jackson, *Letters*, 1:35.

12. Jefferson to Bernard Lacépède, July 14, 1808, in Jackson, *Letters*, 2:443.

13. Samuel L. Mitchill, *A Discourse on the Character and Services of Thomas Jefferson* (New York, 1826), 27-28.

14. *The Conrad Prospectus* (Philadelphia, c. April 1, 1807), in Jackson, *Letters*, 2:395. Although the prospectus was printed by Conrad, it was written by Lewis while the explorer was staying in Philadelphia.

15. Jefferson to Lewis, July 17, 1808, in Jackson, *Letters*, 2:445; Jefferson to Lewis, August 16, 1809, in ibid., 2:458.

16. C. and A. Conrad and Co. to Jefferson, November 13, 1809, in Jackson, *Letters*, 2:469.

17. Jefferson to F. H. Alexander von Humboldt, December 6, 1813, in Jackson, *Letters*, 2:596.

18. John L. Allen, "'Of This Enterprize': The American Images of the Lewis and Clark Expedition," in *Enlightenment Science in the Pacific Northwest: The Lewis and Clark Expedition*, ed. William F. Willingham

and Leonoor S. Ingraham (Portland, 1984), 29-45, reprinted in this volume, 255-80.

19. Paul R. Cutright, *A History of the Lewis and Clark Journals* (Norman, Okla., 1976), 98.

20. Thw, 1:lvi.

21. Ibid.

22. Thwaites, *A Brief History of Rocky Mountain Exploration, with Especial Reference to the Expedition of Lewis and Clark* (New York, 1904), 187.

23. Reuben G. Thwaites and Calvin Noyes Kendall, *A History of the United States for Grammar Schools* (Boston, 1912), 236.

24. Edward Channing, *The Jeffersonian System, 1801–1811* (New York, 1906), 94.

25. David S. Muzzey, *American History* (Boston, 1911), 210.

26. Frederic L. Paxson, *History of the American Frontier, 1763–1893* (Boston, 1924), 137.

27. Dan E. Clark, *The West in American History* (New York, 1937), 405-8.

28. Walter Prescott Webb, *The Great Plains* (1931; reprint, Lincoln, Nebr., 1981), 143-44.

29. John Bartlett Brebner, *The Explorers of North America, 1492–1806* (New York, 1933), 464-65.

30. Elijah H. Criswell, "Lewis and Clark: Linguistic Pioneers," *University of Missouri Studies: A Quarterly of Research*, 15 (April 1940), vii.

31. Cutright, *History of the Lewis and Clark Journals*, 208. See also a brief biographical sketch of Criswell by Cutright in "Dr. Elijah Harry Criswell (1888–1967)," *We Proceeded On*, 5 (February 1979), 6-7.

32. Bernard DeVoto, "Passage to India: From Christmas to Christmas with Lewis and Clark," *Saturday Review of Literature*, 15 (December 1936), 3-4, 20, 24, 28, reprinted in this volume, 89-100.

33. Bernard DeVoto, *Year of Decision: 1846* (Boston, 1943), xi.

34. DeVoto to Commager, April 30, 1944, in *The Letters of Bernard DeVoto*, ed. Wallace Stegner (Garden City, N.Y., 1975), 271.

35. Bernard DeVoto, untitled essay in "The Easy Chair," *Harper's Magazine*, 190 (March 1950), 312.

36. Bernard DeVoto to Samuel Eliot Morison, December 1946, in Stegner, *DeVoto*, 273.

37. Mattingly's memorable phrase is recorded in DeVoto to Mattingly, November 1, 1945, in Stegner, *DeVoto*, 273.

38. DeVoto to Catherine D. Bowen, [n.d.], in Stegner, *DeVoto*, 285-86.

39. Bernard DeVoto, *The Course of Empire* (Boston, 1952), 426, 429, 430-31, 443. See also DeVoto's much neglected "An Inference Regarding the Expedition of Lewis and Clark," *Proceedings of the American Philosophical Society,* 99 (August 1955), 185-94, for his most pointed treatment of the expedition's role in American western imperialism.

40. DeVoto to Mattingly, March 14, 1948, in Stegner, *DeVoto,* 293.

41. John Bakeless, *Lewis and Clark: Partners in Discovery* (New York, 1947).

42. Milo M. Quaife, ed., *The Journals of Captain Meriwether Lewis and Sergeant John Ordway* (Madison, Wis., 1916).

43. Ernest S. Osgood, ed., *The Field Notes of Captain William Clark, 1803–1805* (New Haven, Conn., 1964).

44. For a full discussion, see Donald Jackson, *Among the Sleeping Giants: Occasional Pieces on Lewis and Clark* (Urbana, Ill., 1987), 55-74.

45. Jackson, *Letters,* 2:497-545; Jackson, *Sleeping Giants,* 71.

46. Jackson, *Letters,* 1:v.

47. Refer to introduction in Donald Jackson, ed., *The Expedition of John Charles Frémont: Map Portfolio* (Urbana, Ill., 1970), 5.

48. Refer to introduction in Bernard DeVoto, ed., *Journals of the Lewis and Clark Expedition* (Boston, 1953), li.

49. Paul R. Cutright, *Lewis and Clark: Pioneering Naturalists* (Urbana, Ill., 1969).

50. John L. Allen, *Passage through the Garden: Lewis and Clark and the Image of the American Northwest* (Urbana, Ill., 1975).

51. Ibid., xv-xvi.

52. James P. Ronda, *Lewis and Clark among the Indians* (Lincoln, Nebr., 1984), xii.

53. Donald Jackson, "Some Advice for the Next Editor of Lewis and Clark," *Bulletin of the Missouri Historical Society,* 24 (October 1967), 52-62.

54. This essay was originally published in 1988. As of 1997, ten journal volumes and the atlas have been completed.

55. Gary E. Moulton, ed., *The Journals of the Lewis and Clark Expedition* (Lincoln, Nebr., 1983–97), 2:viii.

56. Ibid., 2:428-30.

57. Ibid., 2:431.

58. Ibid., 2:438-44.

59. Thw, 1:lvii.

60. Cutright, *Pioneering Naturalists,* 398.

61. John C. Greene, *American Science in the Age of Jefferson* (Ames, Iowa, 1984), chap. 8; See also Roy Porter, "The Terraqueous Globe," in *The Ferment of Knowledge: Studies in the Historiography of Eighteenth-Century Science*, ed. Roy Parker and G. S. Rousseau (Cambridge, England, 1980), 285-324.

62. Richard Dillon, *Meriwether Lewis: A Biography* (New York, 1965).

63. Jerome O. Steffen, *William Clark: Jeffersonian Man on the Frontier* (Norman, Okla., 1977).

64. Robert B. Betts, *In Search of York* (Boulder, Colo., 1985). Two other members of the expedition also have received biographical treatment: Burton Harris, *John Colter* (New York, 1952), and M. O. Skarsten, *George Drouillard* (Glendale, Calif., 1964). The literature on Sacagawea is large and often uncritical. It is summarized in Ronda, *Lewis and Clark among the Indians*, 256-59.

65. Eldon G. Chuinard, *Only One Man Died: The Medical Aspects of the Lewis and Clark Expedition* (Glendale, Calif., 1979).

66. Robert V. Hine, *Community on the American Frontier: Separate But Not Alone* (Norman, Okla., 1980).

67. A. P. Nasatir, ed., *Before Lewis and Clark: Documents Illustrating the History of the Missouri, 1785–1804*, 2 vols. (St. Louis, 1952). See also Warren L. Cook, *Flood Tide of Empire: Spain and the Pacific Northwest, 1543–1819* (New Haven, Conn., 1973).

68. Jackson, *Sleeping Giants*, 12-16.

69. David Mackay, *In the Wake of Cook: Exploration, Science, and Empire, 1780–1901* (New York, 1985); Richard A. Van Orman, *The Explorers: Nineteenth Century Expeditions in Africa and the American West* (Albuquerque, N.M., 1984); and P. J. Marshall and Glyndwr Williams, *The Great Map of Mankind: British Perceptions of the World in the Age of Enlightenment* (Cambridge, Mass., 1982). The best introduction to the period remains Donald Jackson, *Thomas Jefferson and the Stony Mountains: Exploring the West from Monticello* (Urbana, 1981).

Afterword
'A Darling Project of Mine':
The Appeal of the Lewis and Clark Story

James P. Ronda

MERIWETHER LEWIS ONCE CALLED the Corps of Discovery's journey to the Pacific his "darling Project."[1] Nearly two centuries after the expedition, Lewis's sense of pride and accomplishment seems justified. Americans have taken the Lewis and Clark Expedition into the national heart and mind. No exploring party is more famous, no expedition leaders more instantly recognizable. The journey continues to be recounted in books, films, paintings, and museum exhibitions. Those finding the expedition's story especially compelling can join the Lewis and Clark Trail Heritage Foundation, read the foundation's journal *We Proceeded On*, and attend a yearly national convention. And for many of the Lewis and Clark faithful, the trail has become a pilgrim's way, a route that combines both personal and cultural quests for meaning and identity. What was Lewis's "darling" has become a most favored American story.

But it was not always so. In the years after the Corps of Discovery made its way back across the continent, the journey gradually faded from public view. An unfortunate series of changes and chances conspired to make the expedition and its achievements less visible. Lewis's suicide first delayed publication and then ultimately transformed the character of the expedition's printed report. The *History of the Expedition under the Command of Captains Lewis and Clark* appeared some eight years after the event in a modest press run of only 1,417 copies. By the middle of the nineteenth century Lewis and Clark were nearly forgotten, their presence eclipsed by more popular western heroes like John Charles Frémont, Kit Carson, and a horde of dime-novel frontiersmen.

In more recent times the Corps of Discovery has regained some of its original luster. Public attention came initially at the turn of the century with the St. Louis Louisiana Purchase Exposition (1904) and the Portland, Oregon, Lewis and Clark Centennial Exposition (1905). Both spectacular fairs prominently featured Lewis and Clark as pioneers of an expanding American empire. And more of the expedition's vital written record was finally published, thanks to the editorial efforts of Elliott Coues and Reuben Gold Thwaites. But for all its potential importance, the Lewis and Clark story entered the twentieth century as a shallow tale—one that simply celebrated imperial conquest and personal adventure. Until mid-century what the story lacked were narrators able to relate larger stories set on wider stages with bigger casts. And equally important, the Corps of Discovery needed an audience ready to appreciate the journey as more than an action adventure. The fault was not with the story but with its tellers and its audience. But in the last four decades the Lewis and Clark script has been dusted off, polished up, and given a proper on-Broadway revival. Bernard DeVoto, Donald Jackson, Paul Cutright, John L. Allen, Stephen Ambrose, and a whole company of scholars have brought Lewis and Clark to life for a large and appreciative readership. And the patient, thorough labor of documentary editor Gary E. Moulton has given scholars a reliable set of expedition journals.

The expedition's role in American history now seems assured. But the reasons for the hold Lewis and Clark have on the national mind remain largely unexplored. Jefferson's captains have had worthy competitors for pride of place in western exploration. John Charles Frémont was once the quintessential "Pathfinder." Captain James H. Simpson of the Army Corps of Topographical Engineers counted more miles exploring the West than Jefferson's captains. John Wesley Powell's Colorado River adventures were surely more dangerous than anything Lewis and Clark faced on the Missouri or the Columbia. And it was Alexander Mackenzie who made the first continental crossing north of Mexico by a European, a decade before Lewis and Clark. Yet Lewis and Clark are household names, the instantly identifiable symbols of exploration. Theirs has become the emblematic American journey.

As we consider the unfolding historical record, we should ask about the touchstone character of this particular journey. Why has the Lewis and Clark Expedition captured our imagination while others have faded from memory? What does the Lewis and Clark story reveal about the contours of the American past? Why are so many ordinary citizens eager to join—at least by reading books and visiting historic sites—what seems the Corps of Discovery's never-ending journey?

The distinguished photographer Ingvard Henry Eide titled his collection of Lewis and Clark trail images *American Odyssey*. As the Civil War was the nation's *Illiad*, Eide recognized that the Lewis and Clark Expedition had become the fundamental American journey. In one way or another all of American history can be imagined as a journey. From hunting trips across the Bering Strait land bridge made by the first comers, to the voyages of the most recent immigrants, the essential American experience has been the journey, the trek, the quest. Our history has been the story of trails—the Wilderness Trail, the Oregon Trail, the Mormon Trail, the Chisholm Trail, and the Trail of Tears. And in more recent times those trails carry names like Route 66, the Alaska Highway, and Interstate 80. The Lewis and Clark trail has come to represent all American journeys. In the Corps of Discovery's progress across the continent, Americans see reflected thousands of individual passages into a new world.

But in one important way the American odyssey in its Lewis and Clark reading was profoundly different from the one Homer sang. His story about Odysseus was not so much a narrative of outbound discovery as a tale of homecoming. Odysseus was about the business of *recovery*; Lewis and Clark were on an errand of *discovery*. Odysseus hoped for the pleasures of home. Lewis and Clark sought the road—its motion and its challenges. The expedition's route traced the curve of American energy and expansion. The Corps of Discovery's odyssey continues to attract fellow travelers as a powerful reminder of America as an ongoing journey.

For all its considerable appeal as archetypal journey and personal pilgrimage, the expedition story offers more than the tale of solitary wayfarers trudging through an empty landscape. More than three decades ago, Donald Jackson wrote that "it is no longer useful to think of the Lewis and Clark expedition as the personal story of two men."[2] Jackson understood that the Corps of Discovery had an expanding roster—one that included men, women, and children from many racial and ethnic backgrounds. The expedition was the "vast enterprise" that Clark once called it. Even if the expedition's story is only that of the Corps of Discovery proper— and it was *always* more than that—the cast of characters is large and inclusive. What the captains called "the perminent party" listed men of English, Scots, French, Métis, and African descent. There were soldiers, hunters, craftsmen, and frontier jacks-of-all-trades. The expedition spoke in the accents of New Hampshire, Virginia, Kentucky, and French Canada. And there was an Indian woman who added the inflections of Shoshone and Hidatsa and the sounds of her infant child. No "village on the move" could represent more fully the astounding diversity of American life than the Corps of Discovery. For them, as for us, the journey was to discover not only the land but themselves and each other. In the stories of that community there is a place for every "on the road" American.

The land that Lewis and Clark moved through was not a pristine Eden, untouched by human agency. In the decades before the expedition, native people had colonized the West and changed the land in untold ways. But in the century after Lewis and Clark, change came faster and had far more lasting and visible consequences. We are attracted to the expedition because its records offer a vision of a landscape on the edge of profound transformation.

Lewis and Clark were part of a scientific enterprise aimed at observing, collecting, classifying, and comprehending the "natural world." Words like "ecosystem," "bio-diversity," and "species interdependence" were unknown to the explorers. But in their journal entries, notes, and specimen collections they preserved the raw material from which later generations could fashion such useful and sometimes controversial ideas. The expedition's portrait of

Nature offers us a yardstick for measuring what has been lost and what yet remains. Through Lewis and Clark we can see Nature's West with fresh, and perhaps more discerning, eyes.

∞

AT HIS MOST PHILOSOPHICAL AND REFLECTIVE MOMENTS Thomas Jefferson envisioned the Corps of Discovery in terms of values— values to be preserved and extended. By finding both the garden and the passage, Jefferson's captains would ensure the continued vitality of the republic. Jefferson's thoughts about values ran to the virtues of rural life: simplicity, frugality, and independence. Modern students of the expedition are also attracted to the story for reasons of virtue and value. Even the briefest look at the journey suggests the presence of values with considerable contemporary relevance.

For all its many unique and colorful characters, the Corps of Discovery did not champion the cult of the individual. The expedition lived and moved, survived and prospered as a community. At its beginnings the Corps of Discovery was an infantry company, ordering its days by the official *Articles of War* and by age-old military custom. But over time and through adversity the company became a community. People from different worlds grew to share a common life. The expedition not only exemplified the value of community and cooperative enterprise but the power of perseverance as well. Lewis and Clark never doubted that their journey would be long and hard. They did not expect quick results. Modern readers, conditioned by a popular culture rooted in immediate gratification of nearly every desire, are constantly amazed at the explorers' patience and persistence. The Corps of Discovery did its share of grumbling and grousing, but even when the goal was momentarily lost from sight the travelers kept up the pace. They instinctively knew the meaning of the blues lyric "you gotta keep on keepin' on." By its example, the expedition story makes a powerful case for the values of community and perseverance.

That same story offers unmistakable witness to courage in hard times. Courage has often been defined as a heroic act in the face of great danger. Certainly the expedition saw its share of such perilous moments. Sudden squalls that swept the Missouri, deep snows on the Lolo Trail, and boiling rapids at The Dalles of the Columbia all were nature's tests of courage. And there were personal tests as well. The angry confrontation with the Teton Sioux, the barely concealed tensions at Fort Clatsop, and the explosion of violence and death at the Two Medicine River all measured individual mettle. But dictionary definitions of courage in the face of adversity are unreliable guides to real life. The expedition's authentic bravery came day by day in dozens of little troubles and modest misadventures. It took courage to overcome boredom, overlook hunger, and simply take the next step. Human beings often rise to a great occasion, displaying memorable heroism. Times of great hazard call out the best in bravery and self-denial. But it is the small trials that are the genuine measure of courage. And it was in just such daily routine and numbing labor that members of the expedition showed their undeniable fortitude.

Any history of the Corps of Discovery inevitably becomes a portrait in morals and values—the morals of individual and national behavior and the lasting values of a vast enterprise. But that portrait cannot be sketched in stark blacks and whites, the chiaroscuro of a simpler history. Thoughtful students of the expedition find Lewis's "darling Project" a picture drawn in many shades and tones. The Lewis and Clark story is a study in ambiguity and uncertainty, a subtle interplay of light and shadow. What looks like success may be a mask for abject failure. What seems to call for celebration may in fact be an occasion to mourn. Nowhere can we find more compelling lessons in the shadings of success and failure than in the explorers' struggle to complete their mission to presidential satisfaction. Jefferson was always precise about the journey's central purpose. "The object of your mission," he wrote, "is single, the direct water communication from sea to sea formed by the bed of the Missouri and perhaps the Oregon."[3] By September 1806 Lewis and Clark knew that Jefferson's continental geography was conceptually askew. The president's passage—an easy climb over the western ladder of rivers—seemed as remote as ever.

What Jefferson and his captains confronted in the fall of 1806 was one of the expedition's several paradoxes. The journey had, at least in the eyes of the general public, been a grand success. Public success was measured by survival and a completed passage across the continent. Jefferson had put his own stamp of approval on such a yardstick when he told Congress that the expedition had accomplished all that had been expected from it. But the president knew better, no matter what he reported on Capitol Hill. Jefferson did not want just any journey to the Pacific. Getting to the ocean was, by itself, not enough. He sought a very specific "direct and practicable water communication across this continent for the purposes of commerce."[4] Judged by this statement, the expedition was at best a disappointment and at worst an embarrassing failure. Facing that failure, the president quickly fell back to Levi Lincoln's defense of the enterprise—namely, that the Corps of Discovery had scientific investigation as its central purpose. But when the Nicholas Biddle edition of the expedition report appeared in 1814, it lacked virtually all the scientific findings Jefferson promised. The tension between success and failure, public acclaim and private disappointment, remained to haunt the Corps of Discovery. At least for Jefferson and Lewis, the shadow never fully slipped away. In later life Jefferson became disillusioned with a West that delivered more conflict than promise. And the tension between success and failure in the quest for the passage was just one more burden for Lewis's already burdened life.

The expedition's story has been ambiguous, even contradictory, in other ways as well. Meriwether Lewis's life is surely the story of public accomplishment weighed against personal frustration and tragedy. Unlike Odysseus who came home to a loving wife and a faithful son, Lewis's odyssey brought him to a St. Louis filled with political and personal trouble. Odysseus and his son were able to slay their enemies. As territorial governor, Lewis proved an inept politician, unable to either conciliate or defeat his opponents. And finally there was a steady slide into what the age called "a melancholic disposition." The distance between public attention and private anonymity touched the lives of ordinary members of the expedition as well. Had they done their work and made their "tour" today, they would shuttle from one talk show to another, endlessly rehearsing every moment of the journey, speculating on the personal lives of their commanders, and basking in celebrity limelight. But nearly all those who took part in the nation's most famous journey slipped quietly into obscurity. Only a few—like George Drouillard, John Colter, and John Potts—went west again. And in 1810 Drouillard and Potts paid for that westering with their lives at the hands of Blackfeet Indians.

In the vast enterprise that was the Lewis and Clark Expedition no people better exemplify the complex legacy and the slippery ambiguity of the venture better than those Native Americans who witnessed the journey and were an essential part of it. With few exceptions—important ones to be sure—the Corps of Discovery enjoyed peaceful relations with its native neighbors. That relative harmony was not the result of any special genius Lewis and Clark had for diplomacy or cultural understanding. Rather, the explorers were the beneficiaries of Indian hospitality and goodwill. And most often the expedition did its best to match that hospitality. But for all its efforts at cooperation and friendship, the Corps of Discovery represented the forces of economic dependence and political dominion. Behind the clasped hands on the Jefferson Peace Medal were the harsh realities of invasion, conquest, and dispossession. To travel the Lewis and Clark trail is to take the first steps down a road filled with twists and turns, tears and betrayals. When native people welcomed the expedition, they greeted an uncertain future.

Ultimately, it is the expedition's cast of characters that continues to hold our attention. Names like John Ordway, York, Sacagawea, and Jean Baptiste Charbonneau march across the page in step with Black Buffalo, Black Cat, Cameahwait, and Coboway. In our dreams and in our imaginations we can be like them, walking the same earth and feeling the same sense of wonder in discovery. In the Lewis and Clark journey we find an accessible past, one that—unlike space exploration—neither demands special training nor requires an esoteric language. The explorers' language is ours, the common tongue of everyday experience. We can visit the sites; we can see the sights. Some of the "seens of visionary inchantment" that captivated Lewis and Clark are gone, effaced by the passion for change and profit. But enough remains to remind today's explorers of what once was and what yet endures. As ordinary travelers we can join the Corps of Discovery, learning its lessons and sharing its joys and hardships. So long as we envision life as a journey—one with both hazard and promise—the Lewis and Clark story will have special place in the American imagination. It will remain, as Lewis said, "a darling Project of mine."

Notes

1. Gary E. Moulton, ed., *The Journals of the Lewis and Clark Expedition* (Lincoln, Nebr., 1983–97), 4:10.

2. Donald Jackson, ed., *Letters of the Lewis and Clark Expedition with Related Documents, 1783-1854*, 2d ed. (Urbana, Ill., 1978), 1:v.

3. Ibid., 137.

4. Ibid., 61. Jefferson's instructions to Lewis, June 20, 1803, are reprinted in this volume, 31-38.

Suggested Reading

Jackson, Donald, ed. *Letters of the Lewis and Clark Expedition with Related Documents, 1783–1854.* (2d ed., 2 vols.) Urbana: University of Illinois Press, 1978.

Moulton, Gary E., ed. *The Journals of the Lewis and Clark Expedition,* 11 vols. Lincoln: University of Nebraska Press, 1983–97.

Allen, John L. *Passage through the Garden: Lewis and Clark and the Image of the American Northwest.* Urbana: University of Illinois Press, 1975; reprinted as *Lewis and Clark and the Image of the American Northwest.* Mineola, N. Y.: Dover Publications, 1991.

Ambrose, Stephen E. *Undaunted Courage: Meriwether Lewis, Thomas Jefferson, and the Opening of the American West.* New York: Simon and Schuster, 1996.

Appleman, Roy E. *Lewis and Clark: Historic Places Associated with Their Transcontinental Exploration (1804–06).* Washington, DC: Government Printing Office for the National Park Service, 1975; reprint, St. Louis: Jefferson National Expansion Historical Association, 1993.

Botkin, Daniel B. *Our Natural History: The Lessons of Lewis and Clark.* New York: G. P. Putnam's Sons, 1995; reprint, New York: Berkley Publishing Group, 1996.

Cutright, Paul R. *A History of the Lewis and Clark Journals.* Norman: University of Oklahoma Press, 1976.

——————————. *Lewis and Clark: Pioneering Naturalists.* Urbana: University of Illinois Press, 1969; reprint, Lincoln: University of Nebraska Press, 1989.

DeVoto, Bernard. *The Course of Empire.* Boston: Houghton, Mifflin, 1952; reprint, Magnolia, Mass.: Peter Smith Publications, 1990.

Duncan, Dayton. *Out West: An American Journey.* New York: Viking, 1987.

Furtwangler, Albert. *Acts of Discovery: Visions of America in the Lewis and Clark Journals.* Urbana: University of Illinois Press, 1993.

Goetzmann, William H. *Exploration and Empire: The Explorer and the Scientist in the Winning of the American West.* New York: Random House, 1966; reprint, Austin, Tex.: Texas State Historical Association, 1994.

Jackson, Donald. *Among the Sleeping Giants: Occasional Pieces on Lewis and Clark.* Urbana: University of Illinois Press, 1987.

——————————. *Thomas Jefferson and the Stony Mountains: Exploring the West from Monticello.* Urbana: University of Illinois Press, 1981; reprint, Norman: University of Oklahoma Press, 1993.

Ronda, James P. *Lewis and Clark among the Indians.* Lincoln: University of Nebraska Press, 1984.

Credits

Part One. Genesis

Jefferson's Instructions to Lewis, June 20, 1803, in *Letters of the Lewis and Clark Expedition with Related Documents, 1783–1854,* ed. Donald Jackson, 2d ed. (Urbana, Ill., 1978), 1:61-66.

John L. Allen, "Geographical Knowledge and American Images of the Louisiana Territory," *Western Historical Quarterly,* 2 (April 1971), 151-70.

Donald Jackson, "Jefferson, Meriwether Lewis, and the Reduction of the United States Army," *Proceedings of the American Philosophical Society,* 124 (April 1980), 91-96.

Part Two. The Corps of Discovery

John Ordway to His Parents, April 8, 1804, in *Letters of the Lewis and Clark Expedition with Related Documents, 1783–1854,* ed. Donald Jackson, 2d ed. (Urbana, Ill., 1978), 1:176-77.

James P. Ronda, "'A Most Perfect Harmony': The Lewis and Clark Expedition as an Exploration Community," published as "'A Most Perfect Harmony': Life at Fort Mandan" in *We Proceeded On,* 14 (November 1988), 4-9, and reprinted in Lewis and Clark Trail Heritage Foundation, *Westering Captains: Essays on the Lewis and Clark Expedition,* WPO Publication no. 9 (Great Falls, Mont., 1990), 85-88.

Bernard DeVoto, "Passage to India: From Christmas to Christmas with Lewis and Clark," *Saturday Review of Literature,* 15 (December 1936), 3-4, 20, 24, 28.

Part Three. The Journey

Meriwether Lewis, Journal Entry, August 13, 1805, in *The Journals of the Lewis and Clark Expedition*, ed. Gary E. Moulton (Lincoln, Nebr., 1983–97), 5:76-84.

John L. Allen, "Lewis and Clark on the Upper Missouri: Decision at the Marias," *Montana The Magazine of Western History*, 21 (Summer 1971), 2-17.

Silvio A. Bedini, "The Scientific Instruments of the Lewis and Clark Expedition," in *Mapping the North American Plains: Essays in the History of Cartography*, ed. Frederick Luebke, Frances W. Kaye, and Gary E. Moulton (Norman, Okla., 1987), 93-110.

Part Four. Mutual Discovery

Benjamin Rush to Lewis, May 17, 1803, in *Letters of the Lewis and Clark Expedition with Related Documents, 1783–1854*, ed. Donald Jackson, 2d ed. (Urbana, Ill., 1978), 1:50.

John C. Ewers, "Plains Indian Reactions to the Lewis and Clark Expedition," *Montana The Magazine of Western History*, 16 (Winter 1966), 2-12.

James P. Ronda, "Exploring the Explorers: Great Plains Peoples and the Lewis and Clark Expedition," *Great Plains Quarterly*, 13 (Spring 1993), 81-90.

Part Five. Homecoming

"Arrival of Captains Lewis and Clark at St. Louis" (St. Louis Welcomes Lewis and Clark), Frankfort, Kentucky, *Western World*, October 11, 1806.

Anthony G. Bettay to Thomas Jefferson, January 27, 1808, in *The Territory of Louisiana-Missouri, 1806–1814*, vol. 14 of *The Territorial Papers of the United States* (Washington, D.C., 1949), 165-66.

Donald Jackson, "The Race to Publish Lewis and Clark," *Pennsylvania Magazine of History and Biography*, 85 (April 1961), 163-77.

Part Six. Looking Back

John L. Allen, "'Of This Enterprize': The American Images of the Lewis and Clark Expedition," in *Enlightenment Science in the Pacific Northwest: The Lewis and Clark Expedition*, ed. William F. Willingham and Leonoor S. Ingraham (Portland, Ore., 1984), 29-45.

Gary E. Moulton, "On Reading Lewis and Clark: The Last Twenty Years," *Montana The Magazine of Western History*, 38 (Summer 1988), 28-39.

James P. Ronda, "'The Writingest Explorers': The Lewis and Clark Expedition in American Historical Literature," *Pennsylvania Magazine of History and Biography*, 112 (October 1988), 607-30.

Contributors

John L. Allen, Professor of Geography at the University of Connecticut at Storrs, is the author of several books, including *Passage through the Garden: Lewis and Clark and the Image of the American West*.

Silvio A. Bedini, Keeper of Rare Books of the Smithsonian Institution, is the author of many books and articles, including *Thinkers and Tinkers: Early American Men of Science*.

Bernard DeVoto (1897–1956), author of over fifteen books and innumerable articles, is best known as the author of *The Year of Decision*, *Across the Wide Missouri*, and *The Course of Empire*.

John C. Ewers (1909–1997) was the director of the National Museum of American History and the author of twelve books, including *The Blackfeet: Raiders of the Northwestern Plains* and *Plains Indian Sculpture*.

Albert Furtwangler is the author of five books, including *Acts of Discovery: Visions of America in the Lewis and Clark Journals* and *Answering Chief Seattle*.

Donald Jackson (1919–1987) was the editor and author of several books, including *Letters of the Lewis and Clark Expedition with Related Documents, 1783–1854* and *Thomas Jefferson and the Stony Mountains*.

Gary E. Moulton, Professor of History at the University of Nebraska–Lincoln, is the editor of the *Journals of the Lewis and Clark Expedition* and the author of *John Ross: Cherokee Chief.*

James P. Ronda holds the H. G. Barnard Chair in Western History at the University of Tulsa and is the author of *Astoria and Empire* and *Lewis and Clark among the Indians.*

Index